AF539544

John Sloan

Spectator of Life

Rowland Elzea and Elizabeth Hawkes
Co-Curators

Library of Congress Cataloging-in-Publication Data
Elzea, Rowland.
John Sloan : spectator of life.
Catalog of a traveling exhibition which opens at the IBM Gallery of Science and Art, New York, April 26–June 18, 1988.
1. Sloan, John, 1871–1951—Exhibitions. I. Sloan, John, 1871–1951. II. Hawkes, Elizabeth H. III. Delaware Art Museum. IV. IBM Gallery of Science and Art. V. Title.
N6537.S57A4 1988 760′.092′4
87-37979
ISBN 0-8122-8149-7 (University of Pennsylvania Press)
Cloth edition distributed by University of Pennsylvania Press
Blockley Hall, 418 Service Drive
Philadelphia, PA 19104

This exhibition has been made possible by a grant from the IBM Corporation.

IBM Gallery of Science and Art, New York
April 26–June 18, 1988

Delaware Art Museum, Wilmington, Delaware
July 15–September 4, 1988

Columbus Museum of Art, Columbus, Ohio
September 17–November 6, 1988

Amon Carter Museum, Fort Worth, Texas
November 19–December 31, 1988

Illustrated on cover:
Sunday Afternoon in Union Square, 1912

Bowdoin College Museum of Art,
Brunswick, Maine (no. 62)

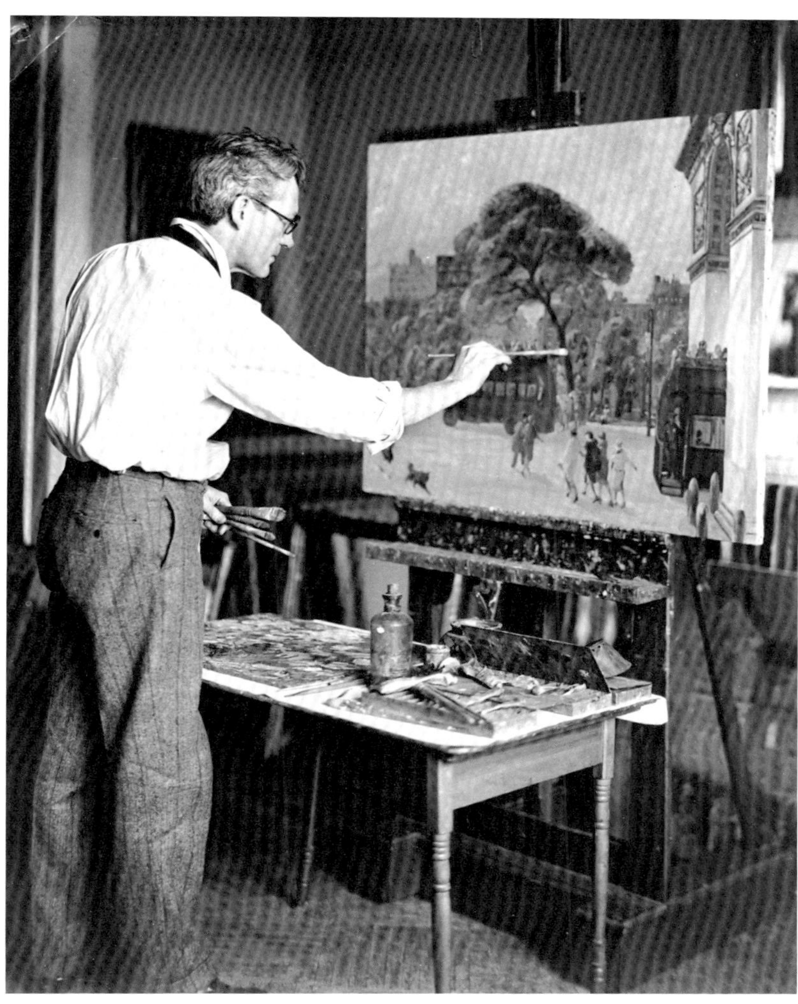

John Sloan at his Easel c. 1925

Delaware Art Museum, John Sloan Collection

"*I* never mingled with the people and the sympathy and understanding I have for the common people, as they are meanly called, I feel as a spectator of life."

John Sloan

This catalog is dedicated to

Bruce St. John (1916–1987)

Director, Delaware Art Museum

(1957–1973)

Curator, John Sloan Collection

(1961–1973)

Contents

6 Acknowledgments

7 Lenders to the Exhibition

8 Preface

10 Essay

11 Introduction

12 Genre Painting and Illustration

14 Painter, Illustrator, and Graphic Artist

23 Color Plates

36 Catalog

150 Photo Credits

Acknowledgments

There have been major comprehensive exhibitions of John Sloan's work in the past, the last being organized by the National Gallery of Art in 1972, and there have been exhibitions that focused on his Gloucester and Santa Fe periods; but, oddly enough, no exhibition has ever been organized that examines his work as a genre painter, draughtsman, and printmaker. This is perhaps the aspect of his work by which he is best known to the public. Less well known is Sloan's work as an illustrator, a profession he followed concurrently with his painting and printmaking for twenty-five years. This exhibition clarifies the intimate relationship between his paintings, prints, and illustrations for the first time.

The organization and mounting of any exhibition, large or small, at the Delaware Art Museum requires a high degree of teamwork from every single member of the staff, which is always cheerfully and unfailingly given. By the time this exhibition completes its travels and the loans are returned to their owners, nearly five years will have elapsed since its conception, and we wish to thank everyone on the staff who has contributed as well as our Board of Trustees for its support of the project. Special thanks is due to Stephen T. Bruni for helping to arrange funding, Mary F. Holahan for seeing to the many details of insurance and transportation, Rebecca E. Lawton for research assistance, Keith Nemlich for planning and executing the installation, Lenora R. White for preparing the catalog manuscript as well as the extensive correspondence necessary to organize the exhibition, Jon McDowell for photography, and Melissa Mulrooney for coordinating all aspects of the production of this catalog.

Special thanks must be given to Helen Farr Sloan for her constant guidance and support at all stages of the exhibition and its planning. We are also indebted to Robert Murdock and Arthur Clark of the IBM Gallery of Science and Art for their advice and counsel, and to Antoinette Kraushaar and Carole Pesner of the Kraushaar Galleries for their unfailing help when called upon.

Finally, we would like to express the gratitude of the Board of Trustees and the staff to the IBM Corporation, Armonk, New York, for its financial assistance and to the individuals and institutions who have lent from their collections to this exhibition. Without their help, the exhibition would not have been possible.

Rowland Elzea
Associate Director
Chief Curator

Elizabeth H. Hawkes
Associate Curator
Curator of the
John Sloan Collection

Lenders to the Exhibition

Addison Gallery of American Art, Phillips Academy, Andover, Massachusetts

Amon Carter Museum, Fort Worth, Texas

Anonymous Lenders

Bowdoin College Museum of Art, Brunswick, Maine

Butler Institute of American Art, Youngstown, Ohio

The Carnegie Museum of Art, Pittsburgh, Pennsylvania

The Cleveland Museum of Art, Cleveland, Ohio

Columbus Museum of Art, Columbus, Ohio

The Corcoran Gallery of Art, Washington, D.C.

Mr. and Mrs. Leonard Daly

The Dayton Art Institute, Dayton, Ohio

Delaware Art Museum, Wilmington, Delaware

Detroit Institute of Art, Detroit, Michigan

Elvehjem Museum of Art, University of Wisconsin, Madison, Wisconsin

Georgia Museum of Art, The University of Georgia, Athens, Georgia

Mr. Albert Hackett

Mr. and Mrs. Ralph E. Hansmann

Harvard University Art Museums, Cambridge, Massachusetts

Mrs. Edwin H. Herzog

Mr. and Mrs. Draper Hill

Hirshhorn Museum and Sculpture Garden, Smithsonian Institution, Washington, D.C.

Hood Museum of Art Dartmouth College, Hanover, New Hampshire

Collection IBM Corporation, Armonk, New York

Indianapolis Museum of Art, Indianapolis, Indiana

Jim and Judi Kaiser

Kraushaar Galleries, New York, New York

McNay Art Museum, San Antonio, Texas

Memorial Art Gallery of the University of Rochester, Rochester, New York

Victoria Miller

Milwaukee Art Museum, Milwaukee, Wisconsin

The Montclair Art Museum, Montclair, New Jersey

Munson-Williams-Proctor Institute, Utica, New York

National Gallery of Art, Washington, D.C.

National Museum of American Art, Smithsonian Institution, Washington, D.C.

A New Jersey Collection

The Parrish Art Museum, Southampton, New York

The Pennsylvania Academy of the Fine Arts, Philadelphia, Pennsylvania

Philadelphia Museum of Art, Philadelphia, Pennsylvania

The Phillips Collection, Washington, D.C.

Mr. and Mrs. Meyer P. Potamkin

Mr. and Mrs. Scott L. Probasco, Jr.

Gary M. and Brenda H. Ruttenberg

Dr. and Mrs. Michael Schlossberg, Atlanta, Georgia

Deborah and Edward Shein

Sheldon Memorial Art Gallery, University of Nebraska, Lincoln, Nebraska

Victor D. Spark

The Toledo Museum of Art, Toledo, Ohio

The University of Michigan Museum of Art, Ann Arbor, Michigan

Walker Art Center, Minneapolis, Minnesota

Whitney Museum of American Art, New York, New York

Yale University Art Gallery, New Haven, Connecticut

Preface

This exhibition of John Sloan's paintings and illustrations selected on the theme of "genre" subjects has been thoughtfully chosen by curators at the Delaware Art Museum. Pioneering work on the Golden Age of Illustration in this country has been done by Rowland Elzea and Elizabeth Hawkes. Their publications have contributed to the serious study of illustration and poster design which is beginning to find recognition in the academic world.

For many years John Sloan earned the free time to paint for himself by making illustrations for newspapers, magazines, and books. At the time of "The Eight" exhibition at the Macbeth Gallery in 1908, which brought much public attention to the group of artists around Robert Henri, Sloan was still making weekly "word-charade puzzles" for the Philadelphia *Press* to pay his rent in New York City. Living on the top floor of a made-over house on West Twenty-third Street across from the old Hotel Chelsea, he paid fifty dollars a month for an attic studio apartment with coal stoves and gas lights. When John Butler Yeats, (father of the poet) recommended to art collector John Quinn that he should buy Sloan's *Wake of the Ferry,* Quinn thought four hundred dollars was too high a price to pay.

The illustrations were made with an immediate audience in mind. As a dramatist or novelist working for contemporary attention must adapt to the requirements of his format and the understanding of a particular audience, so the illustrator must accommodate to the publisher's clientele if more work is to be obtained. Illustrations made for reproduction may be forgotten for many years if the stories are not reprinted. Many of the best drawings by Glackens, Shinn, Luks and Sloan remained unknown because the "literature" was so trivial. On the other hand, if the author's work was too creative, there was no incentive for the illustrator.

This exhibition displays a cross-section of Sloan's work in graphic media, both illustrations made as commissions and etchings made as independent projects for himself. Illustrations made for reproduction are now enjoying a new life. Because the drawings for illustrations are now seen in their original scale and complete technical presence, they can be reevaluated as drawings. This would have pleased the artist because he was a conscientious craftsman. And, as a teacher, he often stated that all great art contains an element of illustration.

The paintings, however, were made with a different creative point of view, unconstrained by editors, publishers and the limitations of mechanical reproduction. The painted pictures were made for the artist alone. He was his own critic first of all. A rare artist of independent character, continuing work for many years with no expectations of financial success, Sloan had sold only eight paintings by the age of fifty. A few friends, students and rare critics appreciated his work. Duncan Phillips and Gertrude Vanderbilt Whitney were early collectors.

The cross-section of genre paintings in this exhibition includes about half of Sloan's work in that idiom. Many of them have not been seen together before. Sloan did not create this kind of painting unless he had an idea, born of direct observation of life, warmed with a feeling of inspiration that could unite the emotional impulse and the technical process.

Robert Henri had encouraged the Philadelphia newspaper artists of the Nineties to start painting memory-pictures of the American scene, the city and country which Whitman had called on poets and painters to celebrate. The illustrators, like the reporters, had developed a kind of "standard prose," a visual vocabulary. When they started to paint for themselves, these artists already had the technical skill which could be adapted to more imaginative work in painting pictures. They were inspired by the opportunities to speak to the general public, unique to their time, that illustration presented to them. Genre pictures with emotional humor and beauty cannot be created through mere classroom instruction. When Sloan turned to teaching instead of illustration as a way to pay the landlord and grocer, he did not encourage imitations of his city life paintings. Students, like Sandy Calder, Peggy Bacon, David Smith, and Barnett Newman, were stimulated to go their own ways.

It is now eighty years since the historically important "Eight" show provoked public attention to pictures of everyday people enjoying hours of recreation in city restaurants and parks. The controversy over "aristocratic" and commonplace aspects of American life at the turn of the century no longer interferes with response to the paintings. As women's skirts go up and down, the old-fashioned look does not distract attention from the artist's human interest, concern for the human family, the human environment.

One hundred years ago, there was the famous blizzard of '88. Sloan's sister Marianna remembered her sixteen year old brother warming his etching plate over the kitchen stove. He was teaching himself print-making from Hamerton's *Handbook*. A few weeks later, he was to leave Central High School to become the main support of his parents and two young sisters when his father's health failed. Speaking of this crisis years later, in his wry way and not bitterly, Sloan said: "I sort of drifted into art as a way of earning a living. While working as assistant cashier in a bookstore where there was a fine print department, I was allowed to borrow original work by Rembrandt and Dürer which I copied in pen and ink to sell for fifty cents. Then I made greeting cards with my own drawings and humorous poems. In my youth, we were poor but not underprivileged. We always had books to read. I had read all of Dickens and Shakespeare by the age of twelve. We had tools and materials to work with. My great-uncle Alexander Priestley had a wonderful library with original prints by Cruikshank and Hogarth.... Responsibilities kept me working in this country when my artist friends went abroad to study. I never wanted to be in debt to anyone for help... Reading George Moore and John Ruskin helped me to make the decision to put down roots in my own country. They warned artists against the dangers of becoming expatriates, trying to assimilate the wrong culture, too fast."

One day in the spring of 1951, as Sloan approached his eightieth birthday, we were walking down Eighth Avenue in the old Chelsea district where he had painted and etched during those first years after the move from Philadelphia in 1904. He hated the Ash Can label attached to the early New York City work. "I did not examine the life of the poor like a social worker...I saw it with an innocent poet's eye. The subjects I found for the paintings were bits of joy in human life."

Helen Farr Sloan

Essay

John Sloan

Spectator of Life

Introduction

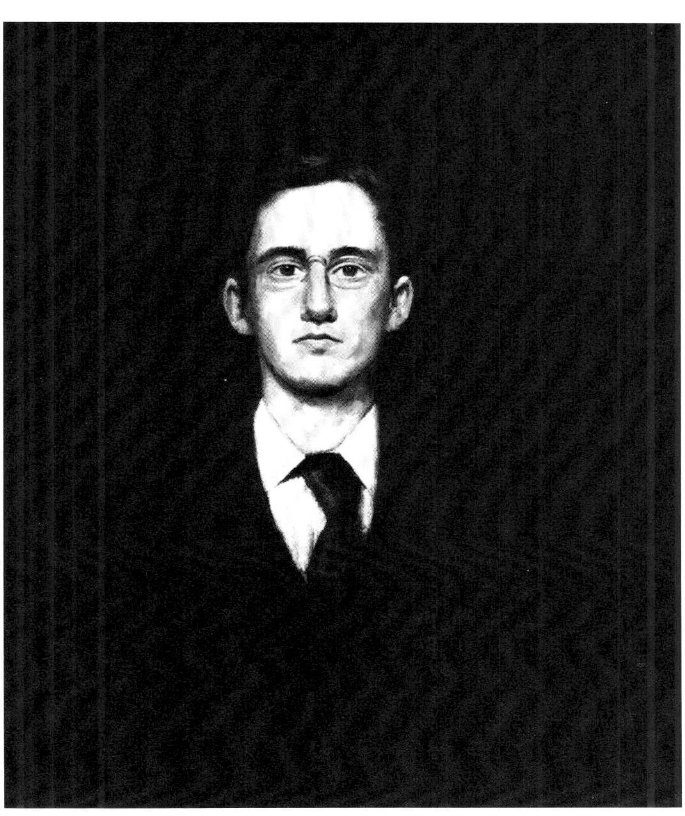

Fig. 1. *Self Portrait,* 1890

Delaware Art Museum, Gift of Helen Farr Sloan, 1970

John Sloan's work is generally associated with his images of New York City; the warm comraderie of McSorley's saloon, the sense of loneliness the city inspires, reflected in *The Wake of the Ferry,* or the rowdy good humor of *South Beach Bathers.* But the life of the people, whether it was in New York, Philadelphia, Gloucester, Massachusetts, or Santa Fe, New Mexico, moved him to paint, draw, or etch it periodically over his long career as an artist, not just in the ten years before the First World War when most of his best-known New York City paintings were done.

Sloan infused the painting of scenes of everyday life, called genre painting, with a zest, humor, and honesty that were new to American painting in the early years of the twentieth century. It was not condescending or satirical, as earlier genre painting had tended to be, nor was it propagandistic, as some later artists would have it; it was a caring but detached view of American life as it was lived by ordinary Americans. As Sloan said of himself, he was "a spectator of life."

For the first twenty-five years of his career, Sloan was an illustrator of books, magazines, and newspapers concurrently with his painting and printmaking. The texts that he illustrated—short stories, poems, and novels—were written for and about ordinary Americans and, in large part, were published in popular family magazines like *Collier's Weekly, The Saturday Evening Post,* or *McClure's Magazine.* The same honest, healthy commentary on life that animated and made real the drawings he made for millions of readers also suffuses his paintings and prints, which could be enjoyed by only a few. Thus, the three aspects of his artistic career form a seamless whole and should be viewed together to understand fully any one of them. In order to do this, some consideration should be given to the states of both genre painting and illustration at the turn of the century.

Genre Painting and Illustration

Genre painting—the painting of narrative scenes of the everyday life of anonymous people in a contemporary setting—in America at the turn of the century had a number of different sources and faces. The most immediately recognizable, perhaps, is that which had its roots in the subjects of the French Impressionists of the 1860s and '70s: ordinary people dressed in their Sunday best enjoying themselves in the fresh summer air after a week's work. The American followers of Impressionism such as Childe Hassam, Joseph De Camp, and Edmund Tarbell translated these subjects from the pleasure gardens of Paris to the sunny morning rooms of Boston, from Trouville to Cape Cod, with enthusiasm if not perfect understanding of the French artists' thinking and motives. However, there was a visual difference. The subjects of the New England Impressionists, called the "Ten," were well-bred and leisured people, usually ladies of wealth who could afford to buy the expensive depictions of their way of life, instead of the shop girls and artisans relaxing in the country at Bougeville that, when painted by Renoir and the other Frenchmen, shocked the bourgeois of the Third Republic, already made uneasy by a rising proletariat. The New England version of the Impressionist subjects we might call "haut genre."

Totally unlike this "haut genre" in style, mentality, and origin was the American school of genre painting, based on English and Dutch prototypes, which was established in the early nineteenth century by John Quidor and continued by William Sidney Mount, Eastman Johnson, and Winslow Homer among many others. The earlier of these artists, at least, perceived their anonymous, underclass models as exemplars of some human verity or virtue in its typically American manifestation—the robust, Rousseauian innocence of George Caleb Bingham's riverboatmen, the earthiness of Johnson's peasants or the simple purity of Homer's schoolchildren—a view that grew increasingly imbued with nostalgia for innocence lost as the century progressed and the pastoral life began to disappear with industrialization. However, a later generation of painters, such as Thomas Eakins, Thomas Hovenden, and Thomas Anshutz, stripped away the nostalgia and substituted a measure of Romantic heroism, seen in Eakins' sportsmen and athletes, Hovenden's farm families, and Anshutz's steelworkers. Despite whatever emotional coloring might be given to pictures of the everyday pursuits of ordinary people, depictions of this subject could be characterized as "bas genre" in contrast to the lives of the elegant and exceptional.

Fig. 2. Fortune Teller's Birds, 1899

Minnesota Museum of Art, Margaret MacLaren Bequest Purchase. 84.4.1

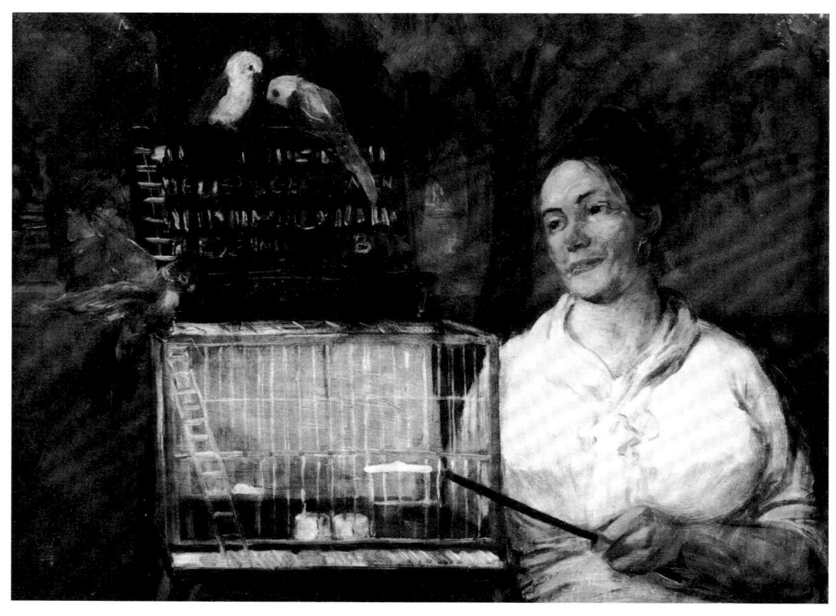

In the last quarter of the century, however, another approach to the "bas genre" subject began to appear: that of the periodical and newspaper illustrator. These artists were trained by the same methods as landscape artists, portraitists, painters of "haut genre," or any others. They found their means of expression, as well as earning a living, by providing pictures for the popular press rather than for the walls of the National Academy of Design or wealthy patrons. Just as the American Impressionist "Ten" knew their audience, so did the illustrators. Commencing during the Civil War, when printing technology began to make generously illustrated periodicals possible, and extending into the 1890s, the purchasing and reading of illustrated books and magazines, and to a lesser extent newspapers, tended to be limited to those who had the ability, leisure, and wherewithal to read as their form of information and pleasure. The illustrations for the publications of the 1880s were designed to appeal to those more cultured readers: Edwin Austin Abbey's stylish drawings for Shakespeare's plays and Herrick's poems; Howard Pyle's historically accurate depictions of American colonial life to accompany the serialized works of such distinguished historians as Thomas Wentworth Higginson, Woodrow Wilson, and Henry Cabot Lodge, to say nothing of his own adaptations of children's classics like Robin Hood and King Arthur; and precise renderings of exotic travel subjects or current events by such artists as Joseph Pennell, Rufus Zogbaum, and Gilbert Gaul, among a host of others, many of them National Academicians.

By the 1890s, however, the picture was changing. Mass production greatly increased income from advertising, and postal distribution of magazines and newspapers widened availability and reduced their cost to consumers. Moreover, the base of literacy had been greatly broadened by compulsory public education. A huge new audience was there to be informed, entertained—and led—by the publishing industry. Beyond that, however, lay an even more golden, if unplanned, opportunity for the publisher: to introduce his readers to visual art. For many this must have been a veritable visual enfranchisement, as the visual arts had heretofore been an even more exclusive preserve of the leisured classes than the literary ones, the general public having had even less exposure to visual art than to literature. Nevertheless, the publisher did not have it all his way in his choice of literary or visual subjects. There was, perforce, a certain *quid pro quo*. People read for entertainment as well as enlightenment, but they knew they wanted to read about and see pictures of the world in which they lived; to find out about people who were just like themselves, involved in familiar situations. In short, what they required was "bas genre" subject matter, and it paid the publisher of these popular magazines to provide it. Certainly historical romances and escapist fiction were part of the entertainment at the turn of the century, but the amount of contemporary subject matter dealt with in the popular literature of 1900 and later was much greater than it had been in prior decades.

Life was changing rapidly from an agrarian to a mercantile and manufacturing society. Young people moving from the farm to the cities to make their ways needed and wanted to know how to deal with their new lives. The publishers could help them with both how-to-do-it nonfiction and encouraging "boy-makes-good" fiction. Millions of immigrants wanted to understand their new home, established Americans needed to understand the newcomers, and the writers, illustrators, and publishers helped to provide the means. The education of children had become a much more serious and time-consuming task than it had been earlier in the century, and the young readers wanted to know about the world in which they were growing up. Magazines like *St. Nicholas* provided articles on current events and science in addition to the more usual children's fare. Photography, growing rapidly by the end of the century, added greatly to the proliferation of images of contemporary life. Some photographs by Jacob Riis and Lewis Hine, among others, had a "bas genre" flavor of anonymity and ordinariness. By the end of the century, it was technically possible to publish the objective truth of photographs in newspapers and magazines, adding weight to *exposes* of political and business corruption by writers like Ida Tarbell and Lincoln Steffens, as well as other so-called muckrakers.

Painter, Illustrator, and Graphic Artist

This, then, was the milieu in which John Sloan found himself when he first began to give serious consideration to the possibility of becoming a painter. He had been working since 1892 as a newspaper illustrator and had achieved national recognition in 1894 at the height of popularity of the Art Nouveau poster for his work in that line (nos. 1–2). His friend and mentor, Robert Henri, urged him to devote himself to painting when they met in 1892, but Sloan could not, his job being the main financial support for his mother, father, and two sisters. For this reason his formal art training was restricted to a night class in freehand drawing at the Spring Garden Institute, Philadelphia, in 1890, and a class in drawing from the antique at the Pennsylvania Academy of the Fine Arts under Thomas Anshutz in 1892. The Philadelphia *Inquirer*, for which he then worked, was an afternoon paper, requiring him to be in his office in the morning and afternoon, leaving only evenings available for study and no daylight for painting. However, he and his friend William Glackens often went landscape sketching in watercolor together on weekends. In 1889 Sloan purchased and studied *A Manual of Oil Painting* (1886) by the British artist John Collier and executed, very competently, his first oil painting, a self-portrait, the following year (fig. 1); but it was not until 1896, when he went to work for a morning paper, the Philadelphia *Press*, which left his mornings free, that he could begin to paint with any regularity at all.

Sloan's work for the newspapers, unlike that of his colleagues William Glackens, George Luks, Everett Shinn, Frederic Gruger, and Wallace Morgan who were artist-reporters, was at first restricted to small humorous drawings in the manner of the English *Punch* artist John Tenniel and to copying photographs for reproduction by line process block. Because he was a slow worker, he was sent out on reporting assignments only in emergencies. Before Sloan went to work for the *Inquirer*, he had worked with A. Edward Newton (later to become a famous bibliophile) designing and etching decorative printed novelties such as calendars and pamphlets in a style influenced by Walter Crane. The newspaper editors saw that this decorative style of drawing would be admirably suited to the daily feature pages, the Sunday supplements, and advertisements.[1]

Sloan was fortunate in meeting Robert Henri in 1892. Henri's magnetic personality and enthusiasm made him a natural teacher and Sloan, Glackens, Shinn, and the other Philadelphia newspaper artists were drawn to him, meeting frequently for informal sketching sessions and critiques as well as social gatherings. On his return to Philadelphia in 1897 after two years of work in Paris, Henri was full of enthusiasm for painting "bas genre" subjects observed in the city streets. This was painting life as it is, rather than life imagined and constructed from studio drawings or painted from a formula such as Impressionism had become by the 1890s. It was not abstract in concept either, like Impressionism with its color theories and consciously arranged composition, which Henri had abandoned after a brief flirtation in the early '90s in favor of the probity and vitality of Hals, Manet, and Velasquez. Henri convinced Sloan for a time that expressing the energy of life honestly and soberly was the sole reason for painting. Henri found Impressionism shallow and predictable, thus setting himself and those influenced by him at odds with the style that was beginning to dominate the American art world of artists, exhibitions, and collectors. However, in 1899 Henri's Parisian street scene *La Neige* was purchased by the French government, a distinction given to few Americans at that time, which confirmed his reputation at home as a leader. Paradoxically, this official recognition gave Henri the influence to make his anti-art establishment views heard, to attract students, and to convince gallery owners and exhibition organizers to show the work of artists painting in an unconventional way.

Most of Sloan's earliest paintings were portraits, a subject he pursued all his life concurrent with whatever other subject happened to engage him at the time. His first painting of a city subject was *The Philadelphia Stock Exchange* (no. 3), painted about 1897, but his early urban subjects, like some of Henri's, were primarily architectural, with human activity either absent or subordinate to the architecture, as in *East Entrance, City Hall, Philadelphia* (no. 6). His first genre painting, *Fortune Teller's Birds* (Minnesota Museum of Art) was done in 1899 (fig. 2). *The Rathskeller* (no. 5) of 1901 combines a decorative art nouveau arrangement of the figures with an expression of human tension between the wealthy, lonely man with his bottle of champagne and the young woman with a beer-drinking escort. However, Sloan's real immersion in the "bas genre" subject (not set in contemporary times, to be sure) came in 1902 when he began two years of work on an extensive series of etchings and drawings to illustrate a deluxe American edition of the collected works of the French humorist Charles Paul de Kock (nos. 9–13). De Kock's farces, set in the early nineteenth

[1] *The Poster Period of John Sloan* (Lock Haven, Pa.: privately printed by the Hammermill Paper Co., 1967), pp. 9-13.

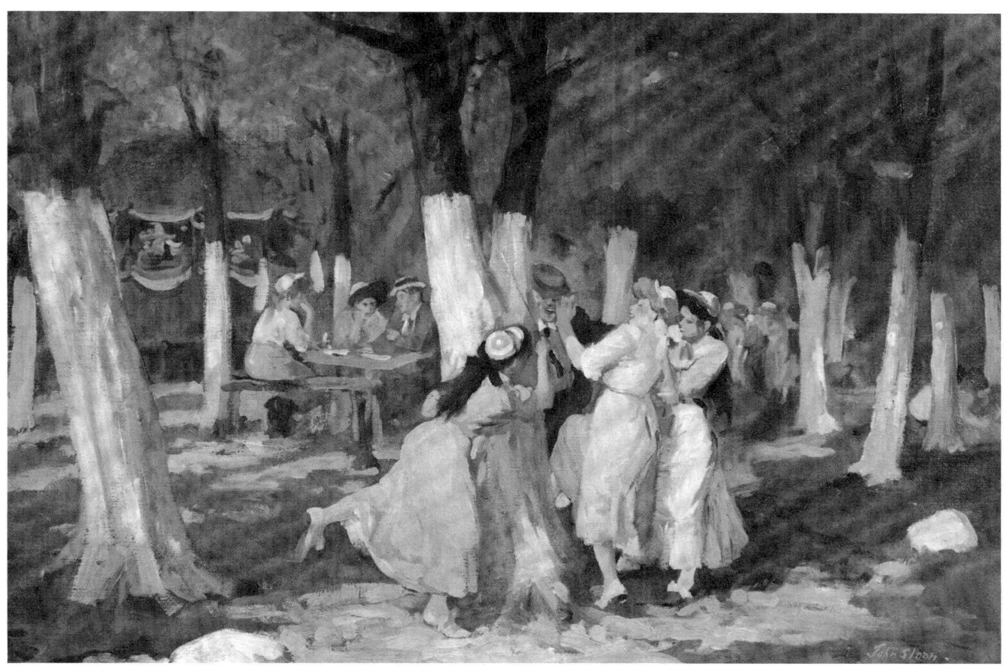

Fig. 3. The Picnic Grounds, 1906

Whitney Museum of American Art,
Purchase 41.34

century, gave Sloan much practice in composing groups of figures interacting with gesture and facial expression. The comic situations appealed to Sloan's sense of humor and compassion for humanity.

In the spring of 1904, Sloan and his wife of three years, Dolly, moved to New York City when he found that his job with the Philadelphia *Press* was to be made redundant except for a weekly word charade puzzle in black and white, a kind of visual pun, which he was to do on a regular basis for the *Press* until 1910. This was his only steady source of income, augmented by frequent freelance illustration commissions for the popular magazines, which he had assured himself he could get before he left Philadelphia. For the first time he was master of his own time and could paint during the days except when he had a puzzle to do or an illustration assignment, to which he always gave priority in a very businesslike way. In September he and Dolly settled in an apartment on West 23rd Street, in Chelsea, on the outskirts of the Tenderloin district of ill-repute. The swarming life of the streets, elemental, unpretentious, and vital, fascinated Sloan in the walks his new freedom allowed him to take, as did the vignettes of domestic life he saw at night through the windows of his neighbors. While Sloan had not been an artist-reporter on the Philadelphia newspapers, he had trained his visual memory to the same retentiveness as his reporter colleagues, and all of his genre paintings and etchings of this period where done from memory with the occasional aid of a quick sketch.

As soon as Sloan finished his work on the over 100 de Kock illustrations in January 1905, he began work on his City Life set of etchings (nos. 19–26, 34–5), in which the vitality and earthy humor of the French subjects was extended to contemporary New York. The characteristic that the ten etchings of the City Life set (so called because Sloan tried to market them as a set, though without much success) had in common with the de Kock illustrations, beside the domestic subject matter, was that the interaction of the figures was the focus of the picture, in contrast to the dominance of the architectural setting in most of his previous city paintings; such as *The Coffee Line* (no. 15), painted in New York in 1905, and the atmospheric *Spring, Madison Square* (no. 16), which demonstrates the emotional reserve of the earlier paintings. It took Sloan, an essentially shy man, some time to feel at home in New York; he felt himself to be, as he said, "an unacclimated Pennsylvanian."[2] Finally, in June 1906 Sloan painted *The Picnic Grounds* (Whitney Museum of American Art), in which he realized, emotionally and visually, his "bas genre" subject for the first time in a painting, and the excitement of life and vitality of his etchings and illustrations bloomed into color (fig. 3).

Even with this breakthrough in painting in 1906, Sloan continued to devote most of his attention to his illustrations for the rest of the year, making a number of witty drawings for stories and articles in the mass circulation magazines (nos. 27-32) and for a book of poems in dialect, *Canzoni* (no. 33), by his Philadelphia friend T. A. Daly. However, 1907 was a different matter. In March of that year, Henri served on the jury of the National Academy's annual exhibition. The conservative jury members not only rejected Luks's and Carl Sprinchorn's paintings in spite of Henri's strong support, but also accepted only one of his own entries, giving his other two insultingly low ratings. (Since he had been elected a member the previous year, Henri was entitled by the Academy's rules to have one picture hung). In protest, Henri withdrew his two poorly rated paintings. Besides the blow to Henri's pride and professional reputation, he and his friends were deeply disappointed by the failure of the merger, for which Henri had worked in 1906, of the National Academy and the originally rather liberal Society of American Artists to bring a more open attitude toward innovative painting; this was also reflected in the Academy's refusal to elect Arthur B. Davies and Ernest Lawson to membership in 1907. Consequently, Henri proposed that he, Sloan, Luks, Glackens, Davies, and Lawson (later joined by Maurice Prendergast and Everett Shinn) hold an exhibition of their work the next year at the Macbeth Gallery, one of the few commercial galleries that showed any interest in paintings by American artists.[3]

Fig. 4. *Ludlow, Colorado, 1914*

Cover, *The Masses,* June 1914. Delaware Art Museum, Gift of Helen Farr Sloan, 1978

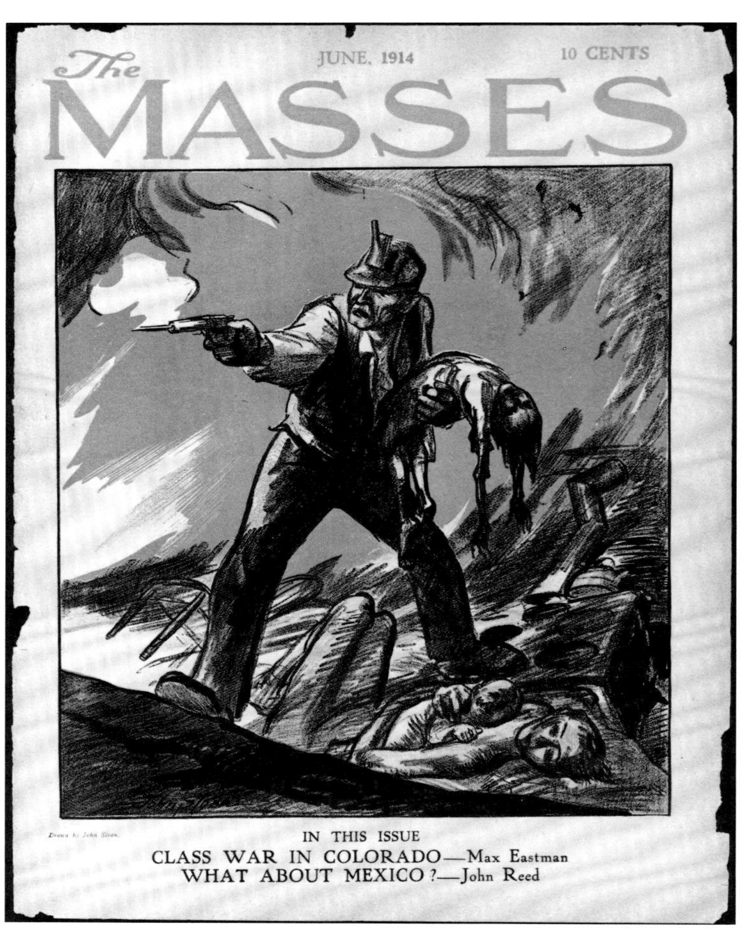

[2]John Sloan, *Gist of Art* (New York: American Artists Group, Inc., 1939), p. 132.

[3]Bruce St. John, ed., *John Sloan's New York Scene* (New York: Harper & Row, 1965), p. 118.

At the time this decision was reached, Sloan had painted only half a dozen canvases in his new "bas genre" style, including *Easter Eve* (no. 36) and *Wake of the Ferry, No. 1* (no. 37). Clearly more were needed to choose from for what Sloan must have suspected would be a momentous exhibition. Produce Sloan did, completing twenty-seven paintings in 1907, nearly half of the number he had done in the preceding sixteen years. The nature of his subjects also underwent a subtle change, becoming as frank as his illustrations, more challenging, more "in bad taste" than his previous paintings like the sensitive *Easter Eve* or the elegiac *Wake of the Ferry, No. 1.* The drunken woman staggering along with her bucket of beer and the ebullient sexuality of the young women laughing at her (duly noted by the male bystanders) in *Sixth Avenue and 30th Street* (no. 38) was a provocative dose of reality to an age where decorum and a shyly downcast eye were thought the ideal of feminine behavior. A similar and equally joyous celebration of the relation between the sexes can be seen in *South Beach Bathers* (no. 39) as well as in the earlier etchings of the City Life series, especially *Man, Wife and Child* (no. 26) and *Turning out the Light* (no. 25), which were probably among those refused showing by the American Watercolor Society in 1906 on the grounds that they were "vulgar." A similar challenge to "good taste" can be seen in the paintings of 1907 that were included in the Macbeth Gallery exhibition of the next year but are not in the present exhibition, such as *Hairdresser's Window* (Wadsworth Athenaeum) and *Election Night* (Memorial Art Gallery of the University of Rochester). While it might be tempting to see Sloan as being deliberately provocative, it is probably closer to the truth to say that since he knew that no jury would be passing judgment on his work, he was free to state exactly what his increasing confidence as a painter and understanding of New York dictated. This kind of freedom to paint and exhibit American subjects in an American way was precisely what the 1908 exhibition of the work of Henri and his friends, known as The Eight, celebrated, nothing more and nothing less.

The exhibition, which had been anticipated in the press by both supporters and detractors of the new realism for a year prior to the opening, was a great success in publicizing the arrival of a new vitality in American art. The conservatism of the Academy, which had been grumbled about in the press for some time, had suffered a serious blow from eight artists of recognized ability, working with a variety of styles and subjects but united in their desire to paint and exhibit as they saw fit. It might be observed quite parenthetically that such an attitude was not limited to America but was in the air internationally. Probably unaware of developments in America, the English artist Walter Sickert wrote in 1910: "The more our art is serious, the more it will tend to avoid the drawing room and stick to the kitchen. The plastic arts are gross arts, dealing joyously with gross material facts."[4]

The number of dealers willing to exhibit American art began to increase, and exhibition possibilities independent of the art establishment soon proliferated. Further declarations of independence followed in rapid succession with the exhibition of the Independent Artists, led by Henri, in 1910 and the first of many annual exhibitions of the Society of Independent Artists in 1917. All of this was concurrent with the introduction of modern art from Europe through the establishment of the Photo-Secession Gallery by Alfred Stieglitz in 1905, the Armory Show in 1913, and the Forum Exhibition of American modernist painters in 1916, among others.

Prior to 1908, Sloan had not shown much interest in politics, but in the election of that year he voted for the Democrats and William Jennings Bryan, who lost to Taft, Roosevelt's handpicked successor, which elicited the following comment in his diary: "The cancerous growth is to have four more years. I'm not a Democrat, I am of no party. I'm for change—for the operating knife when a party rots in power."[5] Several comments he had made in the diary earlier in the year showed his growing indignation with the social injustices that he observed in his daily life. Finally, in December 1908 he wrote in his diary: "Charles Wisner Barrell (a friendly art critic) called. He has become a Socialist and talked with me on the subject—wants me to attend a Sunday meeting in Jersey City some time. It sounds well to me. I believe my next vote will go to their candidates."[6] Although the diary for the winter and spring of 1909 does not dwell on Sloan's growing commitment to Socialism, it was clear by May that he had to reach a decision as to what extent his art would serve his politics. Early in his career he had determined that he would never put himself in a position where his independence as an artist would be threatened by depending on patronage for his livelihood. In this resolve he was successful, selling only eight paintings by the time he was fifty years old. His income came from his illustrating and, beginning in 1916, his teaching.

---

[4]Walter Sickert quoted in *Sickert* (London: Arts Council of Great Britain, 1977.)

[5]St. John. *John Sloan's New York Scene*, p. 259.

[6]Ibid., p. 259.

On May 5, 1909, Sloan was approached by Herman Bloch, an art critic for the Socialist newspaper *The Call*, who had evidently suggested that Sloan's work should demonstrate a Socialist point of view. Sloan refused, noting, "Told him that I had no intention of working for any Socialist object in my etchings and paintings though I do think that it is the proper party to cast votes for at this time in America."[7] The significant omission here is drawings. He felt that the proper place to express his political opinion was in his illustrations, like the great French lithographers whose work he so admired, Daumier, Steinlen, and Gavarni. Even so, a social edge can be seen in some of his paintings of 1909, such as the arrogance of the rich in *Fifth Avenue* (no. 46) and *Gray and Brass* (Mr. and Mrs. Arthur Altschul). Sloan felt, somewhat guiltily, that *Recruiting in Union Square* (no. 48) contained a comment about the power of the state over the individual to involve him in an unwanted war, which contravened Sloan's resolve, although this implication is not particularly evident to us today. *Three A.M.* (no. 47), however, painted in late April, is an archetypal Sloan "bas genre" picture full of warmth, affection, and humor with no hint of social comment.

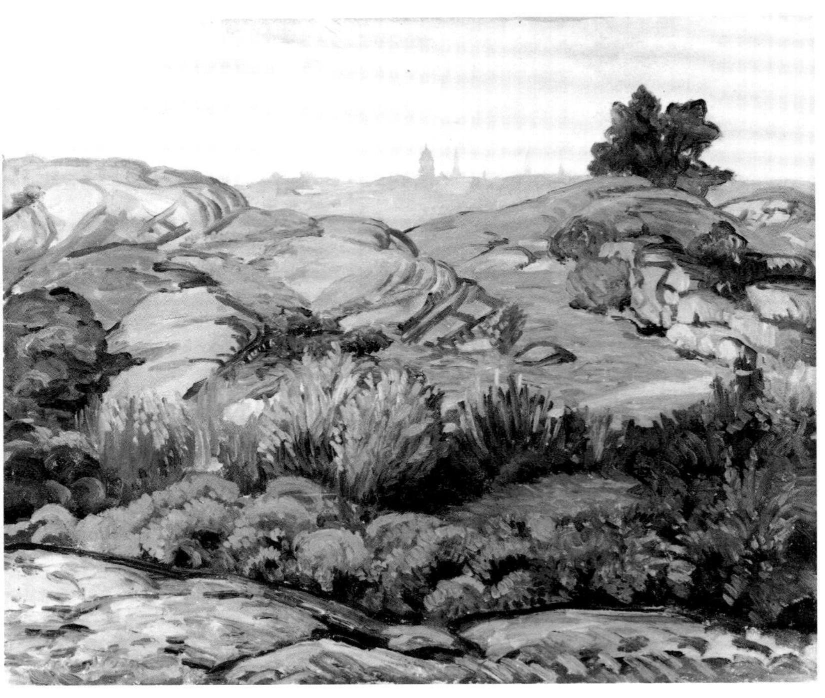

Fig. 5. Path Through Rocks and Bushes, 1914

Delaware Art Museum, Gift of Helen Farr Sloan, 1963

The illustrations Sloan was drawing fairly regularly for magazines such as *Collier's Weekly* dealt with everyday life in many cases, but they could not be an adequate outlet for the growing strength of his Socialist feelings. In August he contributed a cartoon to *The Call* and by October was doing so with some frequency. He continued this in 1910 and also made some drawings for *The Coming Nation*, a Socialist journal. In 1912 Sloan began to direct his efforts to the monthly left wing magazine *The Masses*, serving as its unpaid art editor. At that point in its short life, the magazine published good, advanced literature, poems, and essays that were critical of any foolish excess, whether conservative or liberal. It also published drawings chosen for their quality as art rather than for their propaganda value, executed by a variety of artists, some young and unknown. Sloan's own contributions ranged from the joyous *At the Top of the Swing* (no. 73), through the gentle scorn for the absurdities of fashion of *The Net Result* (no. 77), to the outrage of *Ludlow, Colorado* (no. 83 and fig. 4). Like many other intellectual Socialists, Sloan began to be disillusioned with the international Socialist movement for its failure to prevent the outbreak of war in 1914, and he began to withdraw from the movement, although he never lost his basic compassion for people. The final break with *The Masses* came in 1916 when the magazine became much more politically dogmatic and a new editor, Floyd Dell, insisted on creating political captions for drawings that did not originally have them, or turning humorous captions into ones carrying heavy political freight.

[7]Ibid., p. 268.

In 1909 Sloan was introduced to a system of using color devised by the artist Hardesty G. Maratta. Without going into detail about the rather complex system itself, it had two major benefits for Sloan's work. First, it forced him to extend his palette from the extremely limited one he had learned from Henri (who was also an enthusiastic user of the Maratta system) to a full range of color. A feature of the system was the paint that Maratta prepared and sold. The colors were as pure as possible—a clear, brilliant yellow took the place of the brownish-yellow ochre that Sloan had used, for example. In addition to the primary colors, Maratta also mixed accurately measured secondary and tertiary colors as well as a set of neutral tones. The second benefit to Sloan was that the system imposed a certain abstraction on the process of painting, requiring the use of certain colors and denying that of others according to the permutation of the system chosen for a specific work. Although the quality of the paints Maratta packaged declined in the Teens and Sloan ceased using them, he followed the discipline of the set palette with paints he mixed himself for the rest of his life. The discipline of the system and the somewhat arbitrary use of color prepared Sloan to understand the revelations of modern European art that were to come in 1913 with the Armory Show.

Sloan was in full command of his "bas genre" subject matter. His work for *The Masses* gave him a safety valve for his Socialist emotions, and the years between 1910 and 1914 were among the most fruitful of his genre painting career in both quantity and quality. His work encompassed the humor of *Scrubwomen, Astor Library* (no. 52), the robust vitality of *Sunday Afternoon in Union Square* (no. 62), and the quiet lyricism of *McSorley's Back Room* (no. 57) and *Spring Rain* (no. 60). Still, the New York that had provided those subjects was changing. It was becoming busier and bigger. Cars were filling the streets with noise and the pace of life was becoming faster.

Sloan himself was losing some of the innocence that had infused his earlier paintings as he became aware of the social injustices of city life. He also began to suspect that there was more to painting than he had thought and Henri had taught him. Looking back in later years at this period of his life, Sloan said in his unpublished notes: "With a rather limited palette and through direct and quick work, we made pictures which have design and form because the intention was graphic and honest. Our work done before the influence of the Armory

Fig. 6. Cliff Dwellings, Parajeto (Frijoles), 1922

Delaware Art Museum, Gift of Helen Farr Sloan, 1980

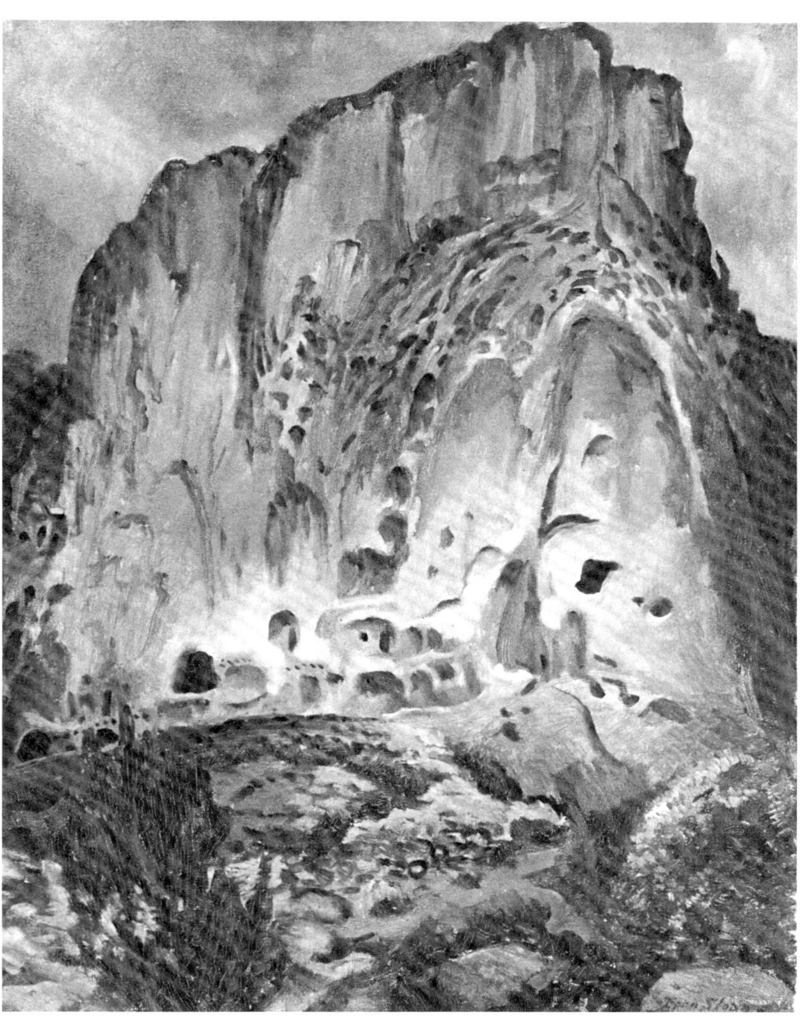

Show was very unself-conscious about plastic motives."[8] Additionally, Sloan was still concerned that none of the feelings that had convinced him to become a Socialist should slip into his painting and make it mere propaganda. Working under such a constraint to the full expression of his thoughts and feelings was a situation which, as an artist, Sloan could not tolerate. After all, constraint of expression, although from an exterior rather than interior source, was what led to the stand of The Eight against the Academy. These subtle discontents led Sloan, in 1912, to obtain a larger studio, one in which he could paint from the figure and begin the study of the nude that would occupy him for the rest of his life. They also led him to leave New York in the summers for concentrated painting sessions in Gloucester, Massachusetts from 1914 through 1918 and then in Santa Fe from 1919 through 1950. After beginning to teach in 1916, primarily at the Art Students League in New York, Sloan had little time or energy left for painting during the school year; this also contributed to the reduction in number of his New York genre paintings. Paper shortages caused by the First World War reduced the number of illustrations that magazines could print, but fortunately Sloan's reliance on illustrating as his source of income had been obviated by his salary as a teacher, practically ending his career as an illustrator.

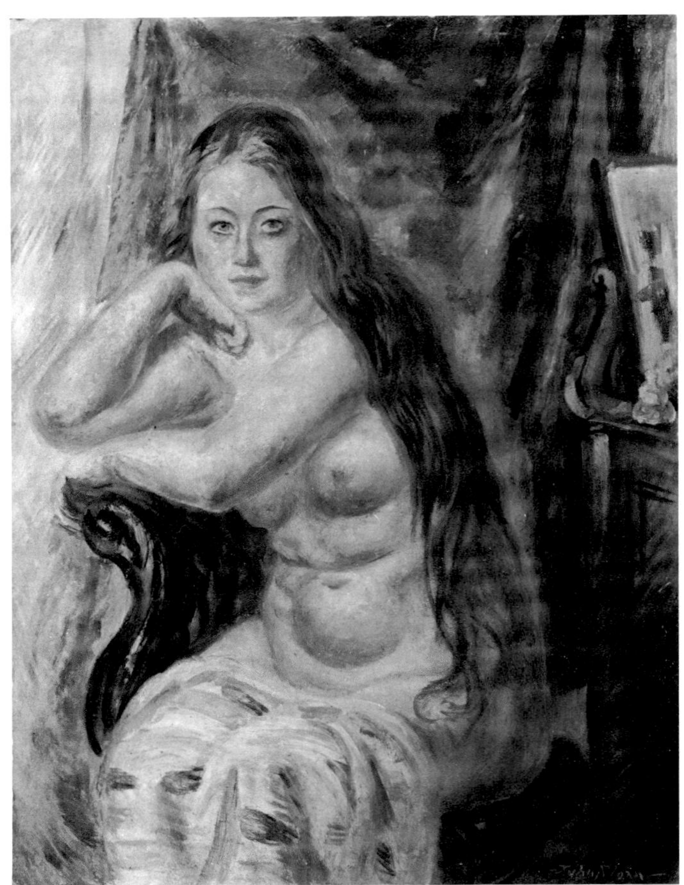

Fig. 7. Semi Nude, Red Hair, 1933

John Sloan Trust

Seeing the work of the European Post-Impressionists and Cubists for the first time in any quantity at the Armory Show of 1913 made a profound impression on Sloan. In his notes he recalled: "For me, this was the beginning of a journey into the living past. The blinders fell from my eyes and I could look at religious pictures without seeing the subjects. I was free to enjoy the sculptures of Africa and prehistoric Mexico because visual verisimilitude was no longer important. I realized that these things were made in response to life, distorted to emphasize ideas about life, emotional qualities of life."[9] The works of Van Gogh and Toulouse-Lautrec particularly impressed him with their brilliant color and the way they modeled solid form with brushstrokes of pure color. He also observed that the subject matter, the narrative, was of secondary importance to the means by which it was expressed by the European artists. They could and did paint anything—an old shoe, a flower, a nondescript landscape.

[8]John Sloan, unpublished notes, 1950. John Sloan Trust, p. 104.

[9]Ibid., p. 146a.

Before this realization Sloan had to have an idea for a picture; he had to see a subject, think about it, and then put it down from memory. After the Armory Show, he saw the need for disciplined and regular work. Speeded by the convenient and logically organized Maratta system of paints, he produced nearly three hundred canvases in his five summers in Gloucester, more than in the preceding twenty-four years of his career. In New York he drew from the model whenever he was not teaching.

Most of Sloan's Gloucester paintings were landscapes or seascapes (fig. 5), but there were a few, like those included in the exhibition (nos. 91–2), that have the busy excitement of Sloan's "bas genre" paintings of New York. These, however, are held in a much more deliberately planned composition, a more abstract structure. This structure is also very evident in his post-Armory Show New York paintings like *Jefferson Market, Sixth Avenue* (no. 90) and *The City from Greenwich Village* (no. 97), which verge on being architectural studies with very little of the "bas genre" quality found in *Bleecker Street, Saturday Night* (no. 94), for instance. A more obvious change, perhaps, than the abstract structure of the post-Armory Show paintings is in the color and paint texture Sloan used. Many of his "bas genre" paintings had been interior or evening subjects and thus inherently dark, but even those fully day-lit subjects like *Spring, Gramercy Park* (no. 59) or *Red Kimono on the Roof* (no. 63) were painted in the middle range of tones and could hardly be described as brilliant in color.

Although he had painted a few portraits and genre subjects between the time of the Armory Show and his first visit to Gloucester in 1914 that show an expanded range of tonality, the use of higher keyed and purer color, and some experimentation in building form by overlaying strokes of contrasting colors, as Van Gogh and Toulouse-Lautrec had done, it was not until he experienced the bright sunlight of Gloucester that his palette brightened considerably and extended its tonal range to include full light and dark. In addition, his brushwork took on a much more graphic quality than it had previously, describing the contours of forms as Van Gogh had done, as seen in *Sally, Sarah and Sadie, Peter and Paul* (no. 86). By the time Sloan transferred his summer allegiance to Santa Fe in 1919, however, he had ceased using paint in such an extreme way.

As in Gloucester, most of Sloan's work in the clear, thin air of New Mexico was dedicated to landscape and figure painting (fig. 6), but he did find the life and customs of the Indian and Hispanic natives of great interest, resulting in paintings like *Threshing Floor, Santa Fe* (no. 101) and *Corpus Christi Procession* (no. 102). However, Sloan's finest genre paintings in Santa Fe continued to be those of a "bas genre" nature like *Bathers in the Acequia Madre* (no. 104), celebrating the simple pleasures of life in which he could also participate. As he had earlier in New York, Sloan reserved his social commentary for his graphic work, as in the etching *Knees and Aborigines* (no. 106), which leads one to wonder which the aborigines were: the Indians or the sightseers.

In 1928 Sloan's painting underwent another profound change, as profound as when he entered his Post-Impressionist phase after the Armory Show. He abandoned the direct method of painting he had used to that time in favor of underpainting and glazing in the traditional manner. His purpose was to obtain a greater sense of solidity in his work and a greater richness of color. By this time the nude had become his chosen subject (fig. 7). His method was to make a fully modeled monochrome drawing of his subject on the canvas or panel first, isolate it from the ensuing layers of color with a gelatin film, and then lay transparent glazes of oil color over the underpaint, gaining translucency in the dark areas and brilliance in the highlights. Obviously, this procedure is much less flexible in allowing changes than the direct painting method, in which one simply scrapes off or overpaints anything one wishes to alter. To make a change using his new method, the glazes have to be dissolved and removed and the underpainting scraped out, repainted, and then reglazed. It is remarkable that such paintings as *McSorley's Saturday Night* (no. 108) and *A Roof in Chelsea* (no. 112) are as lively as they are when one considers the difficulty and meticulousness his technique involved. In fact, those paintings were worked on several times over a period of many years before they satisfied the artist.

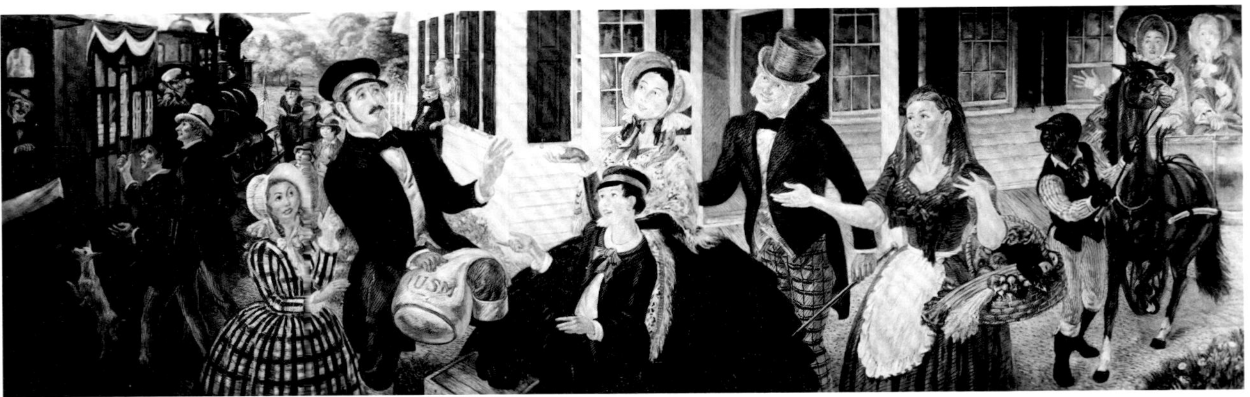

Fig. 8. The First Mail Arriving in Bronxville, 1846, 1939

United States Postal Service

Sloan's last ambitious work as an illustrator came in 1937 when he agreed to produce a set of sixteen etchings to illustrate a deluxe edition of Somerset Maugham's *Of Human Bondage* for the Limited Editions Club (nos. 110–1). The etchings, lively and intimate, show that Sloan's concept of the "bas genre" subject could be translated to a 1930's setting with as much vitality as the City Life set, or the even earlier de Kock illustrations.

In 1938 Sloan was commissioned by the federal government to paint a 5-by-16-foot-long mural for the post office in Bronxville, New York (fig. 8). It was by far the largest work Sloan ever painted and his first essay into decorative painting since his days as a newspaper illustrator in Philadelphia when he, among others, contributed some large scale decorations to the lecture hall of the Pennsylvania Academy of the Fine Arts. As befits a decorative painting, the mural used bright, rich colors and was simplified in form with little modeling to break the architectural plane with an illusion of three-dimensionality. Some of this effect was due, however, to Sloan's study of the work of the masters of the early Italian Renaissance, with their high-keyed colors, light use of chiaroscuro, and simplified planes, resulting in simple but monumental compositions and figures, as much as it was to the architectural purpose of the mural. This simplification and repose began to appear in some of his portraits and figure paintings of the 1940s and was consummated in his last great genre painting, *Monument in the Plaza* (no. 113), which shows citizens of Santa Fe, including the artist and his wife, circulating around the Civil War monument in the central plaza of Santa Fe with Della Francescan poise and dignity.

In 1951 Sloan's doctor advised him to avoid the thin air of Santa Fe because of the strain it put on his heart and, rather reluctantly, he agreed to spend the summer in Hanover, New Hampshire. He had friends in the area and a relative was president of Dartmouth College, which had exhibited and purchased his work in the past. The lush green foliage of a New England summer baffled Sloan as an artist for a short time, but he soon adapted to it and was painting again. He even began to think of building a house in Hanover. In August he was discovered to have a small operable cancer, but the operation proved too much for Sloan's strength, and he died on September 7, 1951.

Rowland Elzea

Color Plates

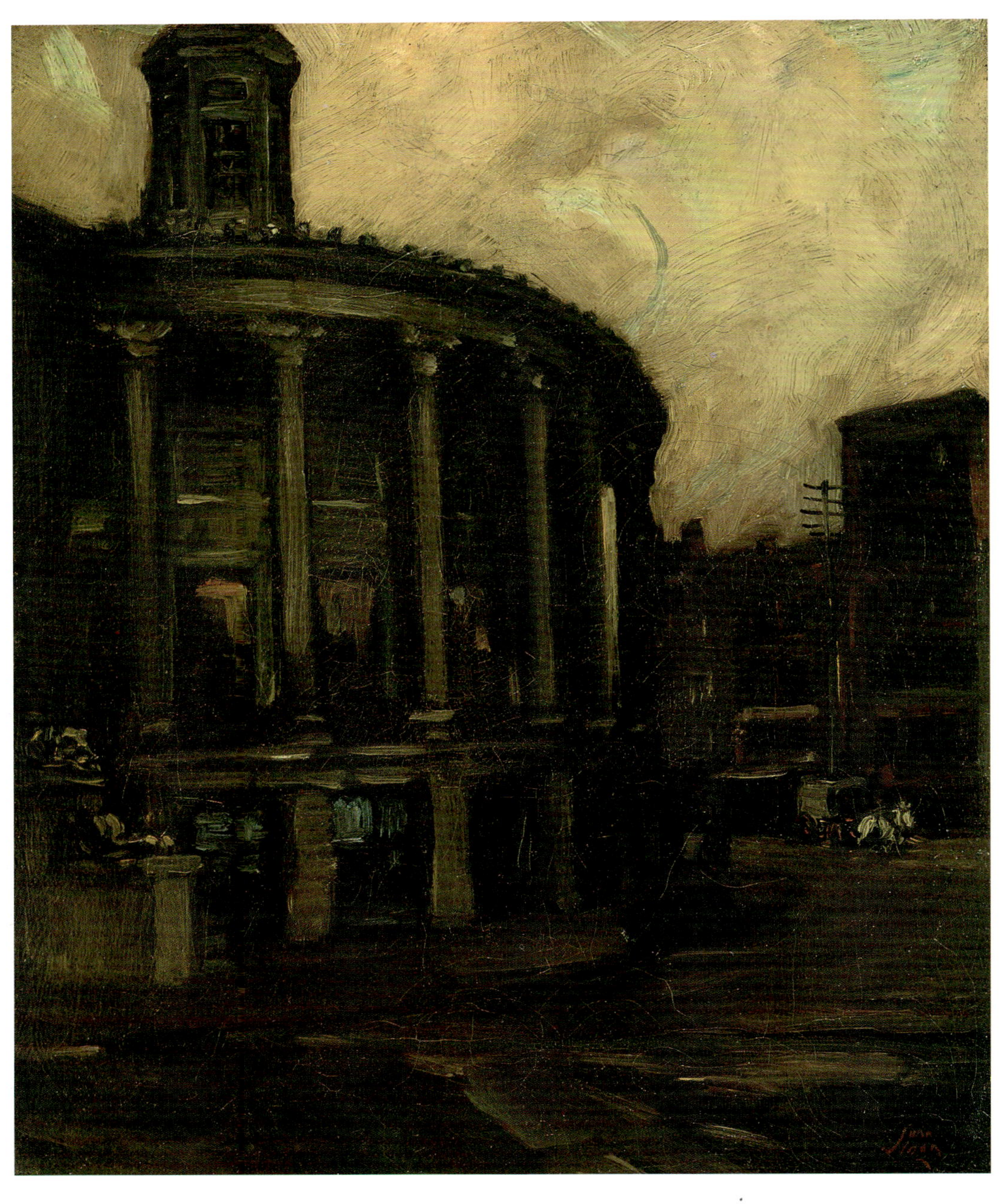

***Philadelphia Stock Exchange,* c. 1897–8**

Delaware Art Museum, Gift of Helen Farr Sloan, 1970 (no. 3)

Easter Eve, 1907

Collection of Deborah and Edward Shein (no. 36)

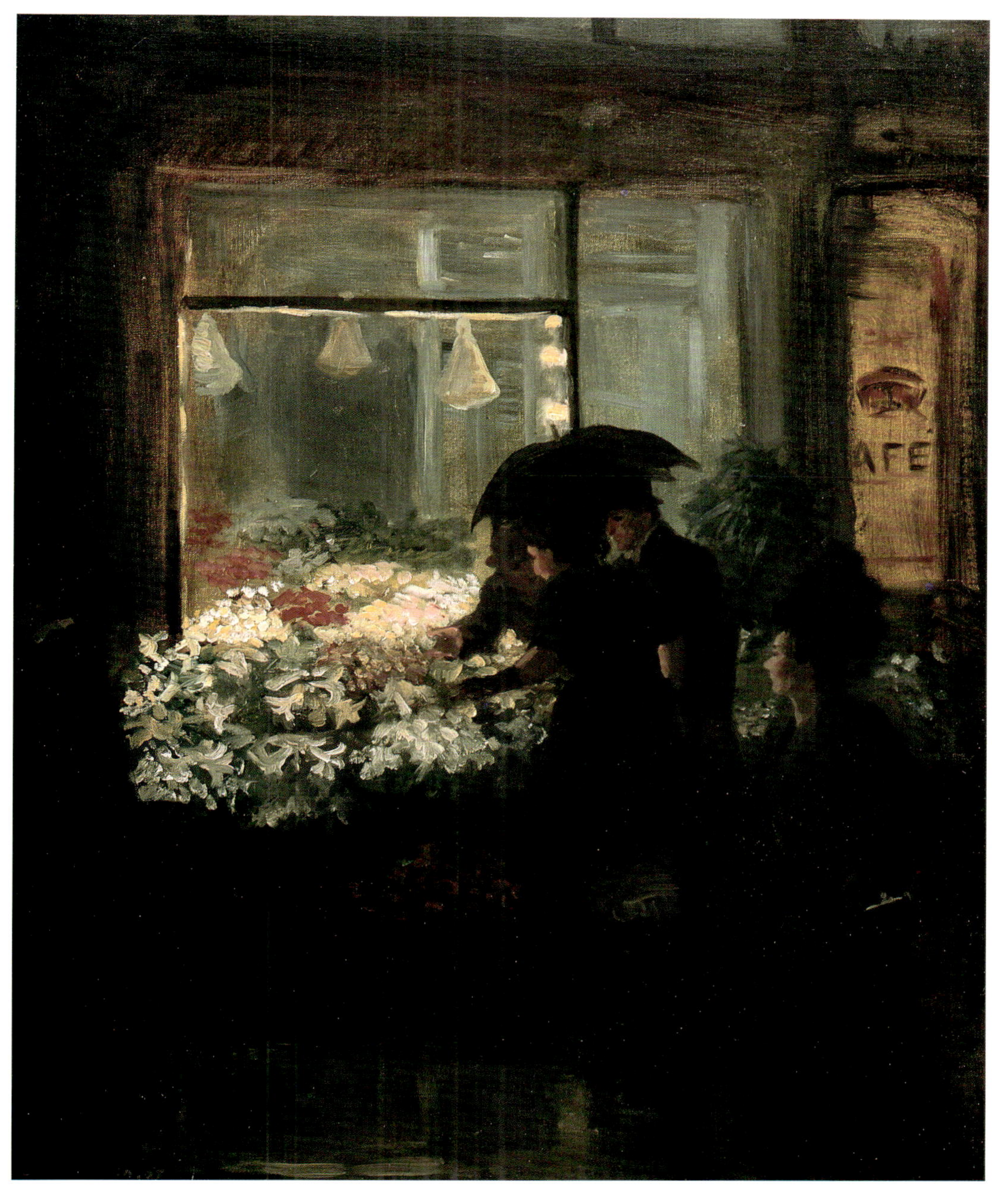

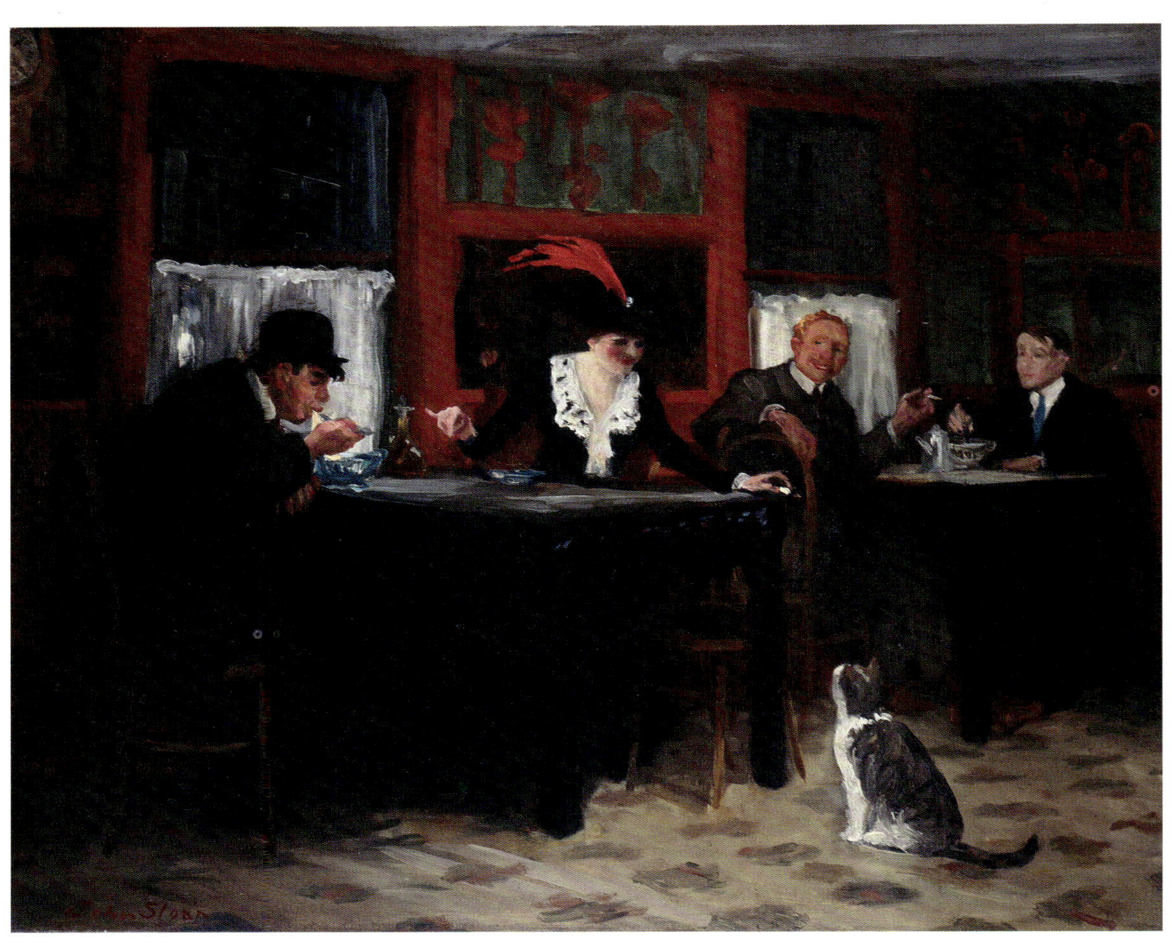

Chinese Restaurant, 1909

Memorial Art Gallery of the University of Rochester, Marion Stratton Gould Fund (no. 45)

Fifth Avenue, New York, 1909, 1911

Private Collection (no. 46)

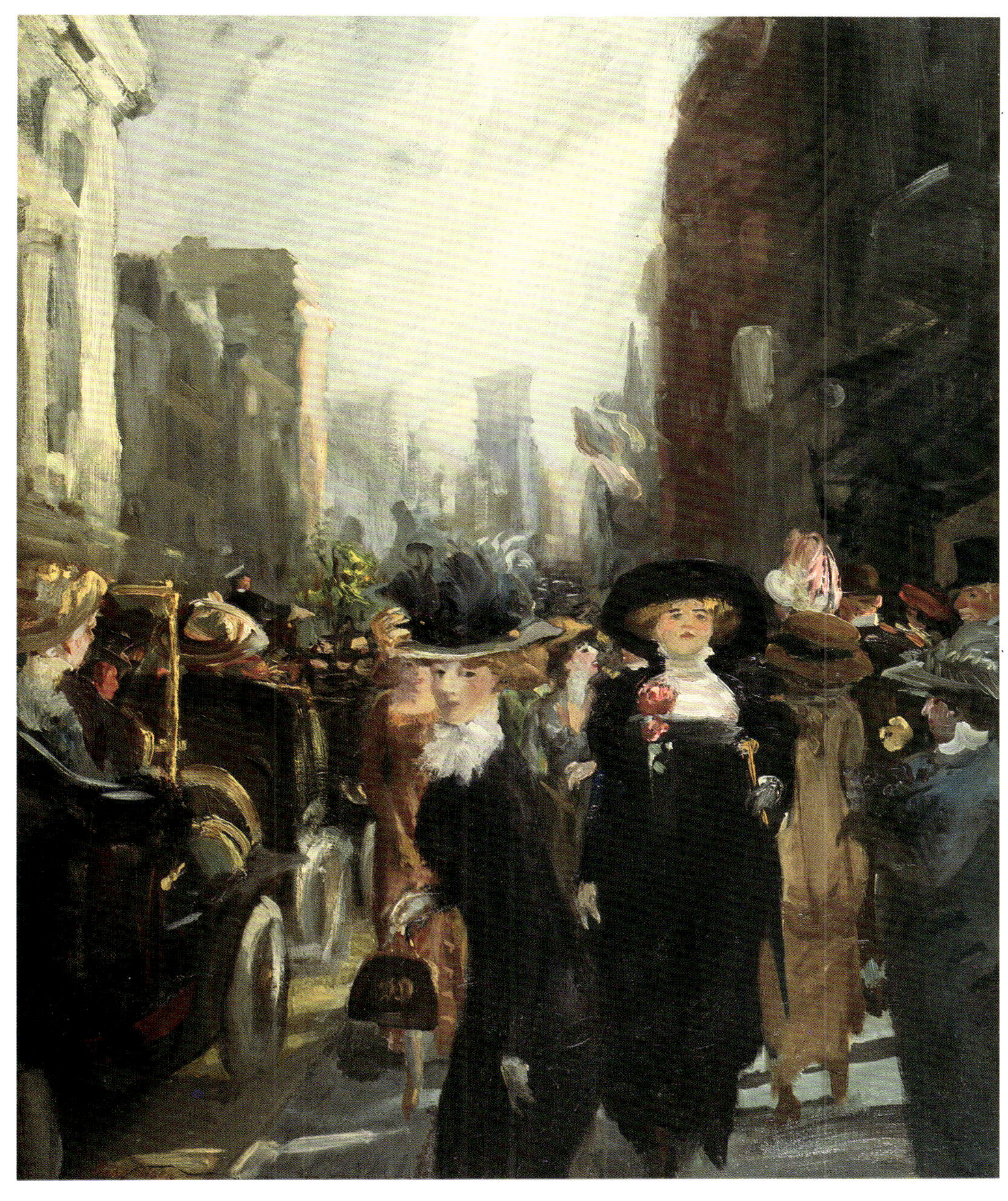

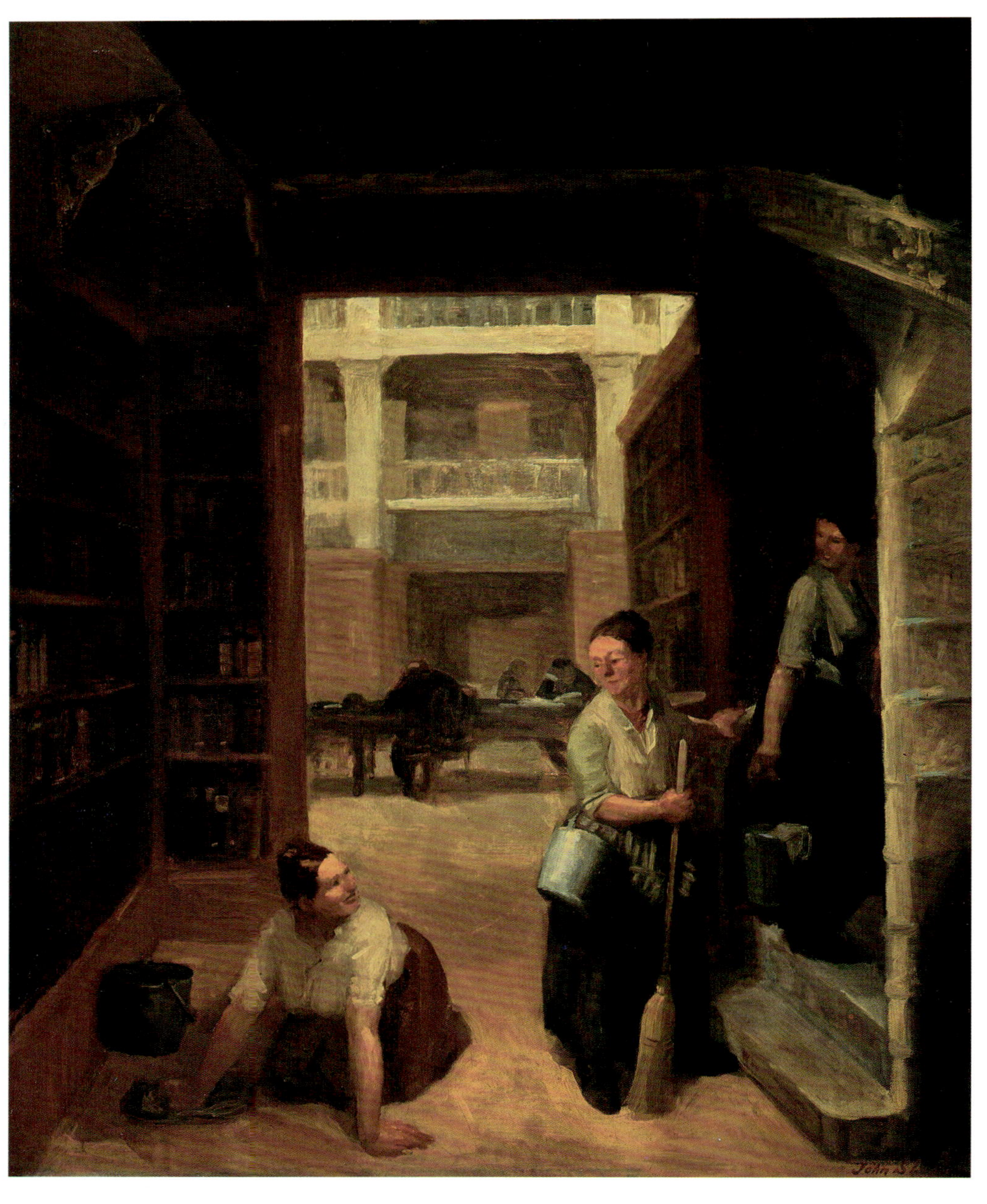

Scrubwomen, Astor Library, 1910–11

Munson-Williams-Proctor Institute
(no. 52)

Six O'Clock, Winter, 1912

The Phillips Collection, Washington, D.C. (no. 56)

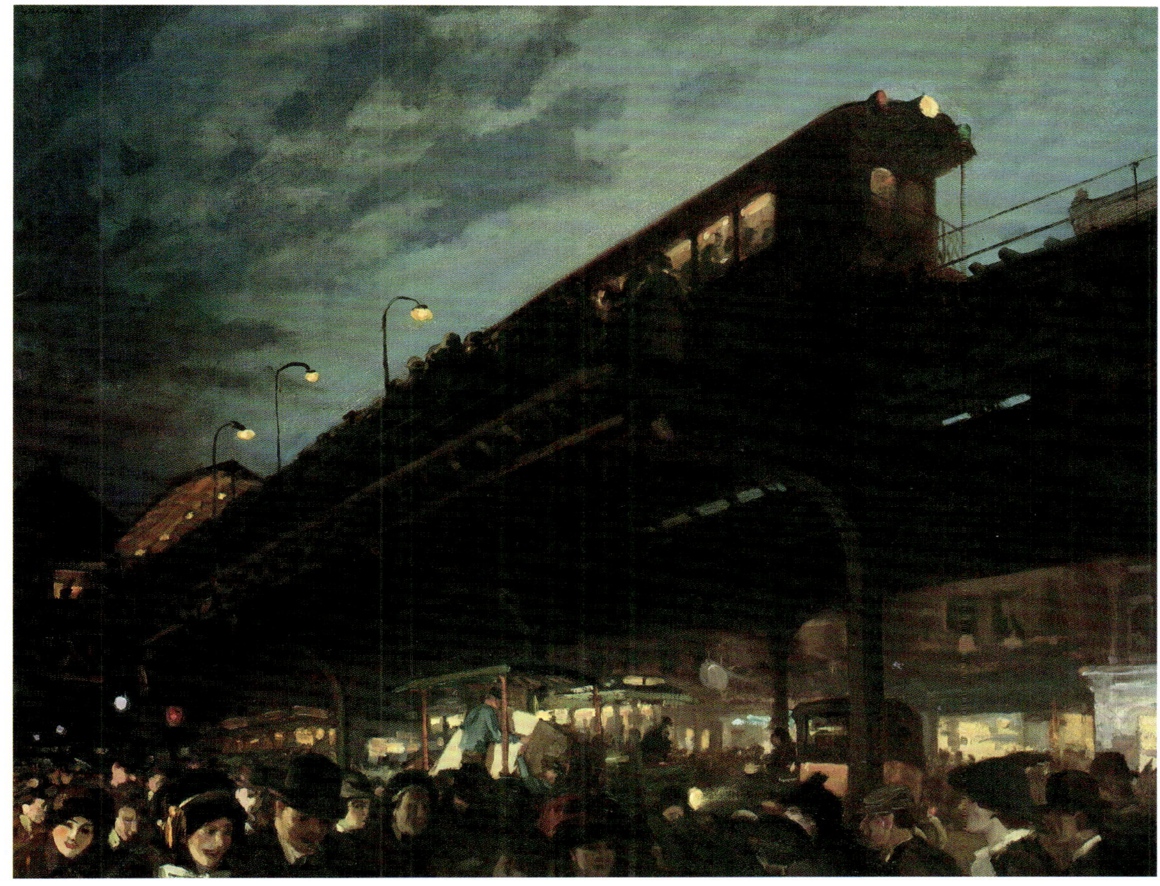

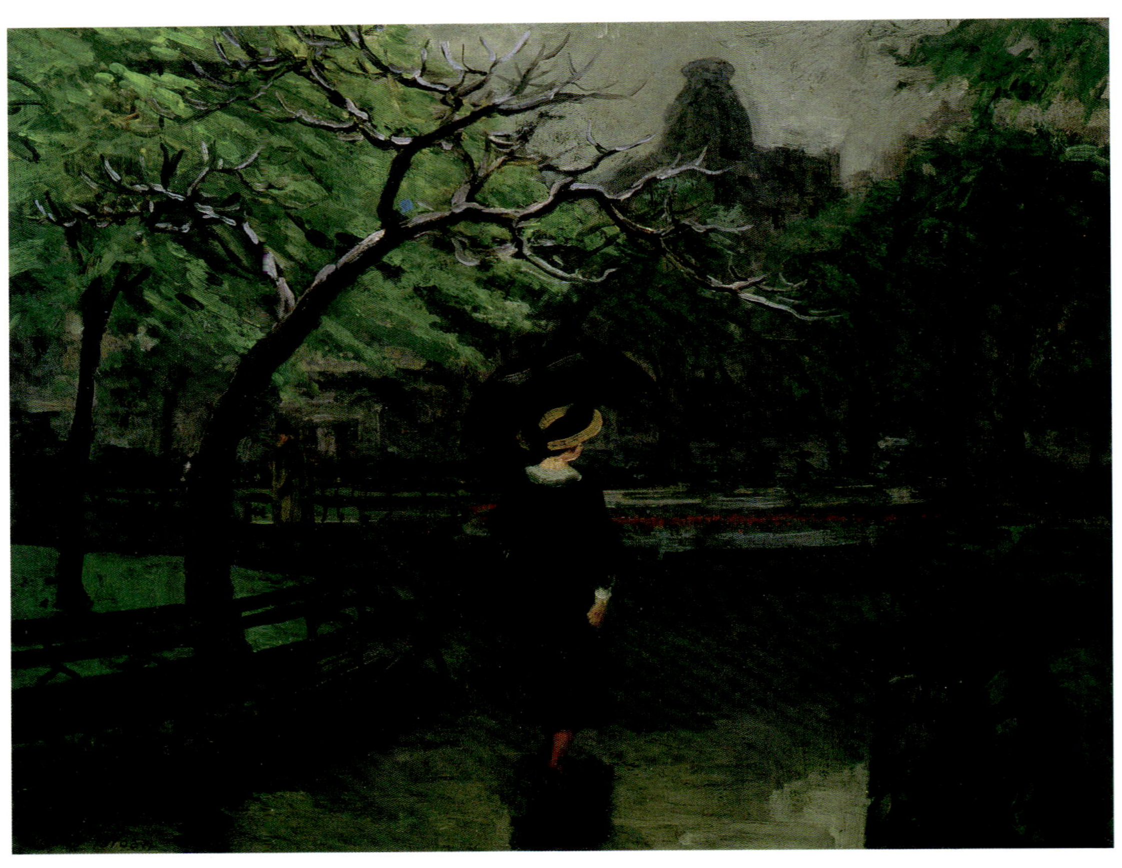

Spring Rain, 1912

Delaware Art Museum, Gift of the John Sloan Memorial Foundation, 1986 (no. 60)

Movies, 1913

Toledo Museum of Art, Museum Purchase Fund (no. 71)

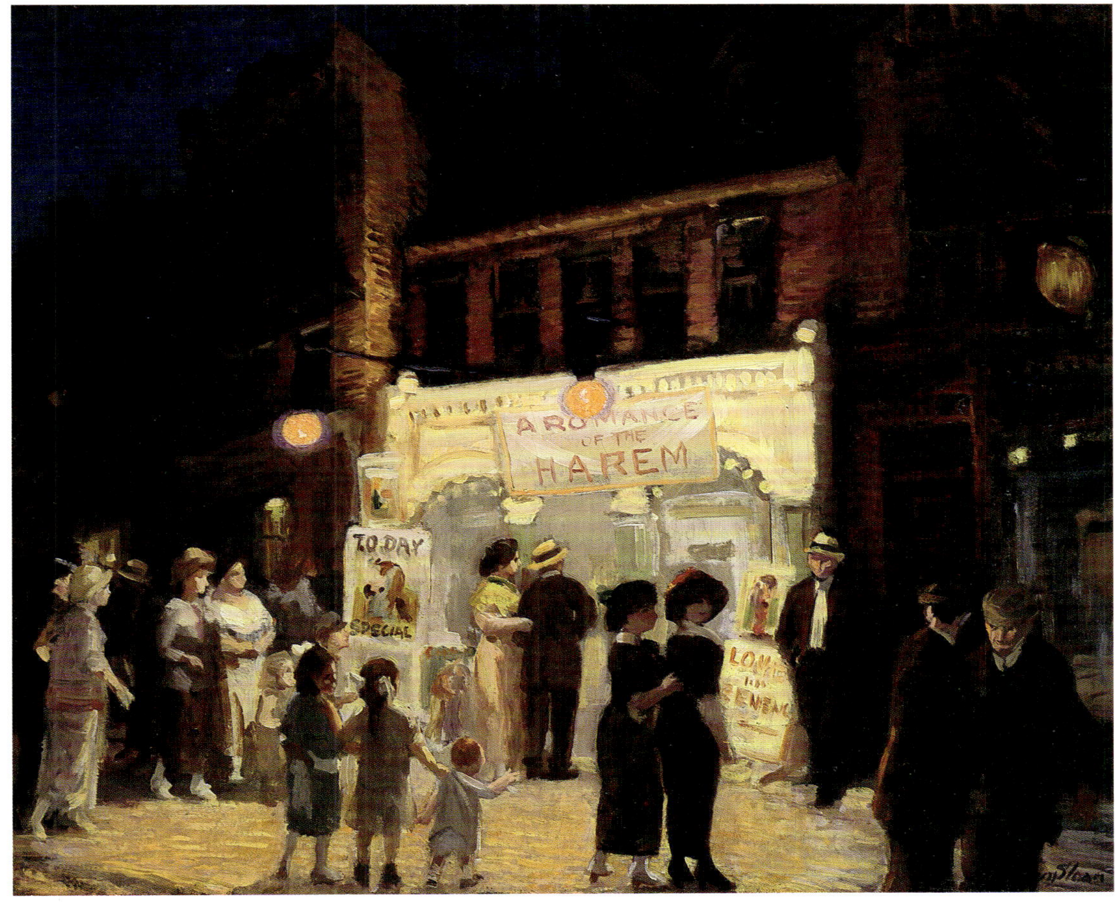

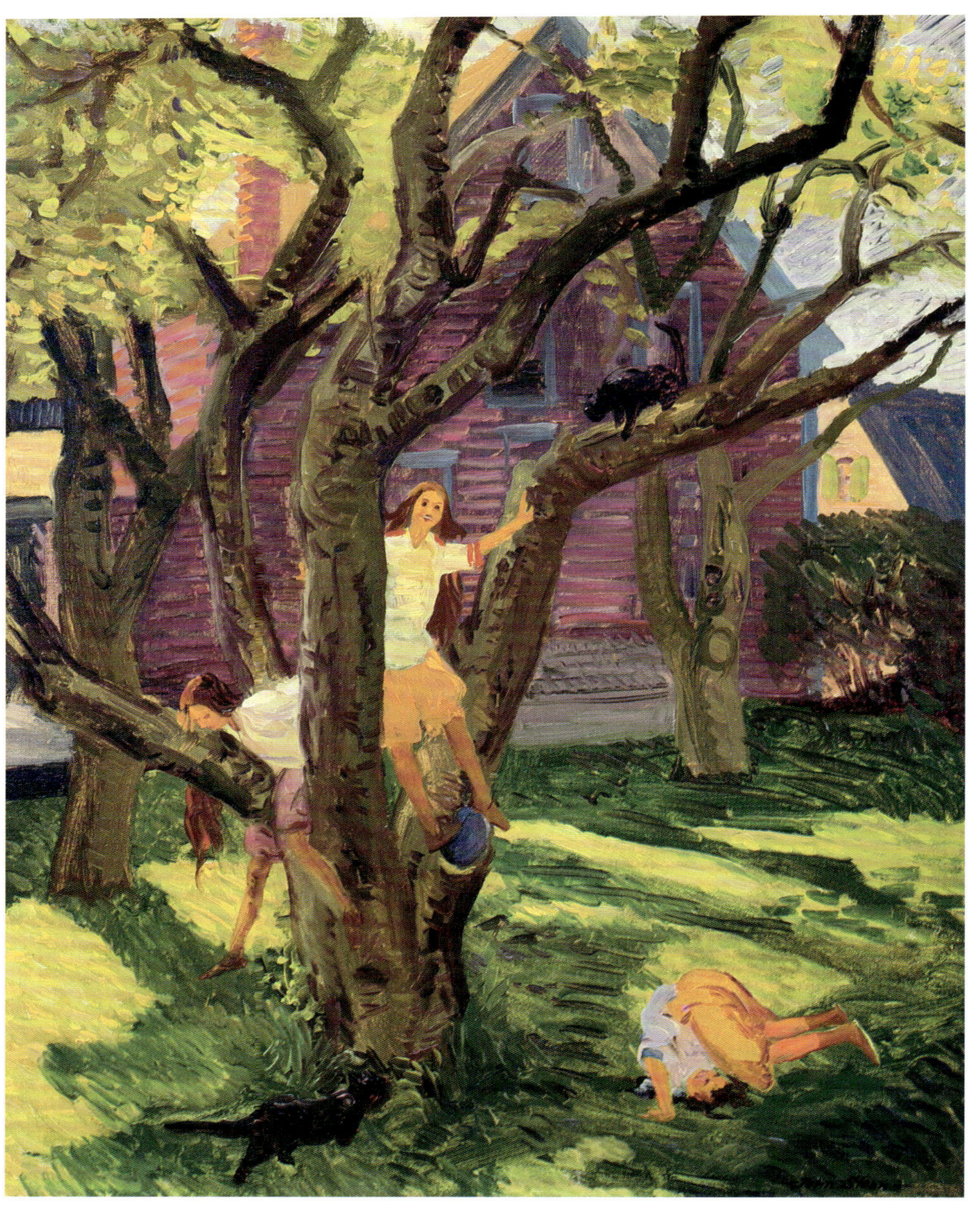

***Sally, Sarah and Sadie, Peter and Paul*, 1915**

Kraushaar Galleries, New York (no. 86)

Bleecker Street, Saturday Night, 1918

IBM Corporation, Armonk, New York
(no. 94)

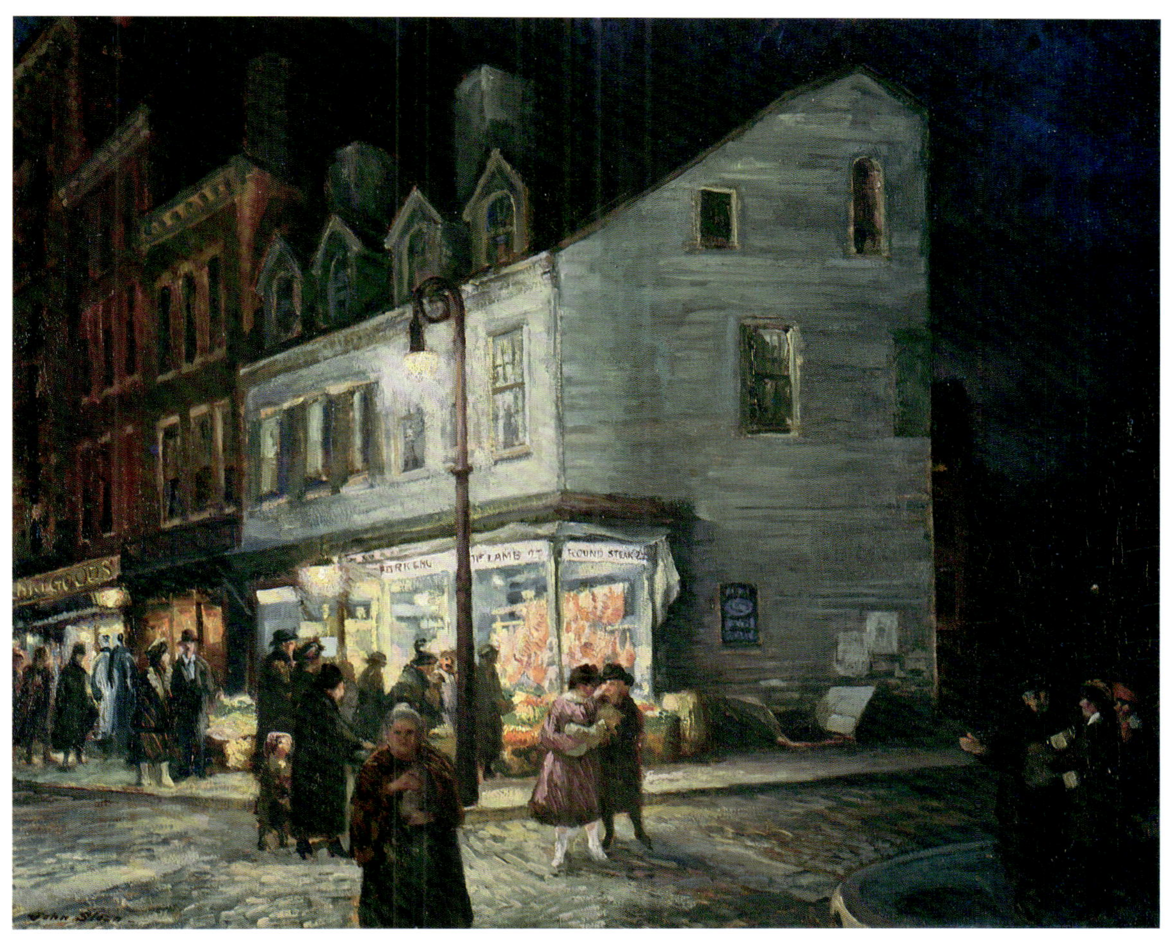

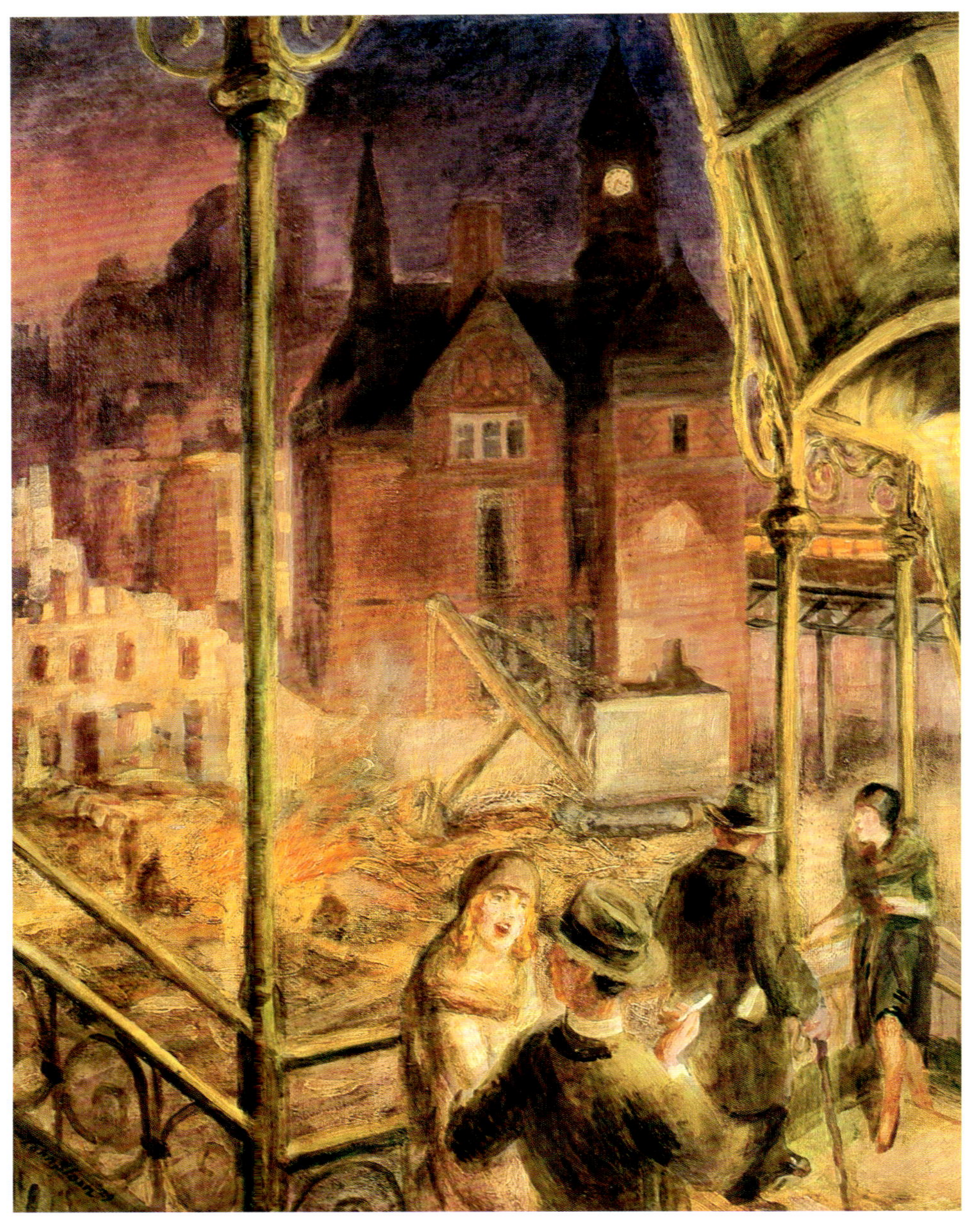

The Fall of the Village Bastille, 1929

Kraushaar Galleries, New York (no. 107)

Monument in the Plaza, 1948, 1949

Kraushaar Galleries, New York (no. 113)

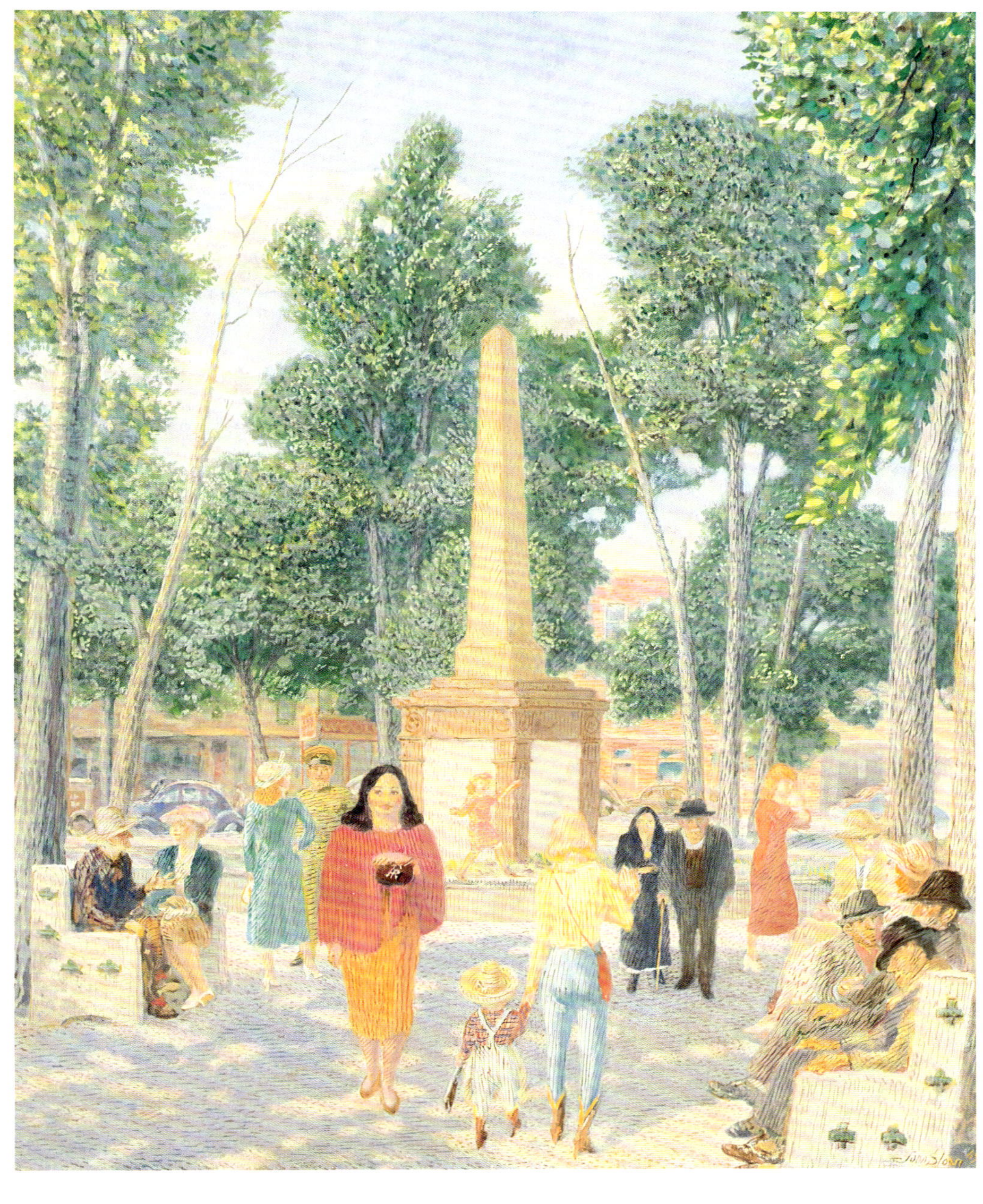

Catalog

Unless otherwise indicated, all quotations are published or unpublished statements by John Sloan. Measurements are given in inches with height preceding width.

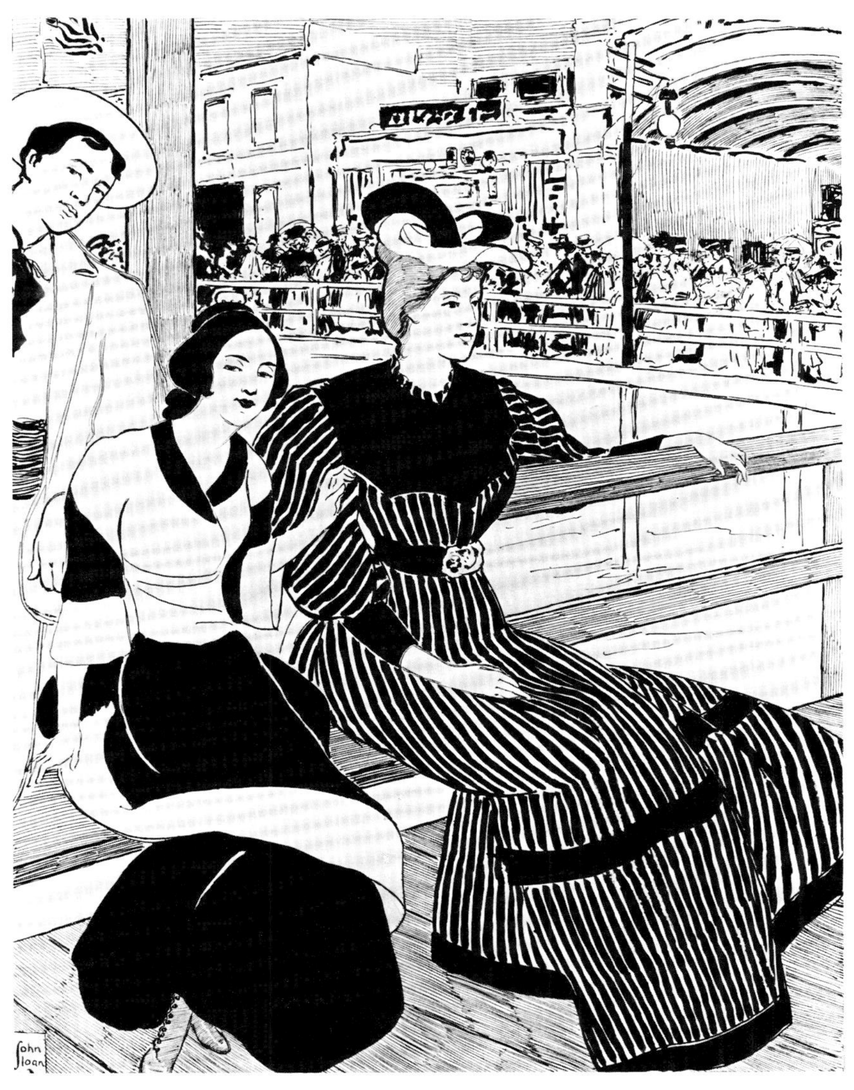

On the Pier, 1894
Ink and pencil on paper
13⅛ x 10⅛ in
Published in the Philadelphia *Inquirer* (Sunday supplement), July 22 and August 12, 1894
Lent by the Delaware Art Museum, Gift of Helen Farr Sloan, 1980

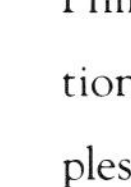

Sloan's poster style drawings for the Philadelphia *Inquirer* brought him national recognition in 1894 when examples were reproduced in the *Inland Printer* and the Chicago *Chap-Book*. This drawing was originally published in an article about Atlantic City in the newspaper's Sunday supplement.

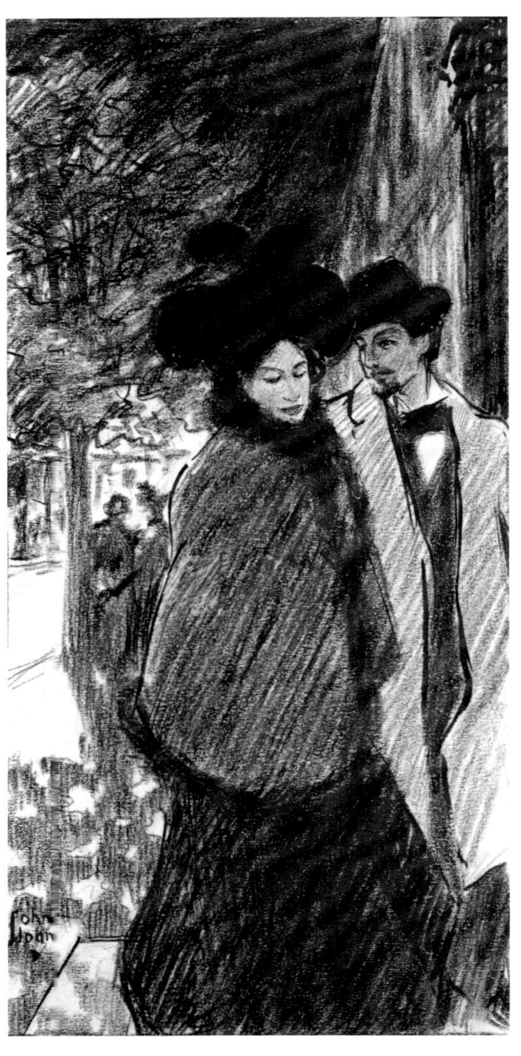

No Caption, 1895
Crayon and ink on paper
15⅞ x 8½ in
Published in *Gil Blas,* November 9, 1895, cover
Lent by the Delaware Art Museum, Gift of Helen Farr Sloan, 1981

2

This drawing accompanied the poem "Love's Kalendar" on the cover of a short-lived magazine *Gil Blas,* published in Philadelphia and modeled after the French illustrated monthly of the same name. Sloan knew the drawings of French artist Theophile Steinlen, whose covers often appeared on the French *Gil Blas.*

Philadelphia Stock Exchange,* *c. 1897–8
Oil on canvas
16 x 13 in
Lent by the Delaware Art Museum, Gift of Helen Farr Sloan, 1970

3 Figures tend to play a minor role in Sloan's early paintings of city subjects, of which this is the first. The earliest paintings are done in cool, low-keyed, almost monochromatic tones similar to those used at the time by his mentor, Robert Henri.

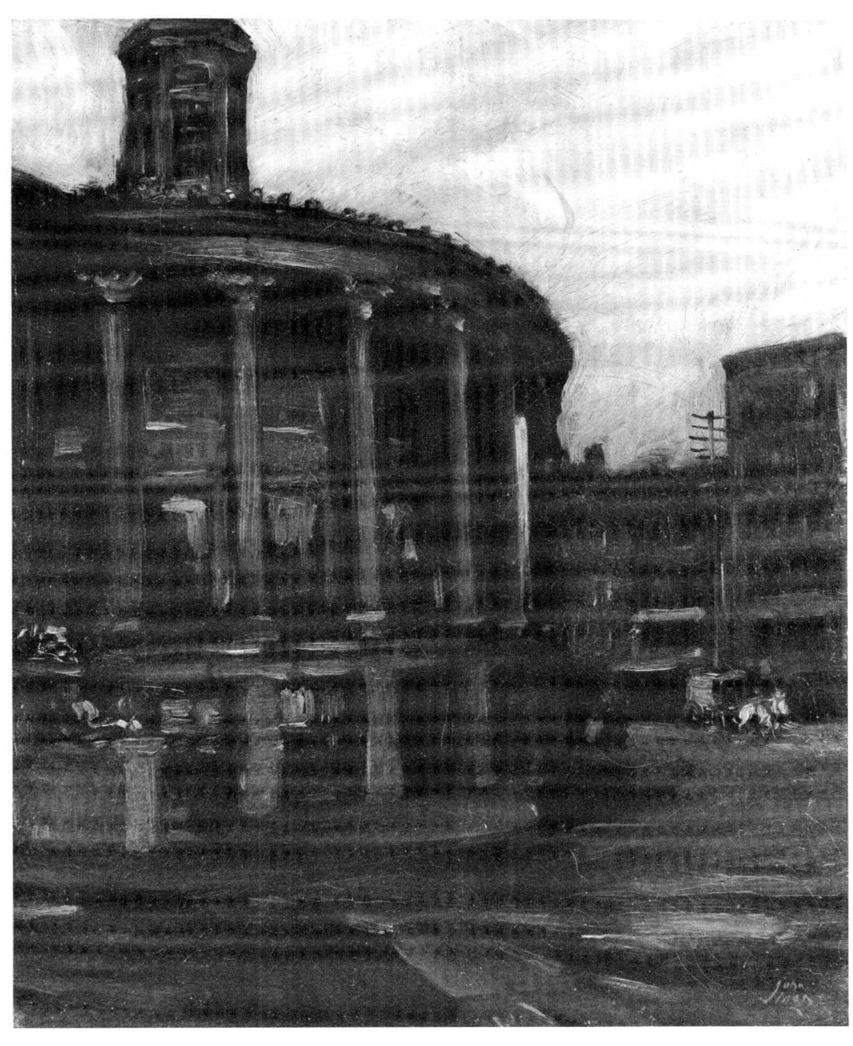

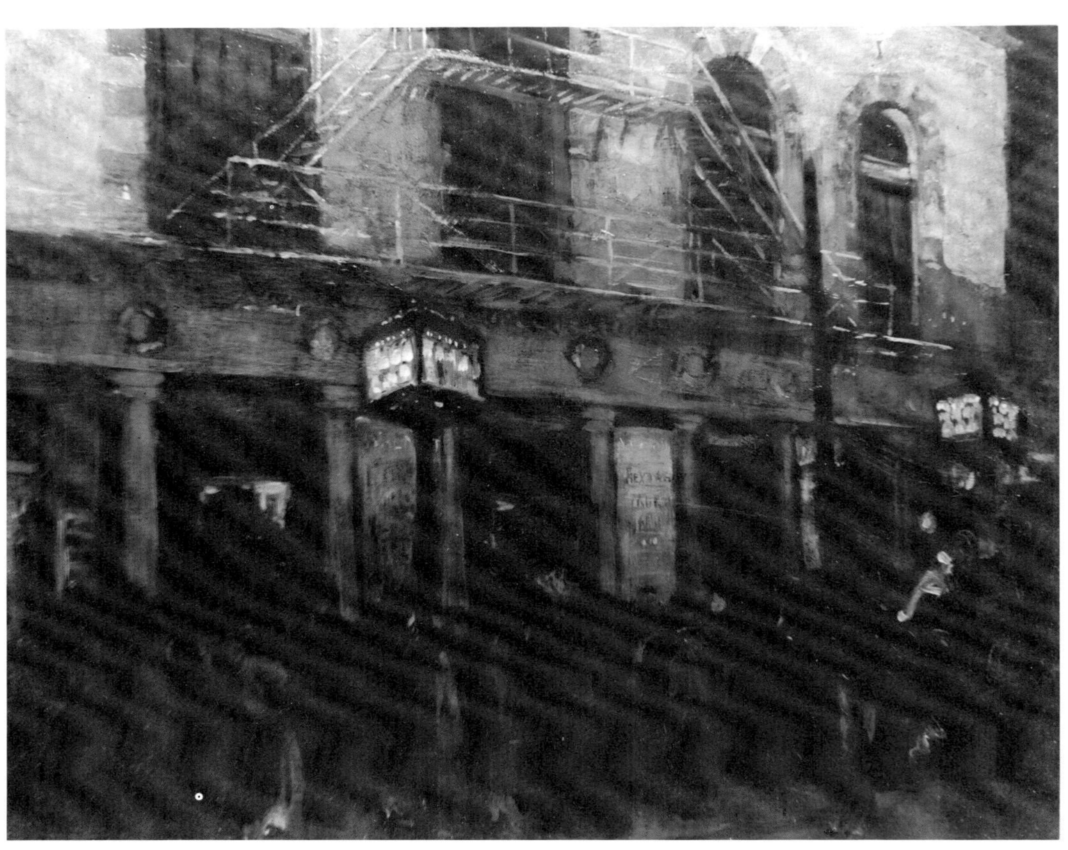

Walnut Street Theatre, Philadelphia, 1900
Oil on canvas
25⅛ x 32 in
Lent anonymously

4

This was the first of Sloan's paintings to be accepted in an important national competitive exhibition, that of the Art Institute of Chicago in 1900. Henri proudly called it "Sloan's debut in paint."

The Rathskeller, 1901
Oil on canvas
35½ x 27¼ in
Lent by the Cleveland Museum of Art, Gift of the Hanna Fund

Human interaction, so evident in Sloan's later genre paintings, is portrayed here for the first time. Sloan observed: "The divided attention noticeable in the young lady with a beer escort whose lonely neighbor is buying champagne, is a symptom that may be observed today."

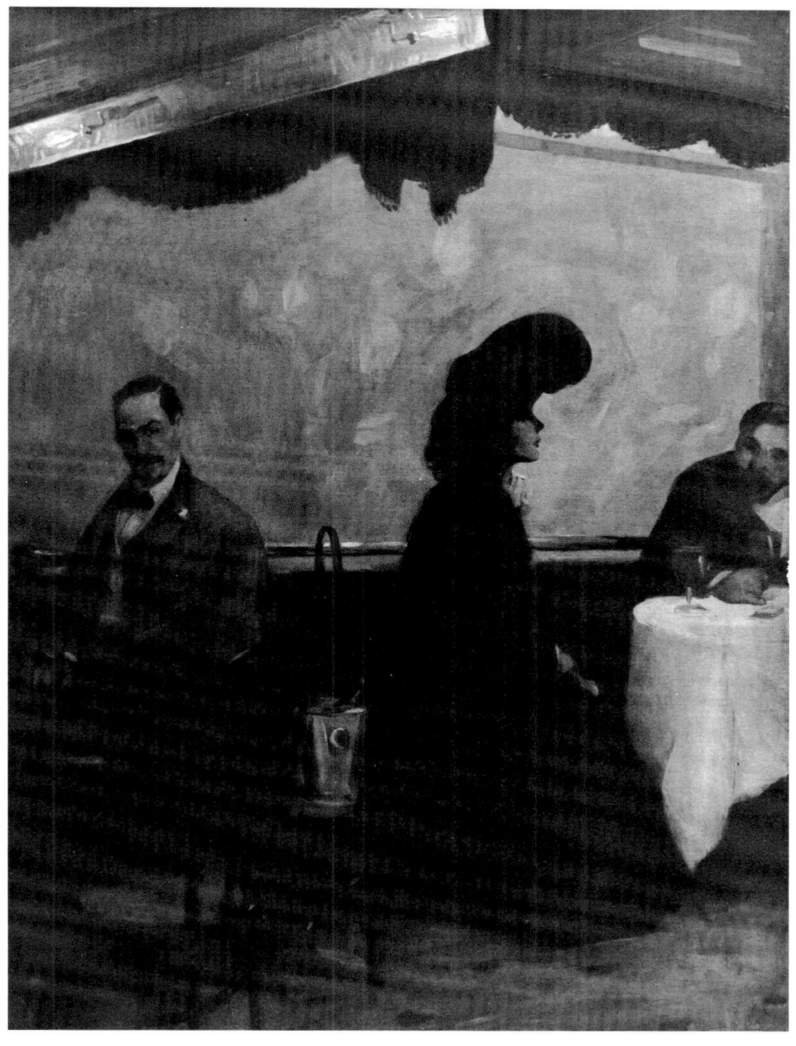

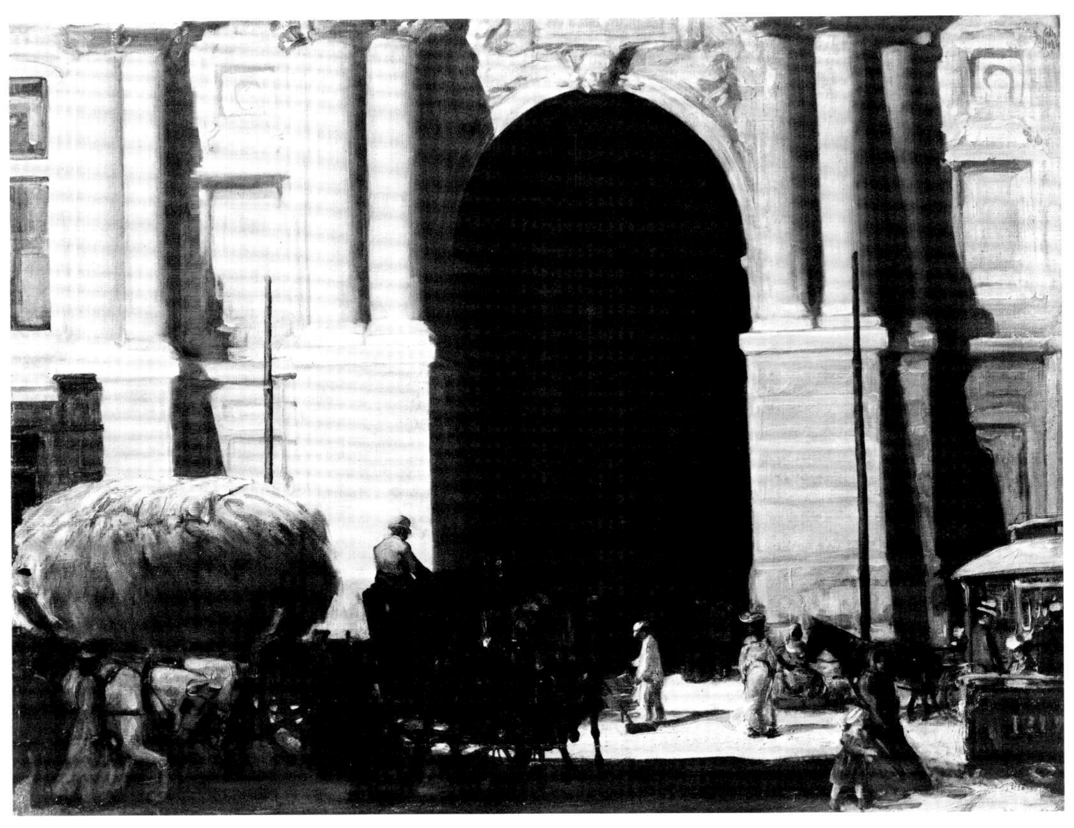

East Entrance, City Hall, Philadelphia, 1901
Oil on canvas
27¼ x 36 in
Lent by the Columbus Museum of Art, Ohio; Museum Purchase, Howald Fund, 1960

"**I** never did any fumbling student work before starting the city pictures. After all, there had been ten years of illustrating before I started, and we were working with very limited palettes, so there was little trouble to get into as far as color was concerned."

***No Caption*, 1903**
Crayon and pencil on illustration board
25 x 19⅛ in
Published in John Kendrick Bangs, "The Genial Idiot," Philadelphia *Press*, 1903
Lent by the Delaware Art Museum, Gift of Helen Farr Sloan, 1980

Sloan did a series of ambitious realist drawings to illustrate John Kendrick Bang's humorous story "The Genial Idiot," in which an eccentric bachelor gives advice on various subjects at mealtime in his boarding house. The story, published in the Philadelphia *Press*, was a takeoff on Oliver Wendell Holmes' *The Autocrat of the Breakfast Table*.

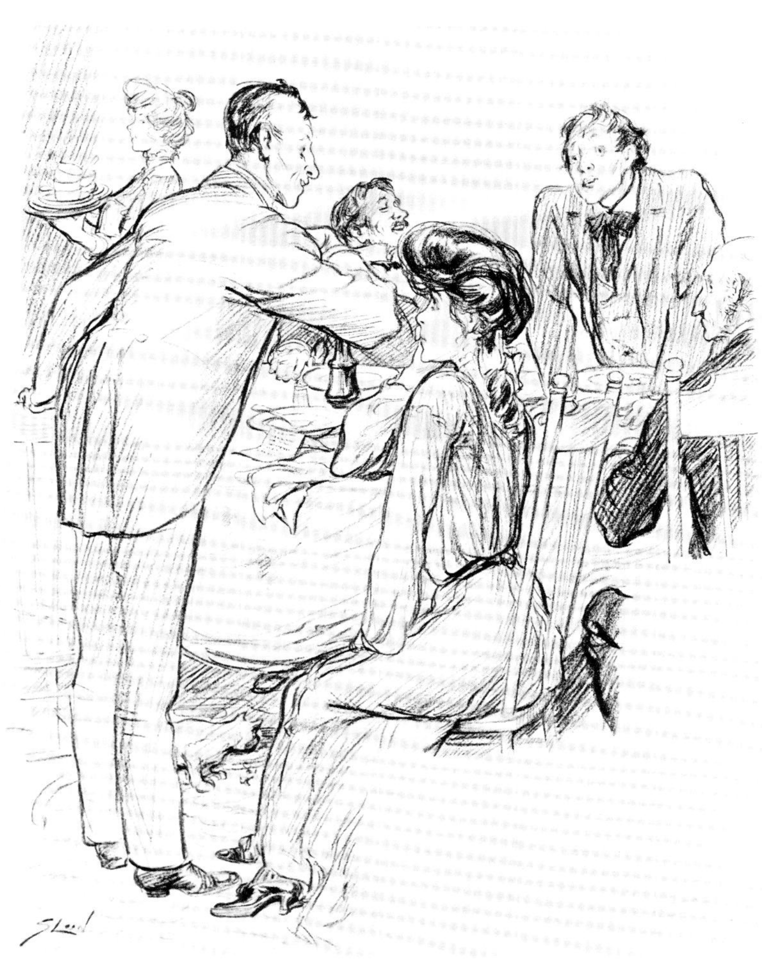

"Dan," she asked, "Phwat be ye doin' on the roof?", 1904
Crayon over pencil on illustration board
12¼ x 14¹³/16 in
Published in Ellis Parker Butler, "The Day on the Roof," *Century*, April 1904, p. 844
Lent by Mr. and Mrs. Draper Hill

In December 1903, Sloan moved to New York to work as a freelance magazine illustrator. His first assignment from *Century Magazine* was this humorous story about a hot-tempered Irish immigrant who was always arguing with his neighbor. He climbed on the neighbor's roof to cut off that part allegedly on the Irishman's property.

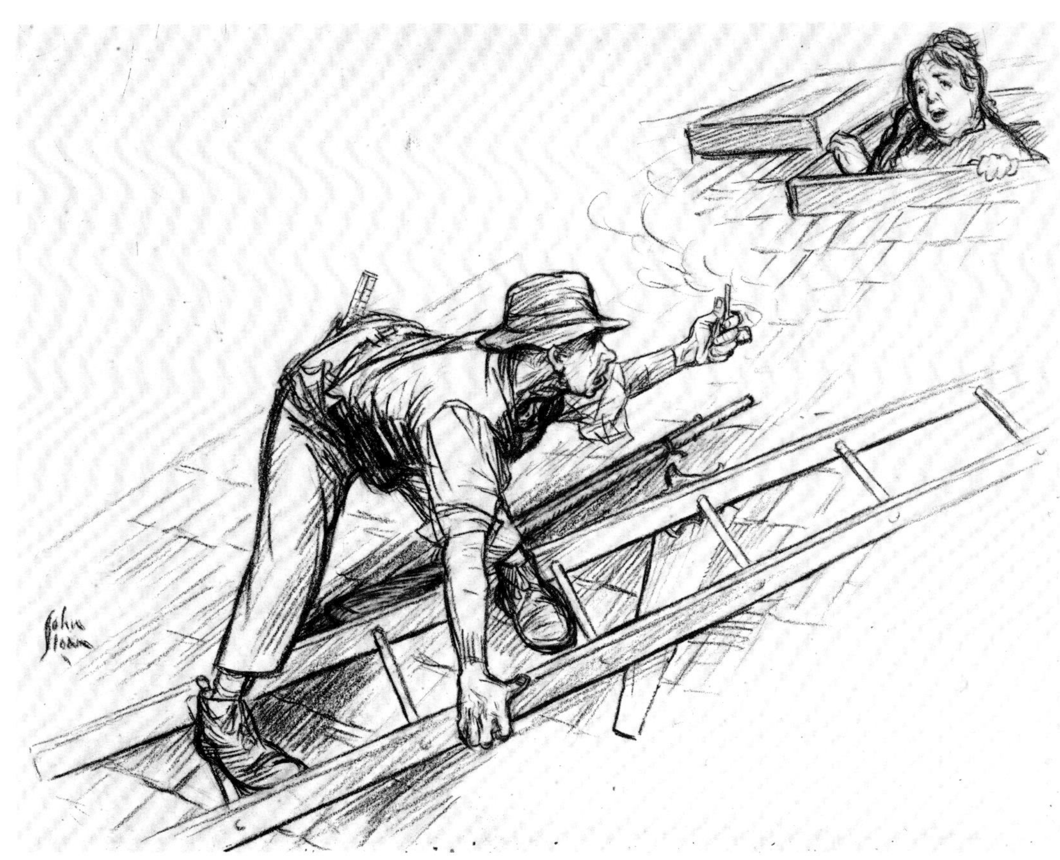

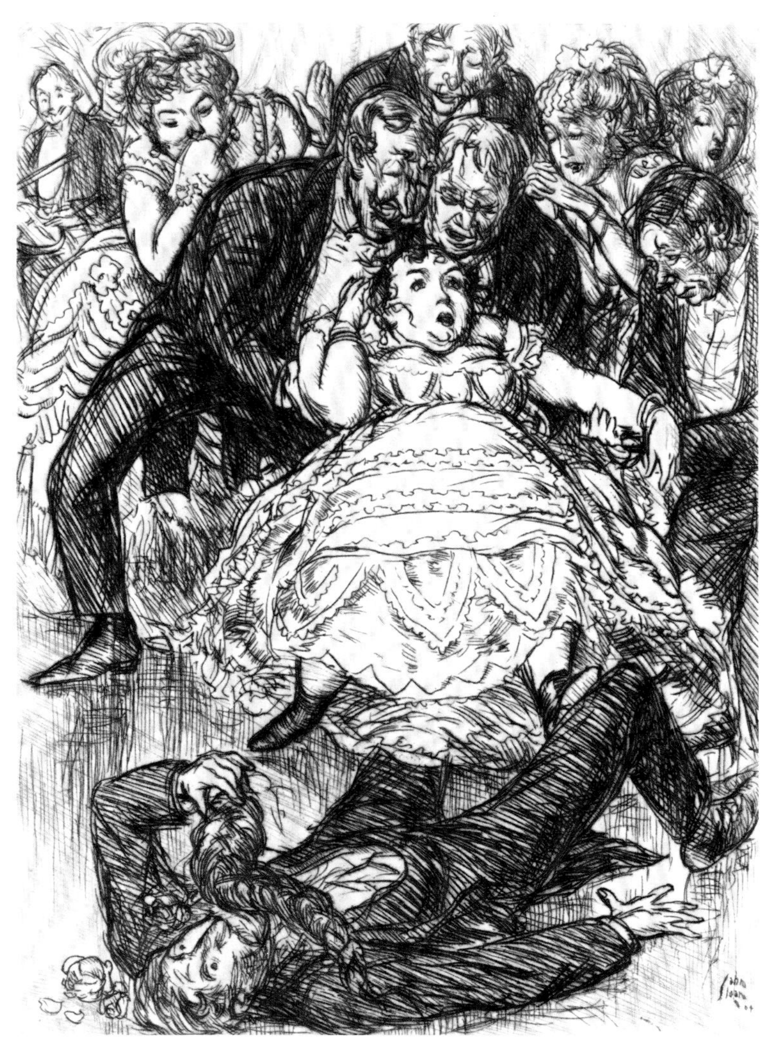

All the waltzers stopped, and hastened to pick up the fallen couple, 1904
Etching
5 x 3½ in
Published in Charles Paul de Kock, *Madame Pantalon* (Boston: Frederick J. Quinby Co., 1904), frontispiece
Lent by the Delaware Art Museum, Gift of Helen Farr Sloan, 1980

Sloan made 53 etchings and 54 drawings for a series of comic French novels by Charles Paul de Kock (1794-1871) published by Frederick J. Quinby Company in Boston from 1903 to 1905. In this frontispiece etching, a plump woman and her inebriated waltzing partner fall on the dance floor.

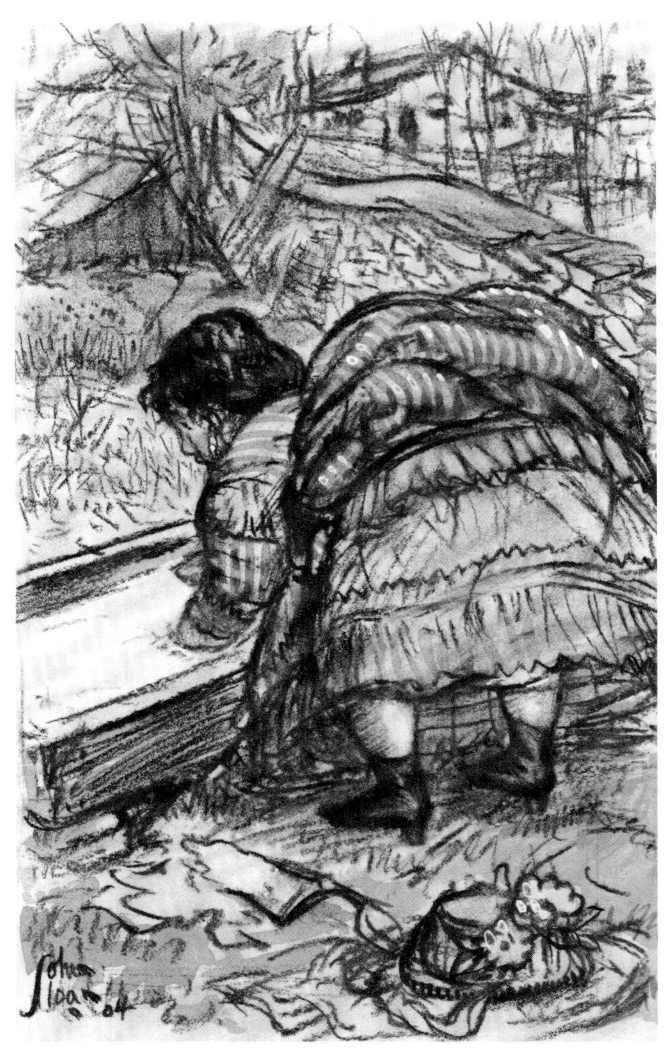

Madame Flambart left both her hands in the mortar, 1904
Crayon, wash, and gouache on paper
14 x 11 in
Published in Charles Paul de Kock, *Madam Pantalon* (Boston: Frederick J. Quinby Co., 1904), oppo. p. 168
Lent by the Delaware Art Museum, Gift of Helen Farr Sloan, 1980

10 In *Madame Pantalon*, a sort of "Taming of the Shrew" story, the women in effect wear the "pantaloons." Trying to do work generally done by men, Madame Flambart mixes cement only to get her hands stuck.

There, my little fellow, what do you think of this step?, 1904
Crayon and ink wash on paper
11⅛ x 15⅜ in
Published in Charles Paul de Kock, *André the Savoyard,* vol. I (Boston: Frederick J. Quinby Co., 1904), oppo. p. 194
Lent by the Delaware Art Museum, Special Purchase Fund, 1960

A young boy, André leaves his widowed mother to venture to Paris to find work. In one adventure, he meets the model Rossignol, who specializes in posing for torsos and cavorts about an artist's studio getting into trouble.

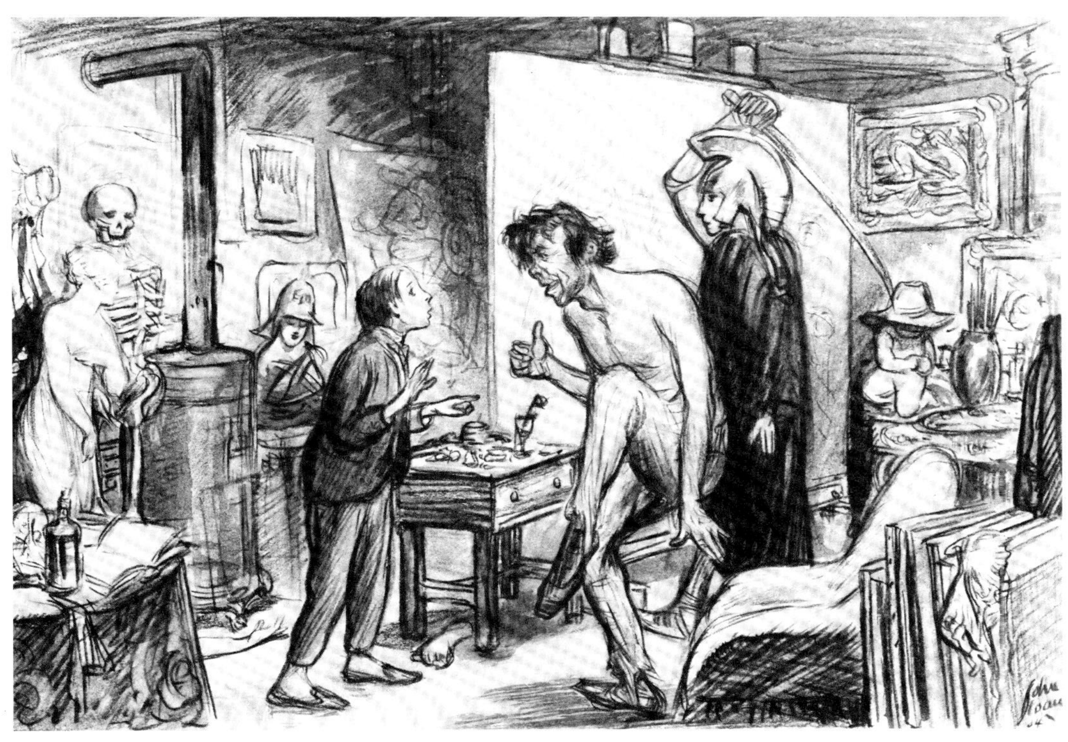

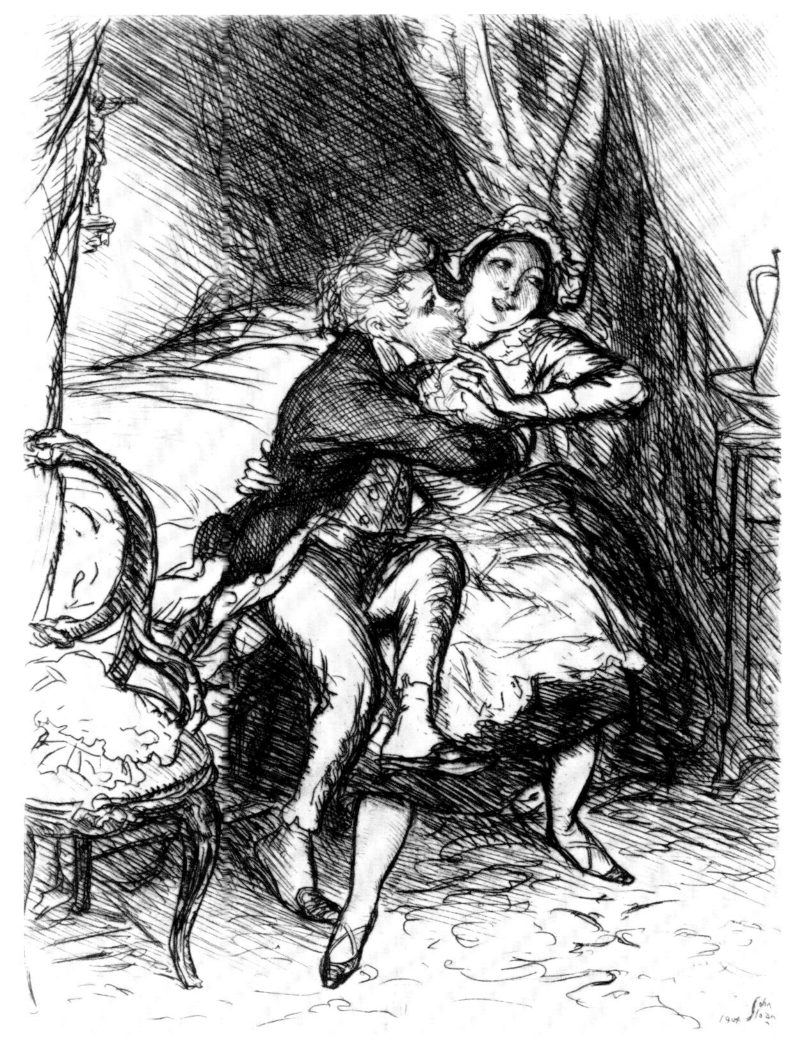

Ah, how pretty—kiss me—stay, I can say that quite readily, 1904
Etching
5½ x 3½ in
Published in Charles Paul de Kock, *André the Savoyard,* vol. II (Boston: Frederick J. Quinby Co., 1904), oppo. p. 26
Lent by the Delaware Art Museum, Gift of Helen Farr Sloan, 1980

The flirtatious French maid entices a young English jockey to her room under the pretense of teaching him French. Sloan made seven etchings and fifteen drawings for the two-volume novel *André the Savoyard.*

Rossignol did full justice to the repast... the corks flew and the bottles were emptied, 1904
Etching
3½ x 5½ in
Published in Charles Paul de Kock, *André the Savoyard,* vol. II (Boston: Frederick J. Quinby Co., 1904), oppo. p. 162
Lent by the Delaware Art Museum, Gift of Helen Farr Sloan, 1980

Rossignol, an artist's model, leads a dissolute life. He and his new friend Pierre drink and dine in excess. "Rossignol threw the dirty plates on a handsome sofa and rolled the bottles on the floor. Pierre...was fast losing all consciousness" (p. 162).

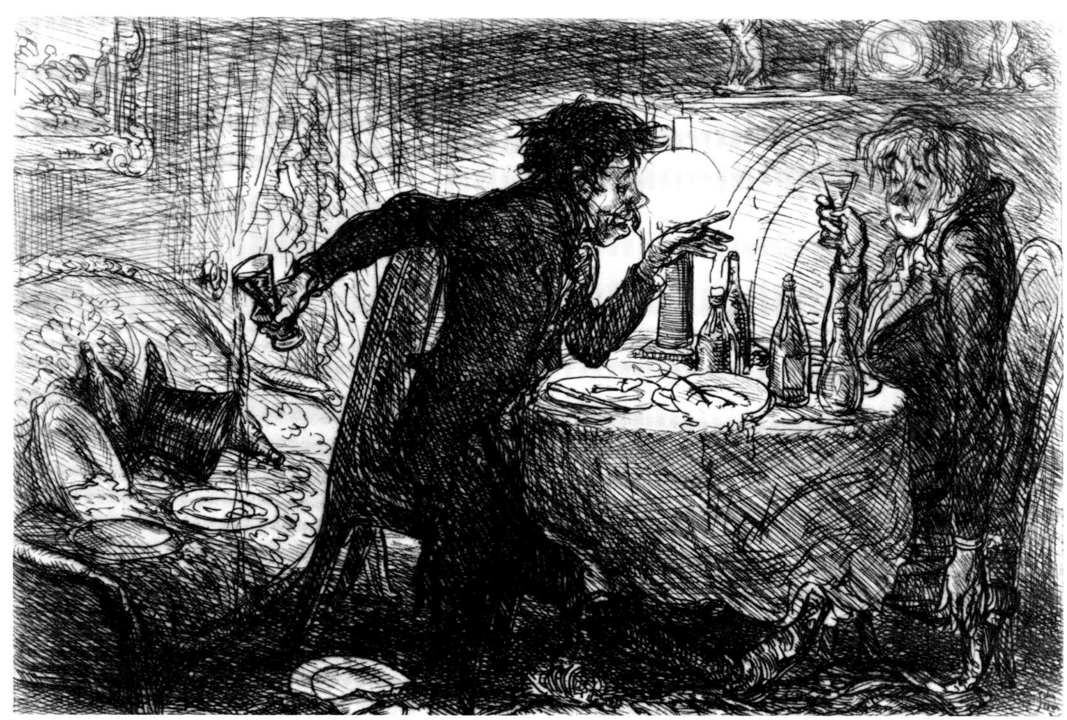

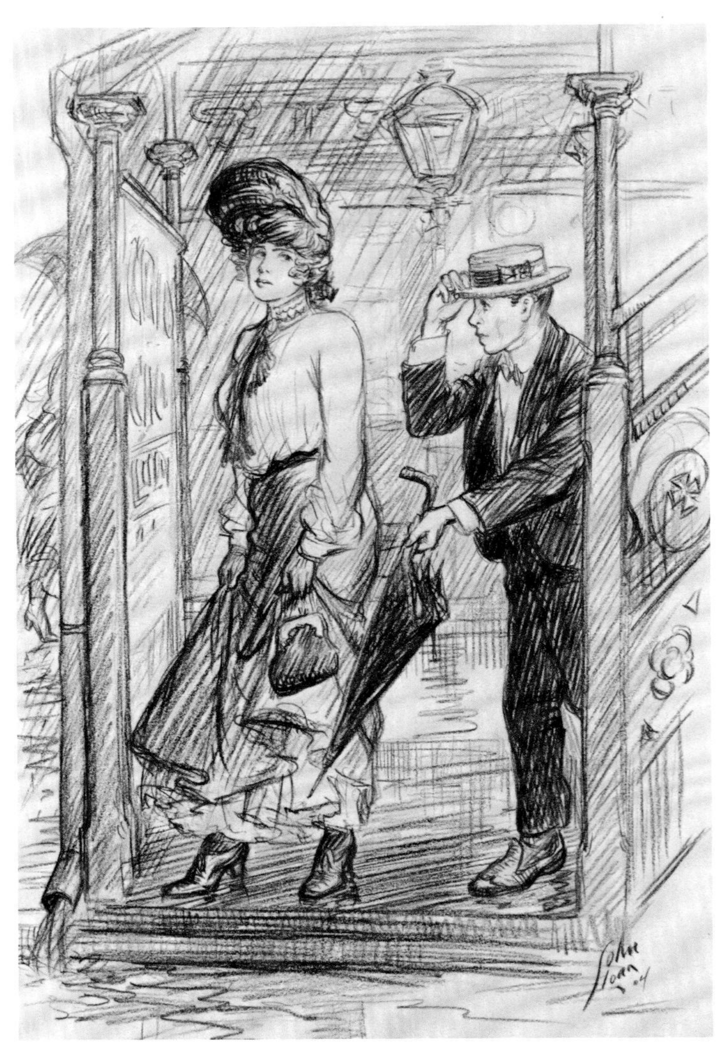

***Don't you want—th' umbrella?*, 1904**
Crayon on illustration board
19⅜ x 14⅞ in
Published in Harvey J. O'Higgins, "The Steady," *McClure's*, August 1905, p. 400
Lent by the Delaware Art Museum, Gift of Helen Farr Sloan, 1980

In the early 1900s, *McClure's* gained popularity for muckraking articles about corrupt politicians and businessmen. However, they also published poetry and short fiction. Harvey J. O'Higgins (1876–1929), a Canadian-born novelist, specialized in short stores about Irish immigrants such as this piece about a shy young boy infatuated with a strapping Irish girl living in New York City.

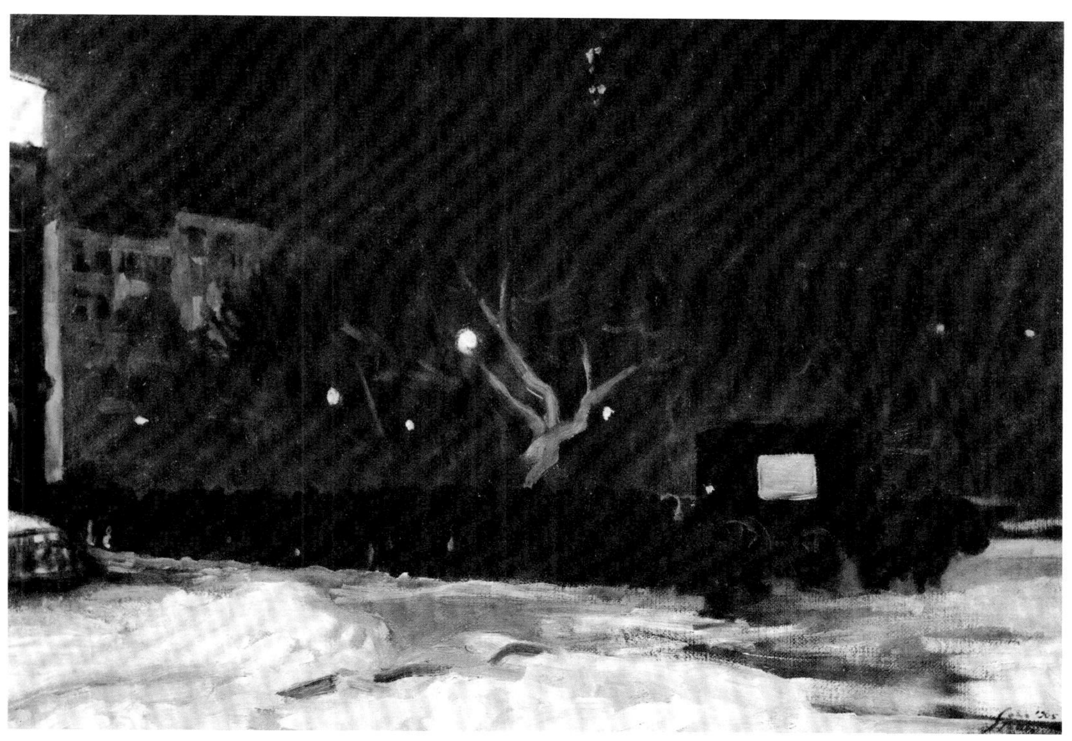

The Coffee Line, 1905
Oil on canvas
21½ x 31⅝ in
Lent by the Carnegie Museum of Art, Pittsburgh; Fellows of the Museum of Art Fund, 1983

One of the first paintings Sloan did after moving to New York in 1904, *The Coffee Line* shows a line of unemployed men waiting in the snow at Fifth Avenue and Madison Square for hot coffee that was being offered by one of the newspapers.

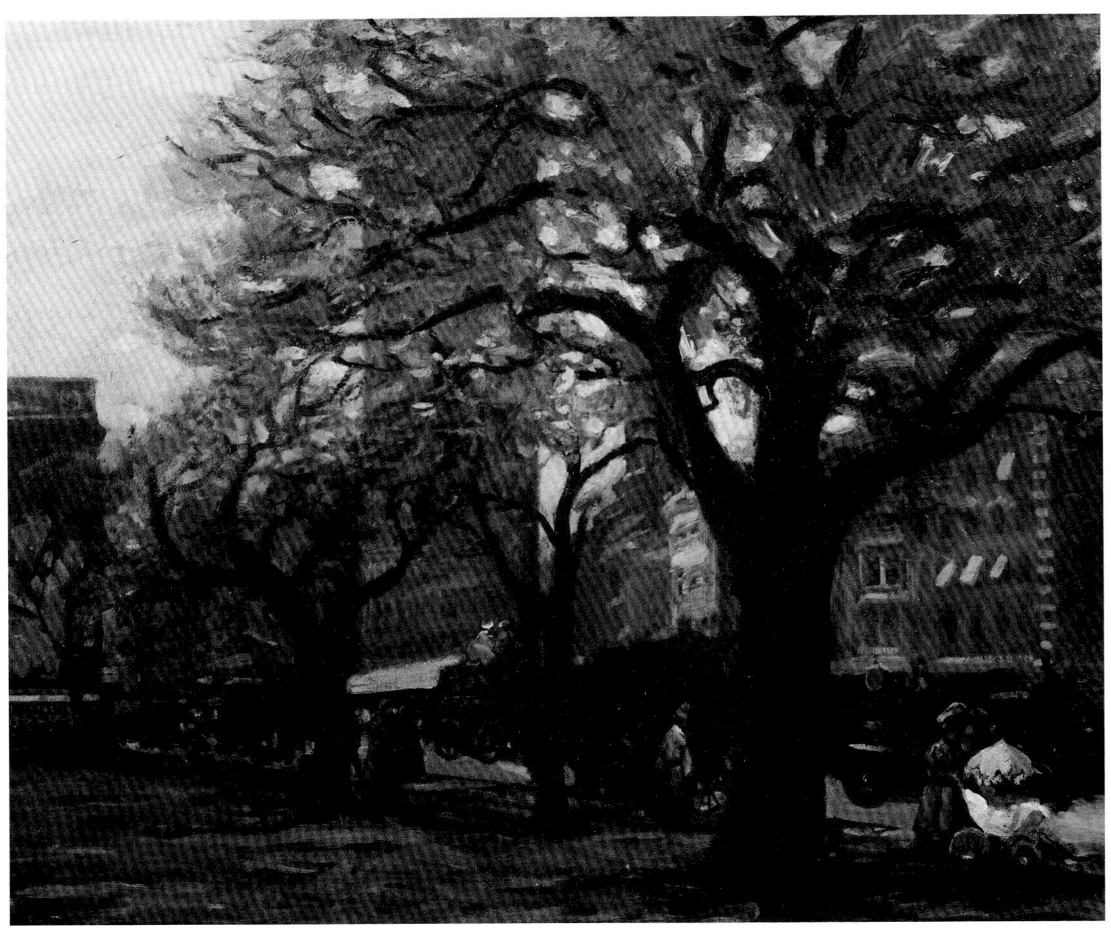

Spring, Madison Square, 1905–6
Oil on canvas
29½ x 35½ in
Lent by the Elvehjem Museum of Art, University of Wisconsin—Madison; Prof. Ruth Wallerstein Fund Purchase

16

"The Flatiron Building and the old Fifth Avenue Hotel are in the background. An old horse-drawn Fifth Avenue bus with one seat perched back of the driver on the roof, cabs and long skirts, and a nearby patch of grass with trees. All but the Flatiron Building, things of the past."

***When they turned a leaf their sleeves brushed or their hands touched* (also called *Their Hands Touched*), 1905**

Crayon on illustration board

11⅝ x 15⅞ in

Published in F. H. Lancaster, "An Eye for an Eye," *McClure's*, November 1905, p. 21

Lent by the Hood Museum of Art, Dartmouth College, Hanover, New Hampshire; Purchased through the Julia L. Whittier Fund

McClure's commissioned Sloan to illustrate two stories in 1905. He made five drawings for this "Romeo and Juliet"-type tale about a classroom romance that blossoms between a young son and daughter of two feuding French-Canadian families.

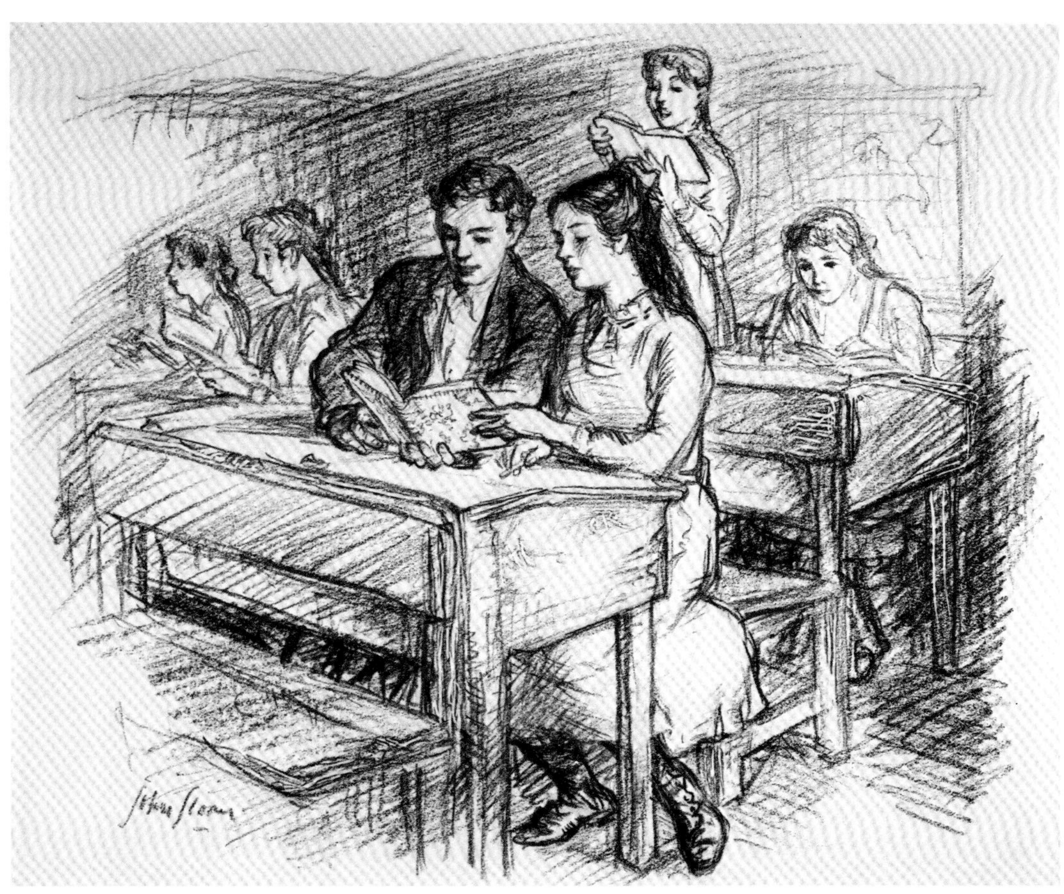

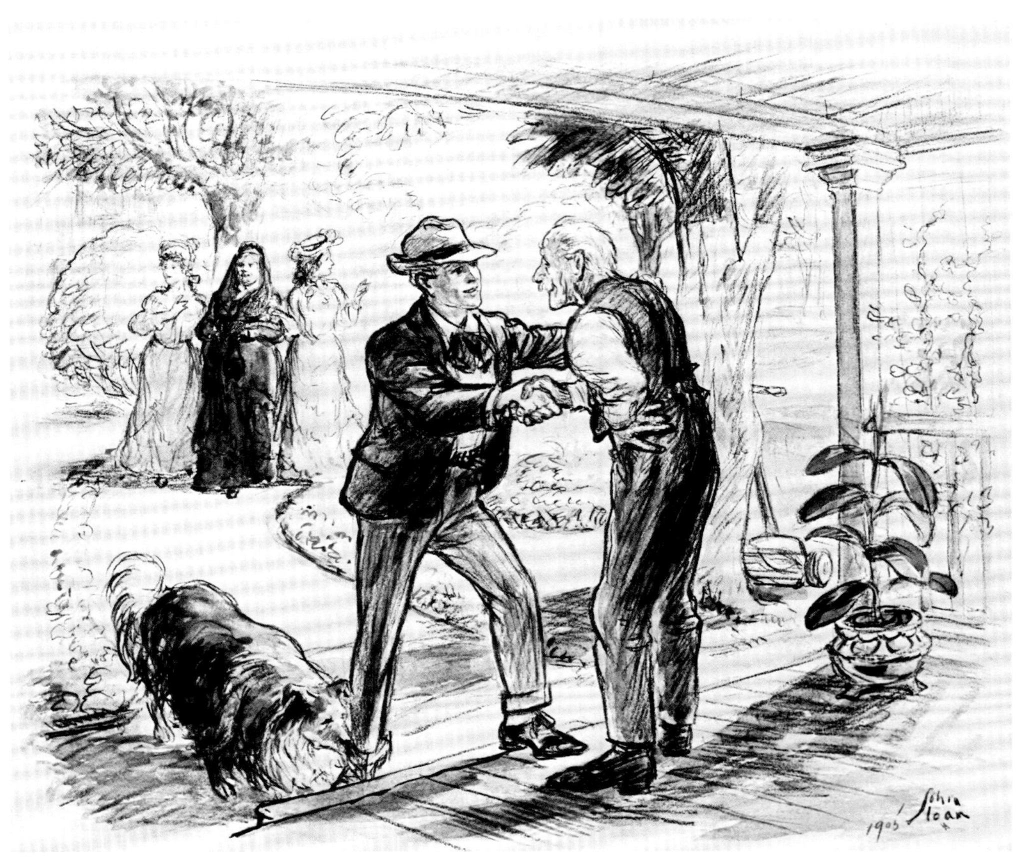

"Come in, come in," said Rixy, an old man's break in his voice, 1905
Crayon, ink, wash, and gouache on illustration board
15¼ x 18 in
Published in George S. Chappell, "The Education of King Jim," *Scribner's*, November 1905, p. 583
Lent by the Delaware Art Museum, Gift of Helen Farr Sloan, 1986

A young man returns to a farm he visited as a child, only to be disappointed by changes that have taken place.

Connoisseurs of Prints, 1905
Etching
4½ x 6¾ in
Lent by the Delaware Art Museum, Gift of Helen Farr Sloan, 1963

In 1905 Sloan planned a series of prints on the subject of connoisseurs, but it was never completed. Instead, this subject, seen in the old American Art Galleries on 23rd Street, became the first of the New York City Life series of prints.

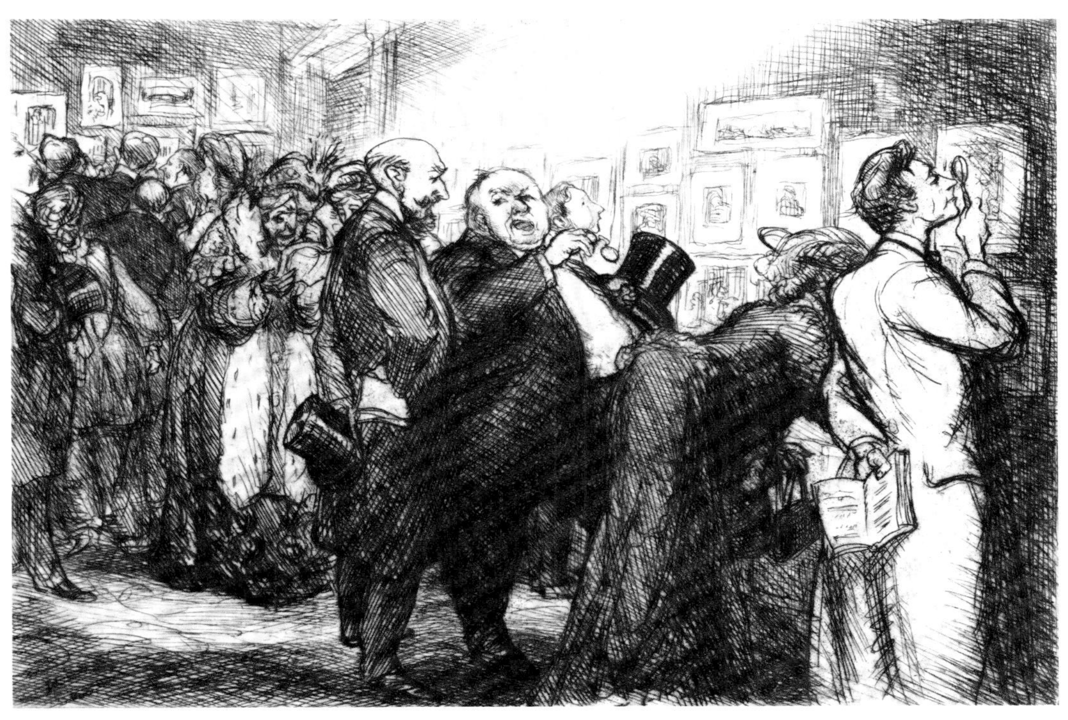

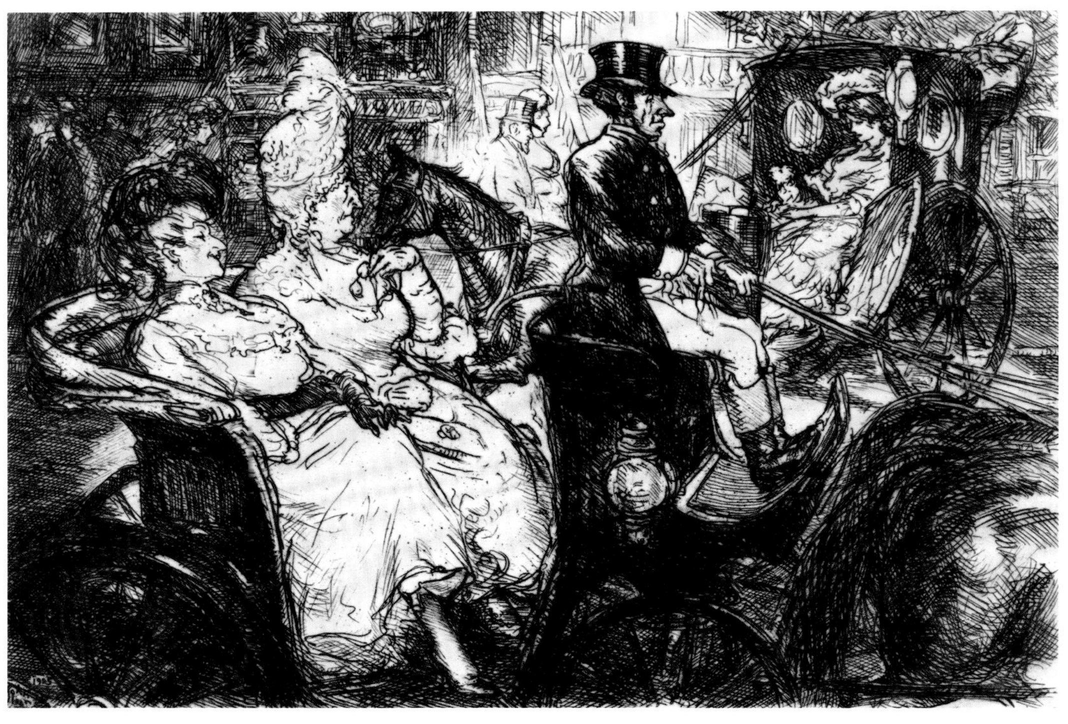

Fifth Avenue Critics, 1905
Etching
4½ x 6¾ in
Lent by the Delaware Art Museum, Gift of Helen Farr Sloan, 1963

20

The original title of this plate for Sloan's projected series on connoisseurs was *Connoisseurs of Virtue.* "These were typical of the fashionable ladies who used to drive up and down the Avenue... showing themselves and criticizing others."

The Show Case, 1905
Etching
4½ x 6¾ in
Lent by the Delaware Art Museum, Gift of Helen Farr Sloan, 1963

First called *Critics on Form,* this plate was the last on the Connoisseurs theme and the three plates were absorbed into the New York City Life series, so called because Sloan tried to market them as a set, without much success.

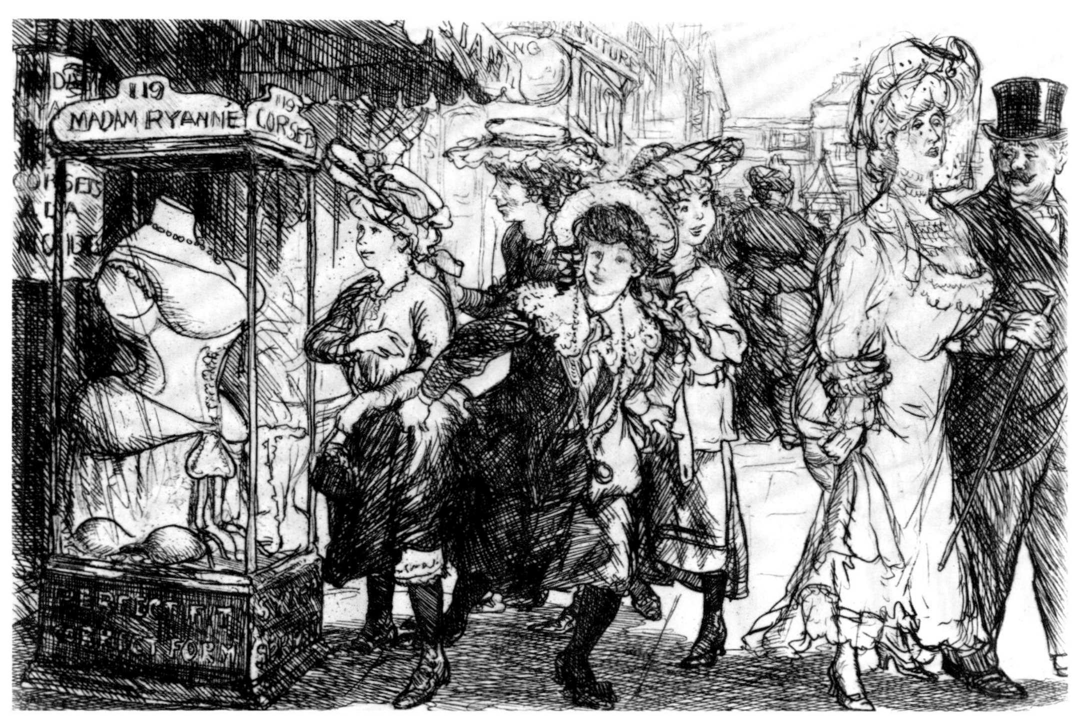

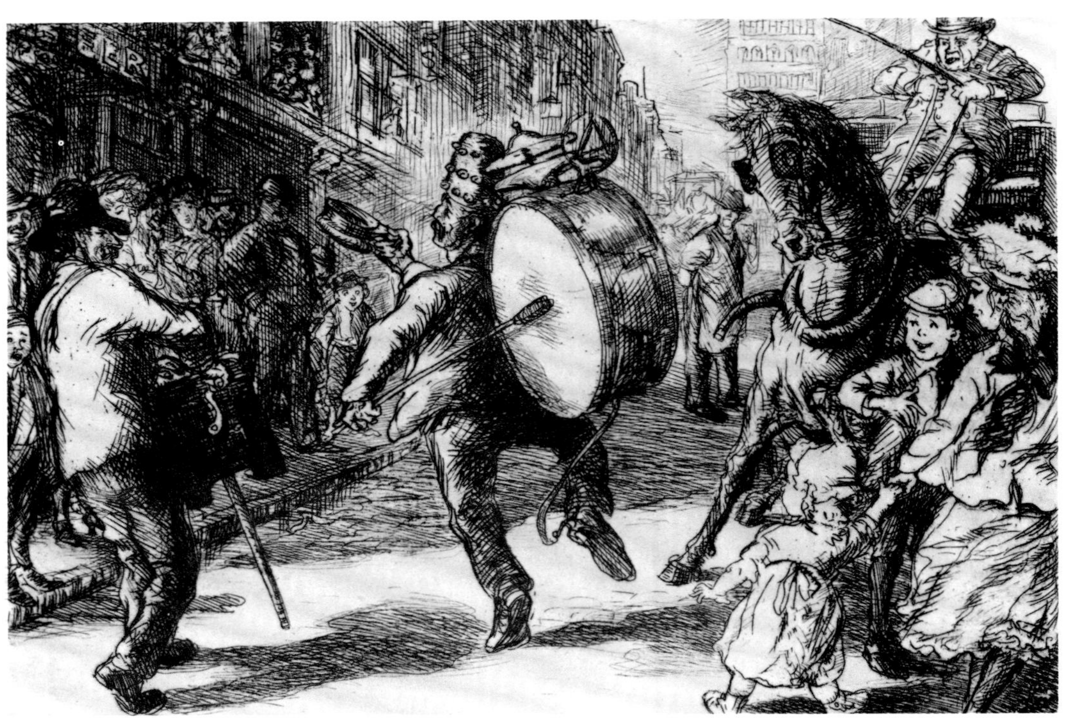

Man Monkey, 1905
Etching
4½ x 6¾ in
Lent by the Delaware Art Museum, Gift of Helen Farr Sloan, 1963

"In the side streets of the Chelsea and Greenwich Village districts, the one man band with hand organ accompanist furnished free entertainment to those who dropped no pennies. He worried the horse-drawn traffic of the time, but before many years the automobile and motor truck cleared him from the streets."

Fun, One Cent, 1905
Etching
4¾ x 6¾ in
Lent by the Delaware Art Museum, Gift of Helen Farr Sloan, 1963

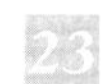

"The Nickelodeon, with its hand-cranked moving photographs, was one of the attractions preceding the moving picture theaters. The one in which I garnered this bouquet of laughing girls was for many years on 14th St. near Third Avenue."

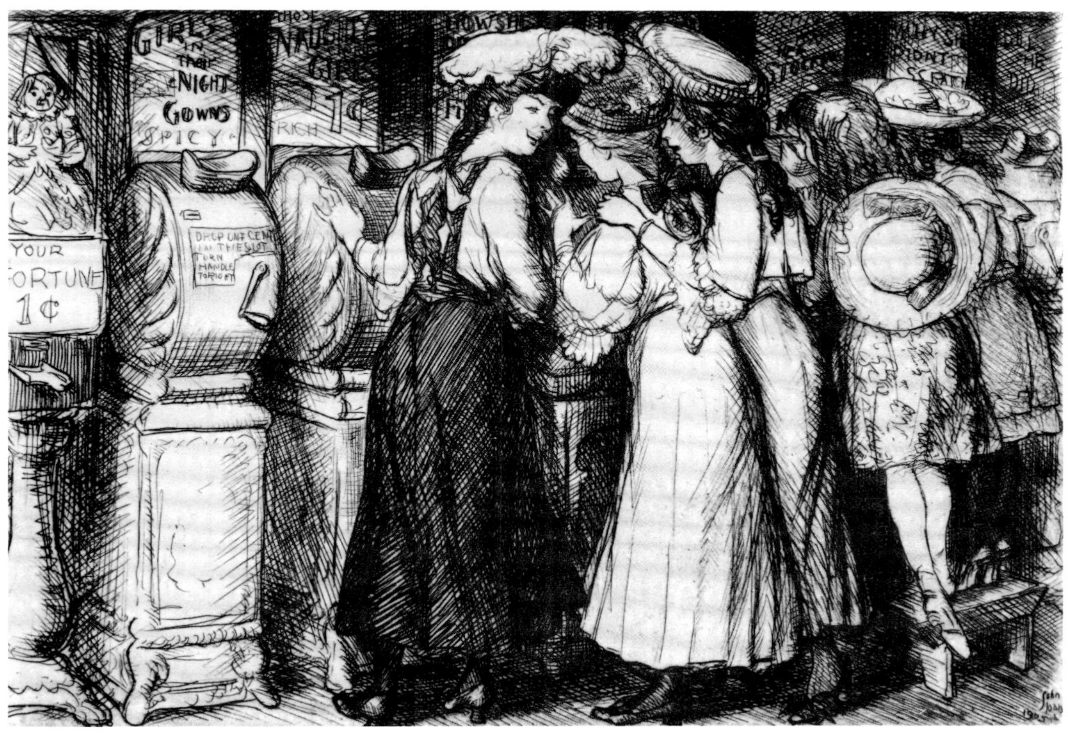

The Woman's Page, 1905
Etching
4½ x 6½ in
Lent by the Delaware Art Museum, Gift of Helen Farr Sloan, 1963

"This woman in this sordid room, sordidly dressed—undressed—with a poor little kid crawling around on a bed—reading the Woman's Page, getting hints on fashion and housekeeping... It's the irony of that I was putting over."

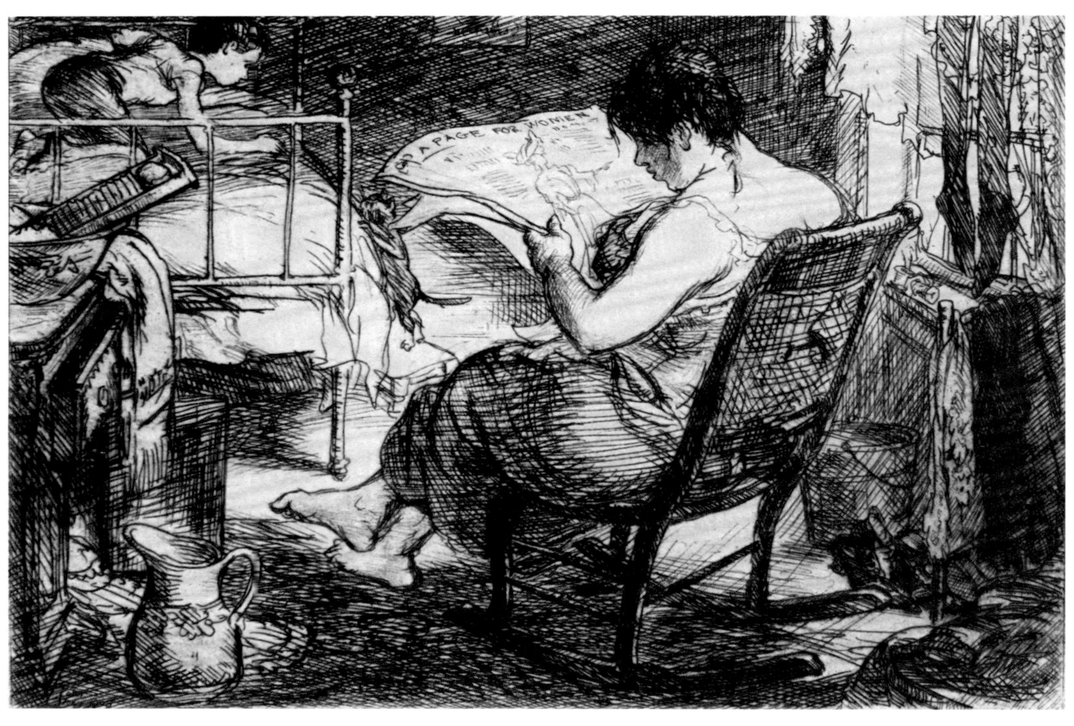

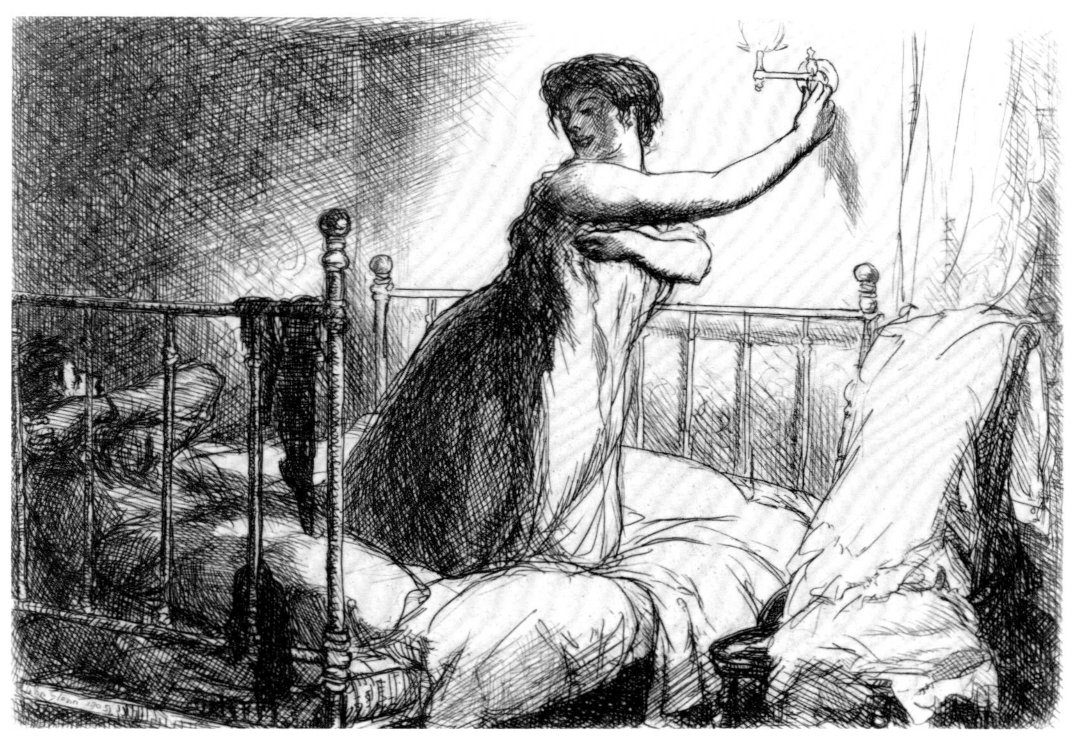

Turning out the Light, 1905
Etching
5 x 7 in
Lent by the Delaware Art Museum, Gift of Helen Farr Sloan, 1963

In 1906, Sloan was invited to send the New York City Life set to the American Watercolor Society exhibition and four of them, doubtless including this one, were returned to him as "vulgar" and "indecent." Furious, Sloan demanded the return of all of them.

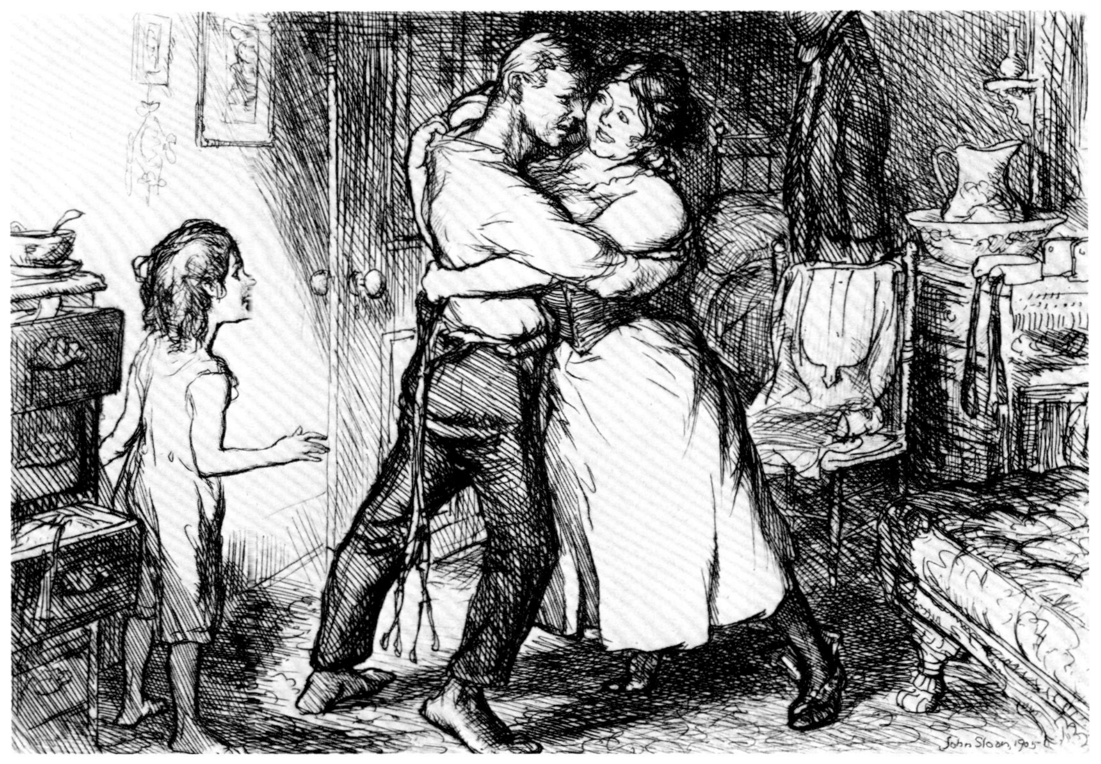

Man, Wife and Child, 1905
Etching
4½ x 6½ in
Lent by the Delaware Art Museum, Gift of Helen Farr Sloan, 1963

26

"The conjugal status given by this title always has, I hope, prevented any improper interpretation being placed on this scene, which rewarded hours spent at my back windows." Even so, it was probably one of those rejected by the American Watercolor Society.

The bundle lay on the white cloth between them, 1906
Crayon and wash on paper
13½ x 16 in
Published in Laura Campbell, "The Inspiration of Perot," *Collier's,* August 11, 1906, p. 15
Lent by Dr. and Mrs. Michael Schlossberg, Atlanta, Georgia

27

The art editor at *Collier's* gave Sloan the "Perot" story to read on February 26, 1906. When he delivered the drawings on March 19, Sloan had to strengthen several of them to improve the contrast for reproduction and printing.

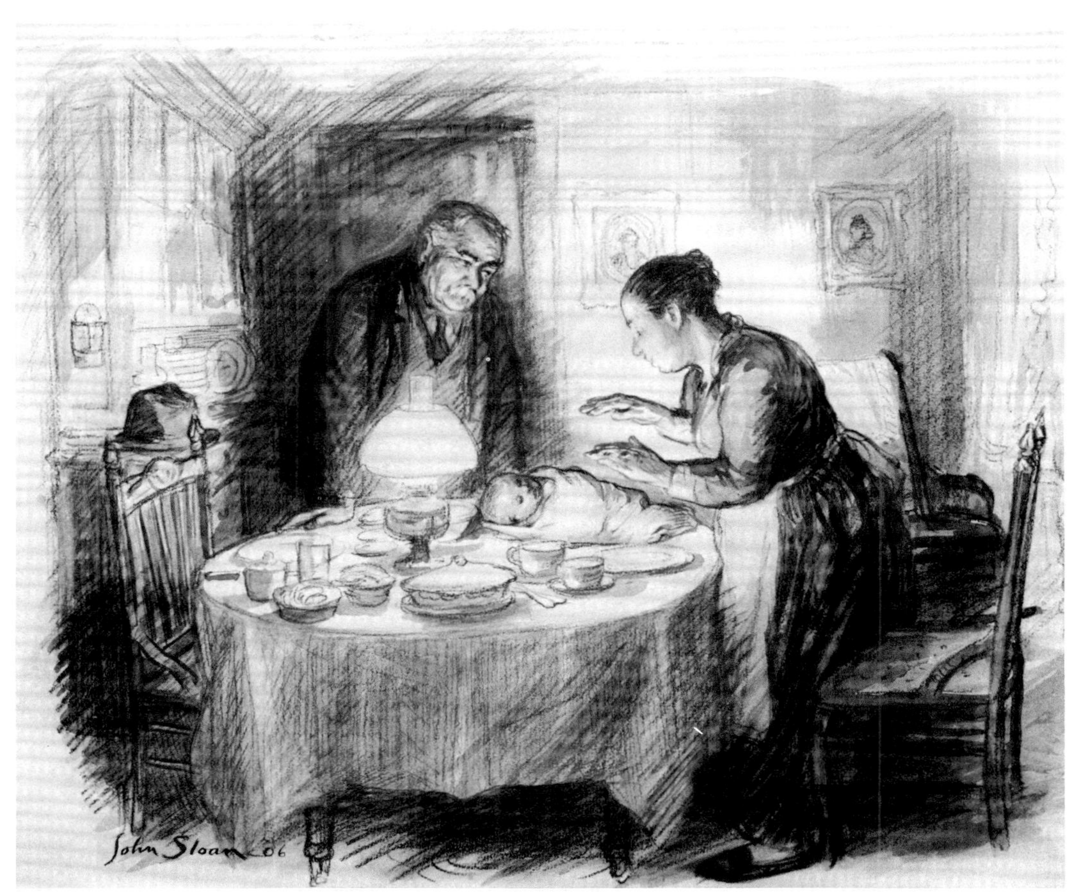

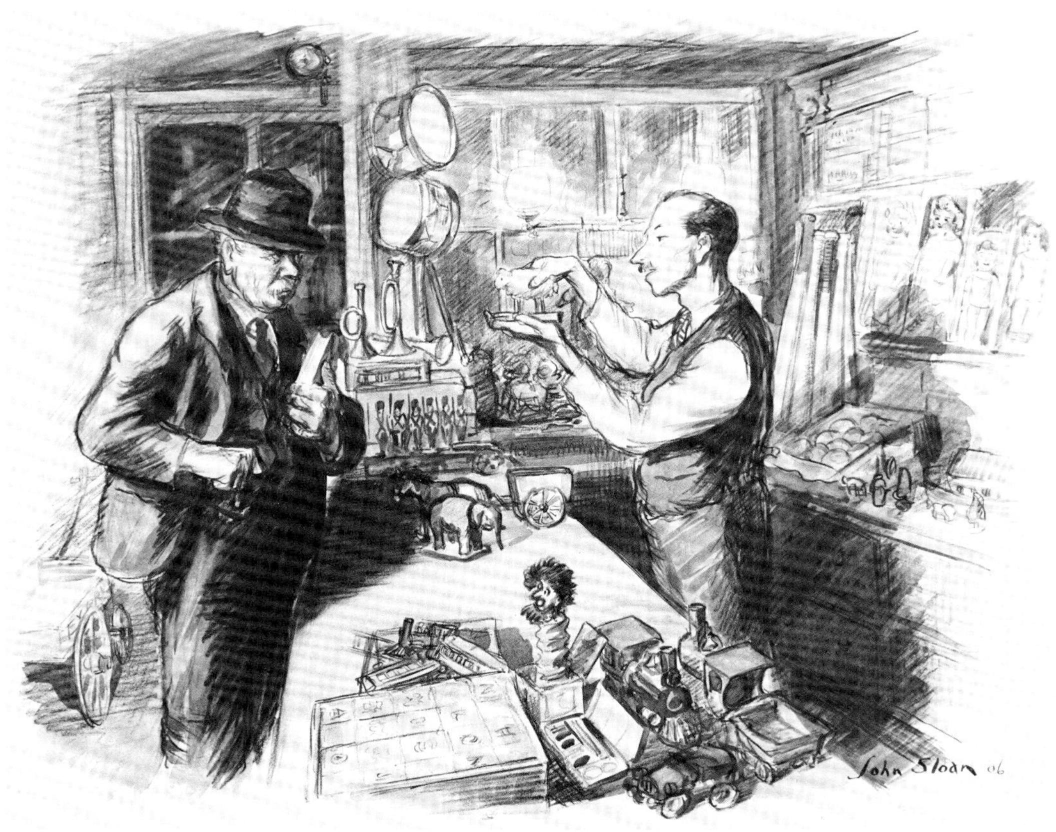

A mechanical "Baa-Baa!" issued from the painted mouth of the toy lamb, 1906

Ink wash and conte crayon on paper

$16\frac{7}{16} \times 21\frac{3}{4}$ in

Published in Laura Campbell, "The Inspiration of Perot," *Collier's,* August 11, 1906, p. 15

Lent by the Amon Carter Museum, Fort Worth

Joseph Perot, a cobbler, worked hard all day in his shop but had no friends. One evening, after having been given a baby's shoe to repair, he began to think of his childhood. On a whim, he bought a toy lamb that cried when squeezed.

I helped him all I could, looking up the worst long words in the dictionary, 1906
Crayon and ink on paper
13 x 18 in
Published in Ernest Poole, "The Queerest Thing in America: Told by Ludwig, the Little German Cobbler," *Saturday Evening Post*, October 20, 1906, p. 8
Lent by Victoria Miller

The cobbler's son, Karl, decides to become a lawyer and attends law school at night. "He worked hard, too—almost every night till twelve or one o'clock, on his law books—to get ready for examinations that would make him a real lawyer. I helped him all I could, looking up the worst long words in the dictionary. And then we talked and smoked our pipes and joked" (p. 10).

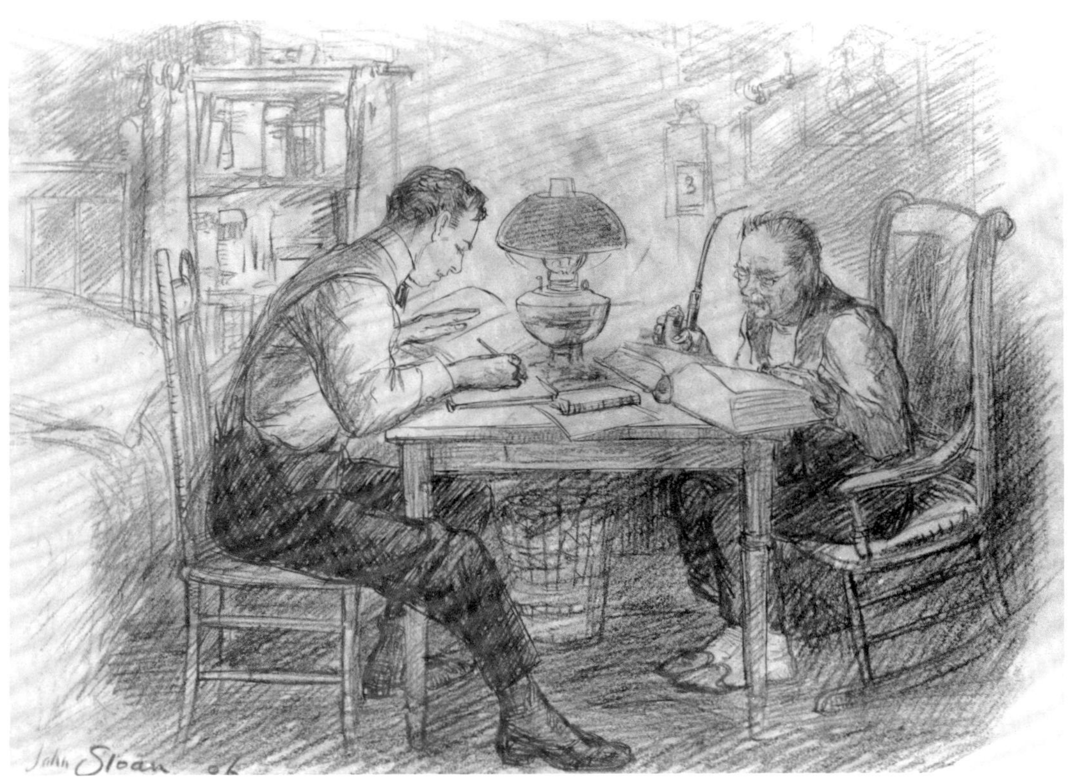

***I punched my long needle into his leg* (also called *Get out of here, I shouted*), 1906**
Crayon and ink on paper
19 x 13 in
Published in Ernest Poole, "The Queerest Thing in America: Told by Ludwig, the Little German Cobbler," *Saturday Evening Post*, October 20, 1906, p. 9
Lent by Victor D. Spark

30

Grafters in the guise of businessmen and lawyers take advantage of New York City's poor immigrants. An unsuspecting Bavarian-born cobbler buys a gold pocket watch on an installment plan and then is swindled out of his money. The angry cobbler chases his accuser out of the shop with his sewing needle. "'Get out of here!' I shouted. 'And I tell you that a fat man went up six steep steps in jumps'" (p. 8).

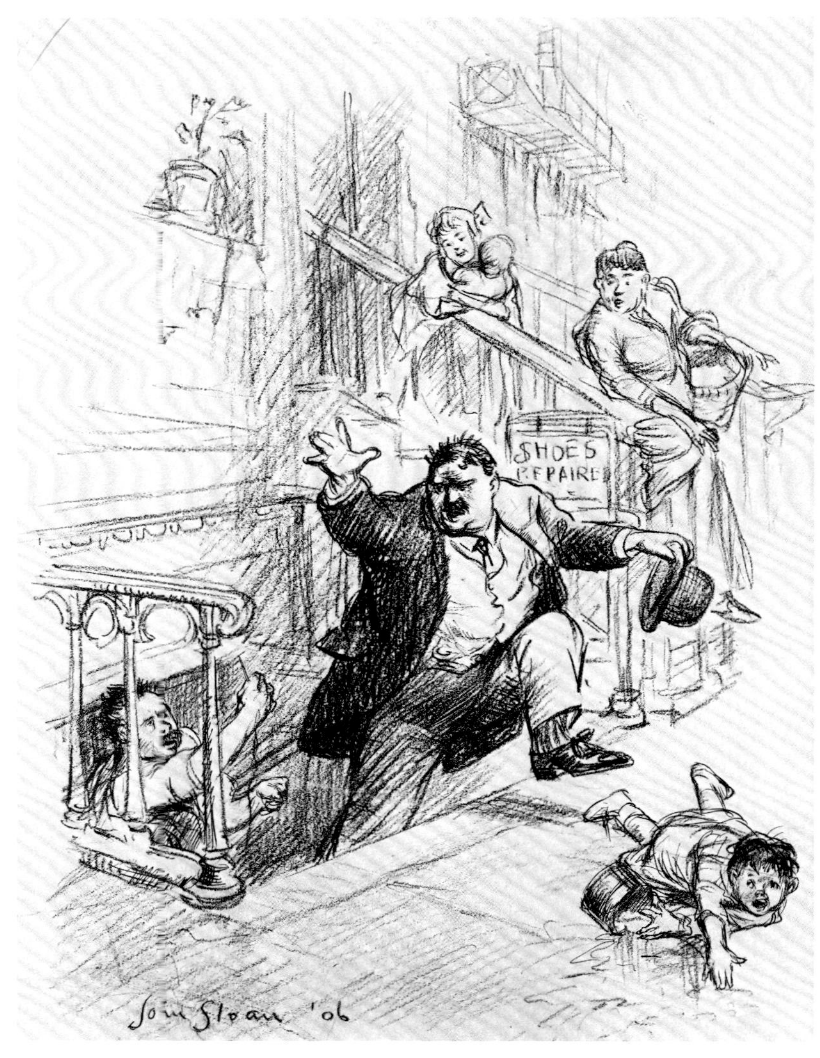

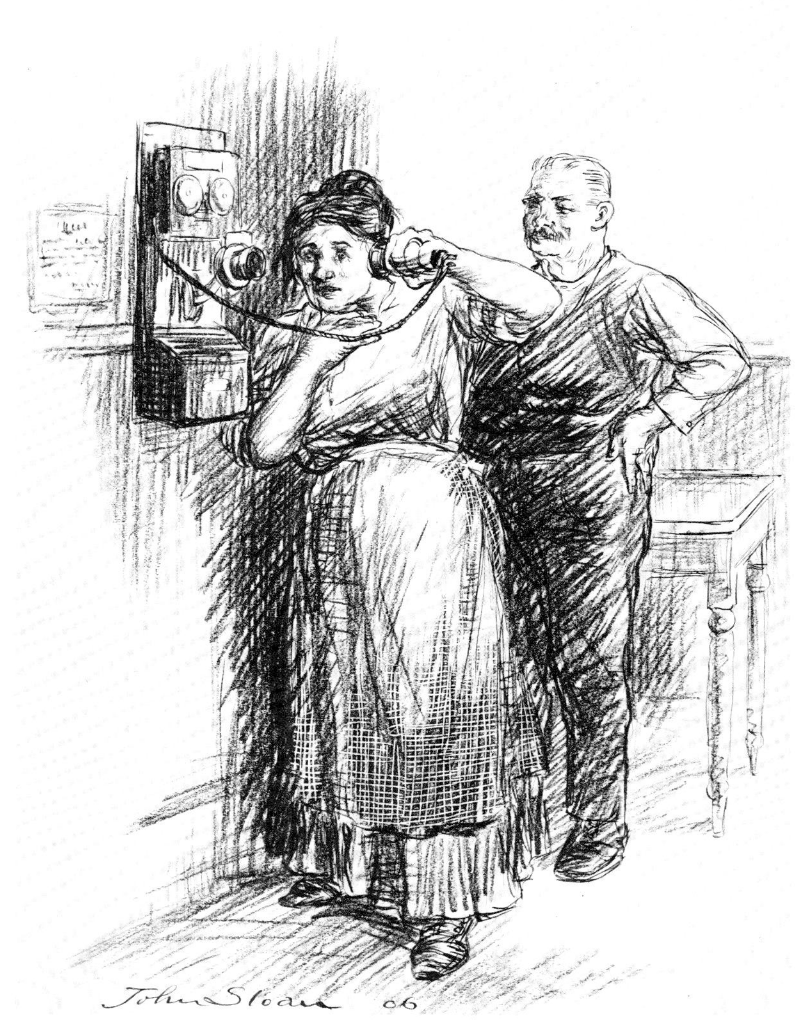

Then one day it was no longer the voice of a stranger to which Mrs. Burke listened, but the voice of her own man* (also called *The Telephone*), *1906
Crayon and ink on paper
16¾ x 14 in
Published in W. B. MacHarg, "The Debts of Antoine," *McClure's*, December 1906, p. 195
Lent by the Butler Institute of American Art, Youngstown, Ohio

31

Mrs. Burke learns of her husband's recovery from smallpox: "Hopeful messages came over O'Rourkes's telephone; then one day it was no longer the voice of a stranger to which Mrs. Burke listened, but the voice of her own man speaking words which healed her, while she leaned against the wall, the receiver at her ear, tears flowing down her cheeks" (p. 196).

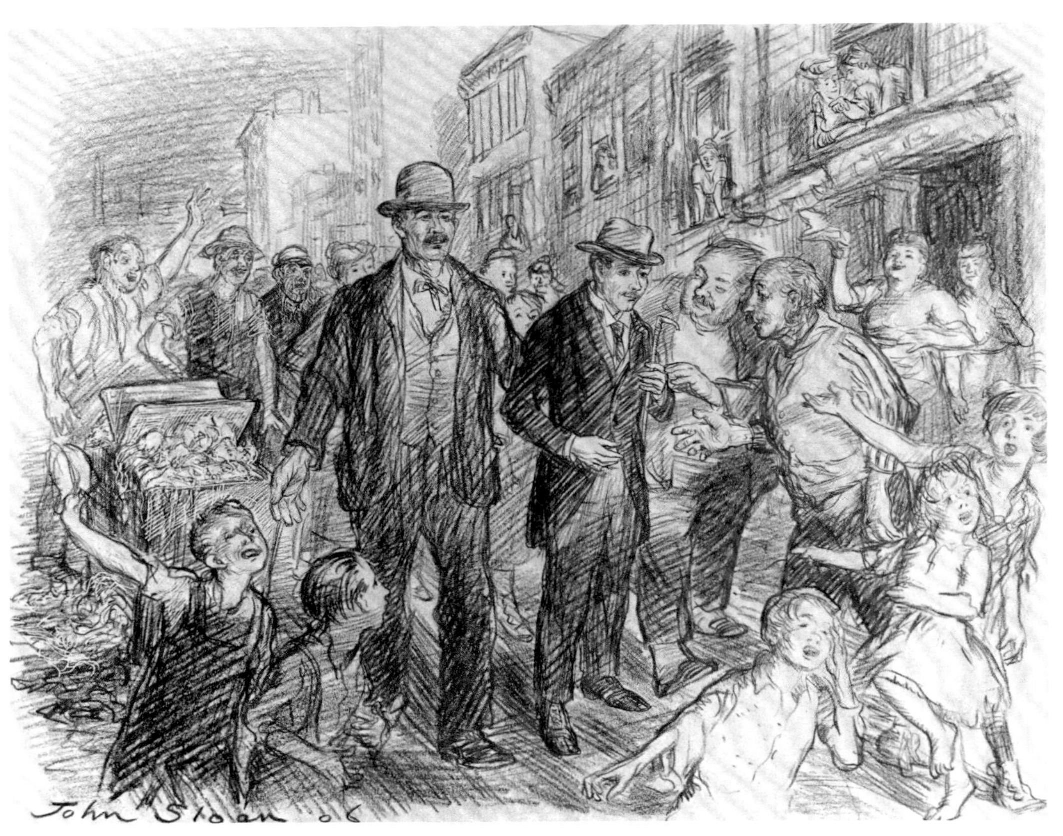

Antoine did not know what to make of it, so often had he passed down this street in loneliness, 1906
Crayon and ink on paper
13¼ x 16¾ in
Published in W. B. MacHarg, "The Debts of Antoine," *McClure's*, December 1906, p. 197
Lent by Mr. and Mrs. Scott L. Probasco, Jr.

32

Living in a Chicago tenement building, a lonely French immigrant Antoine nursed his sick neighbor and then also contracted smallpox. When fully recovered, both Antoine and Burke return home greeted by their neighbors.

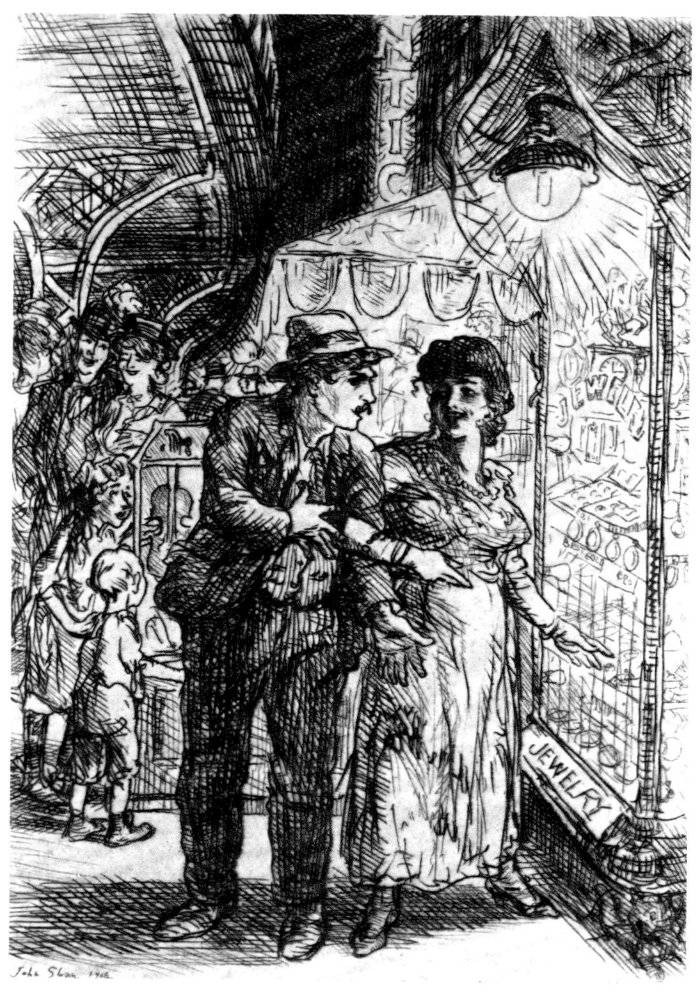

Carlotta's Indecision: "O! com', see des jew'ler store," 1906
Etching
5 x 3½ in
Published in T. A. Daly, *Canzoni* (Philadelphia: David McKay, 1906), frontispiece
Lent by the Delaware Art Museum, Gift of Helen Farr Sloan, 1963

33

To get ideas for this work, Sloan and Dolly went to the Lower East Side one evening; on his return Sloan made a pencil sketch for the etching based on Daly's poem "Carlotta's Indecision" about a coy young woman who won't tell her boyfriend whether she'll marry him.

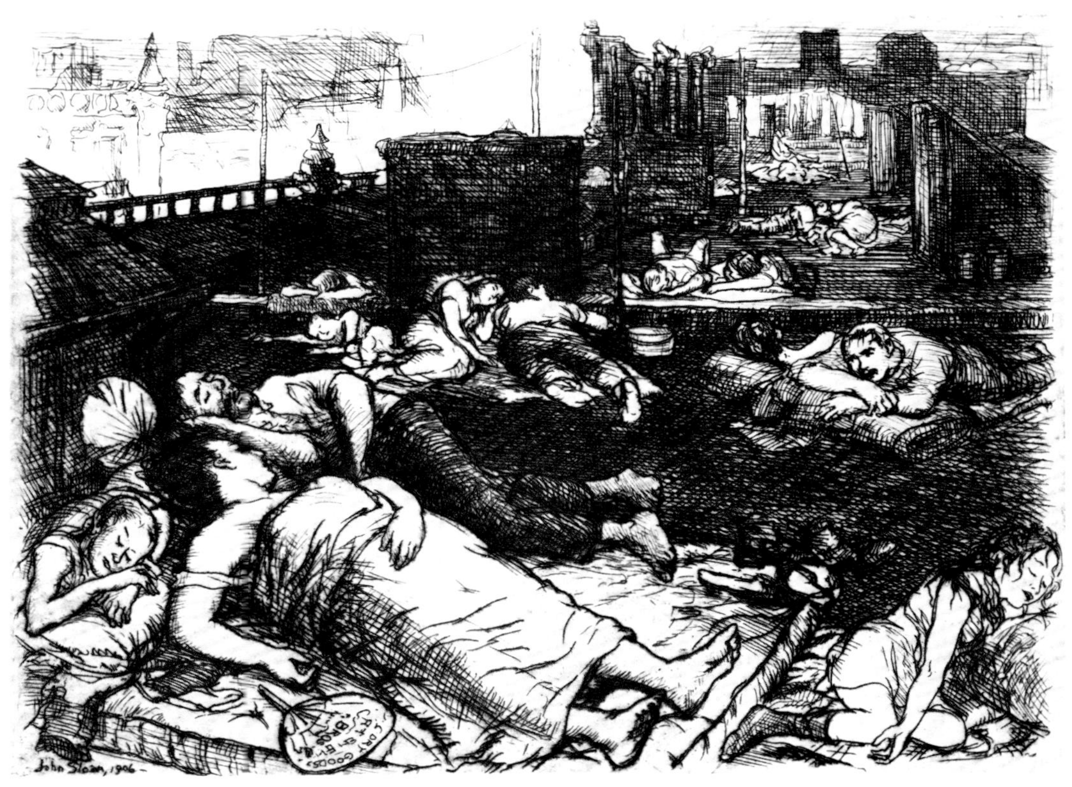

Roof, Summer Night, 1906
Etching
5 x 6¾ in
Lent by the Delaware Art Museum, Gift of Helen Farr Sloan, 1963

"*I* have always liked to watch the people in the summer, especially the way they live on the roofs. For many years I have not seen the summer life of the city [being in Santa Fe], which has perhaps been better for my health than my production of city life etchings."

The Little Bride, 1906
Etching
4¾ x 6¾ in
Lent by the Delaware Art Museum, Gift of Helen Farr Sloan, 1963

35

"Back in 1906 there was a considerable French population north of 23rd Street, and the church near Proctor's Theatre was known as the French Church. The stone steps down which these newlyweds are escaping have since been removed...."

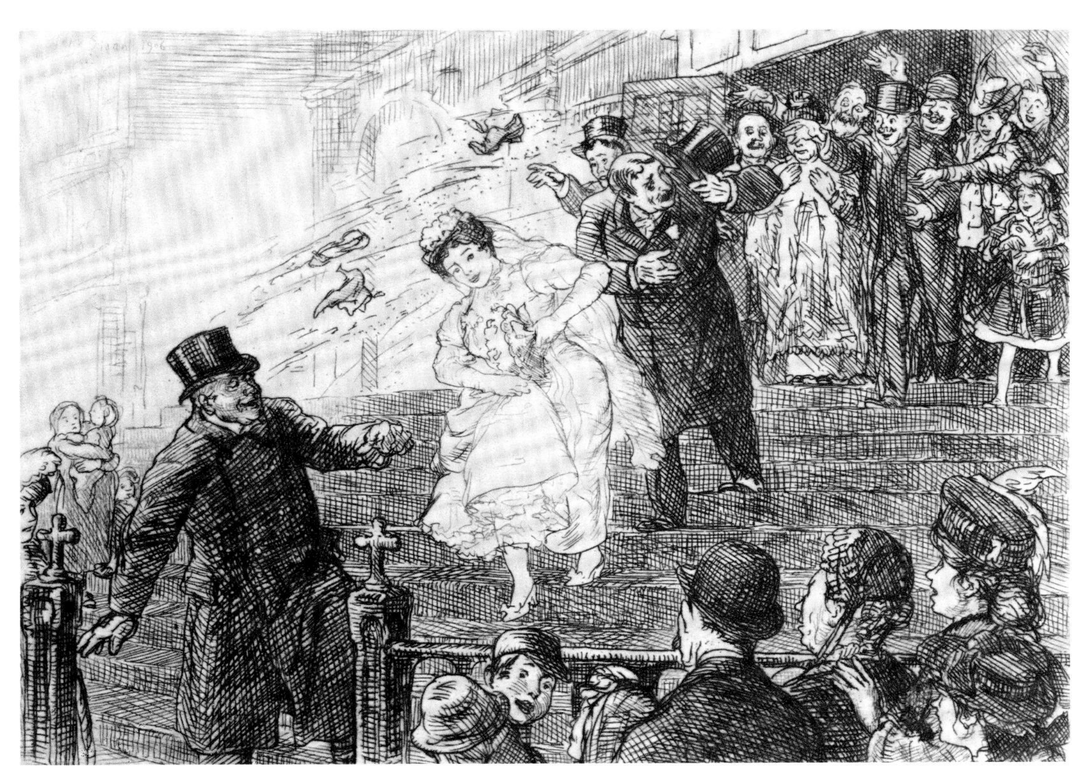

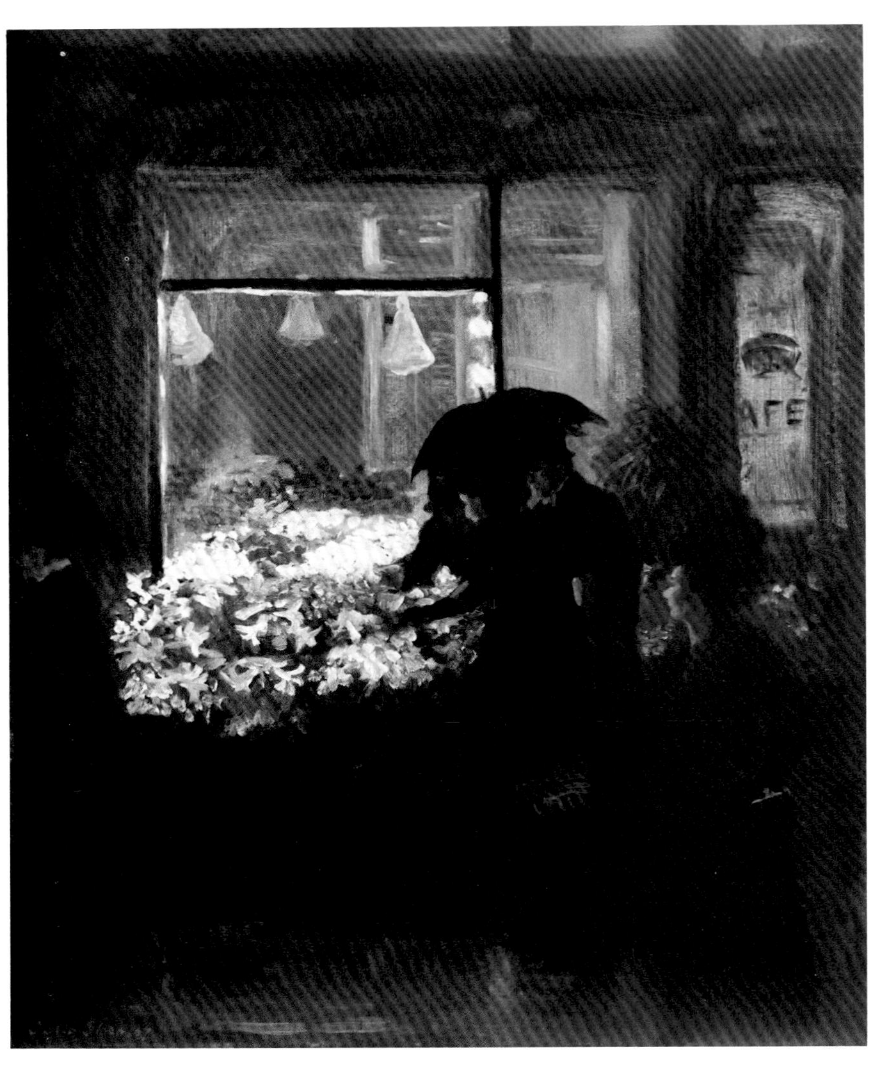

***Easter Eve*, 1907**
Oil on canvas
32 x 26⅛ in
Lent by Deborah and Edward Shein

*I*n his diary Sloan wrote: "Rained in the late evening and I saw an idea for a picture in the Flower Shop across the way. Stock out in front and open all night on account of Easter." He began the painting from memory the next day.

Wake of the Ferry, No. 1, 1907
Oil on canvas
26 x 32 in
Lent by the Detroit Institute of Arts,
Gift of Miss Amelia Elizabeth White

Before the tunnel to New Jersey was finished in 1908, the ferry was the only way to get in and out of Manhattan. One evening in the spring of 1907, Sloan saw a friend to the train in New Jersey and had the idea for this painting.

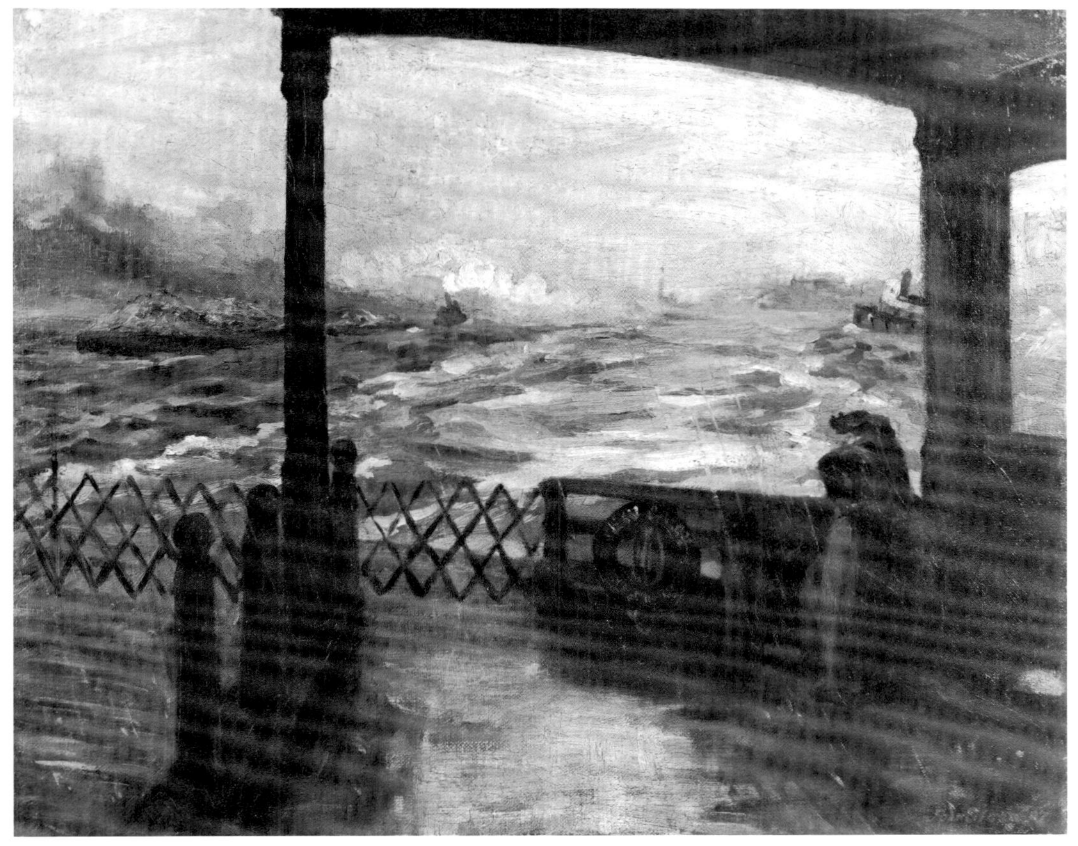

Sixth Avenue and 30th Street, 1907, 1909
Oil on canvas
26¼ x 32 in
Lent by Mr. and Mrs. Meyer P. Potamkin

In 1907 Sloan was living on the outskirts of the Tenderloin district in Manhattan, on West 23rd Street. Many of his subjects occurred to him on walks through the neighborhood. This painting was included in the famous exhibition of The Eight in 1908.

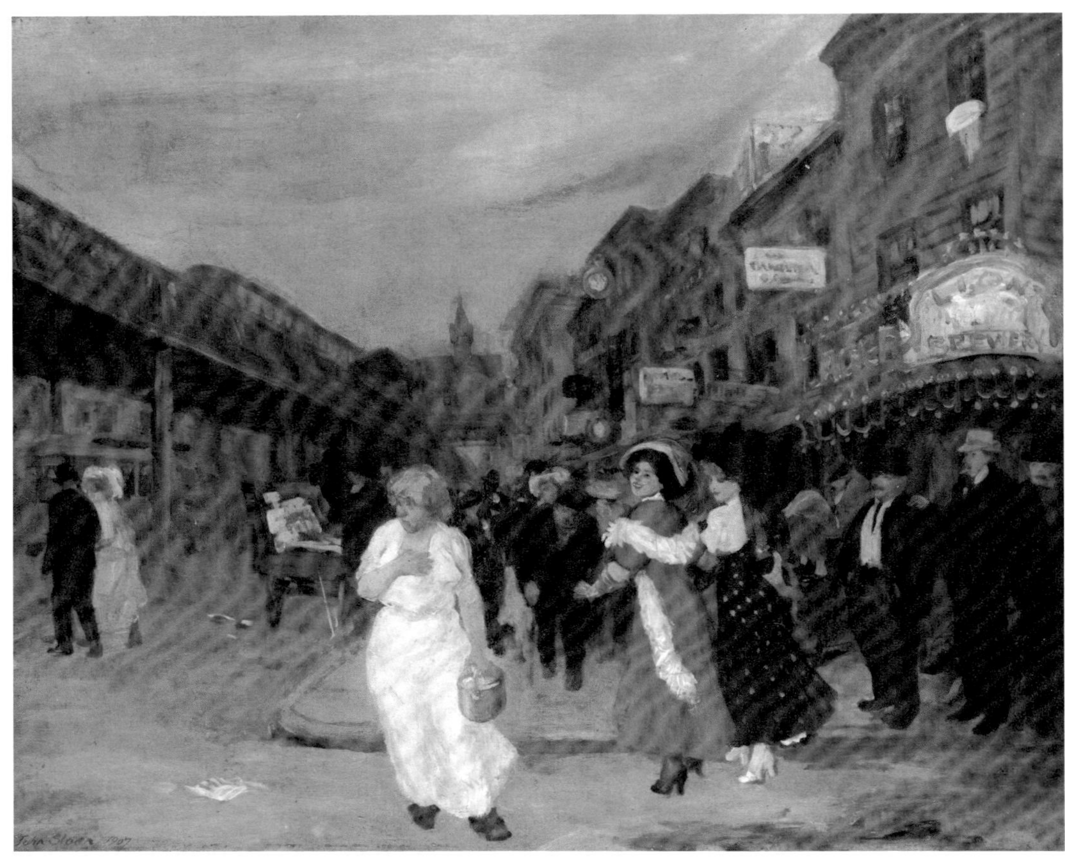

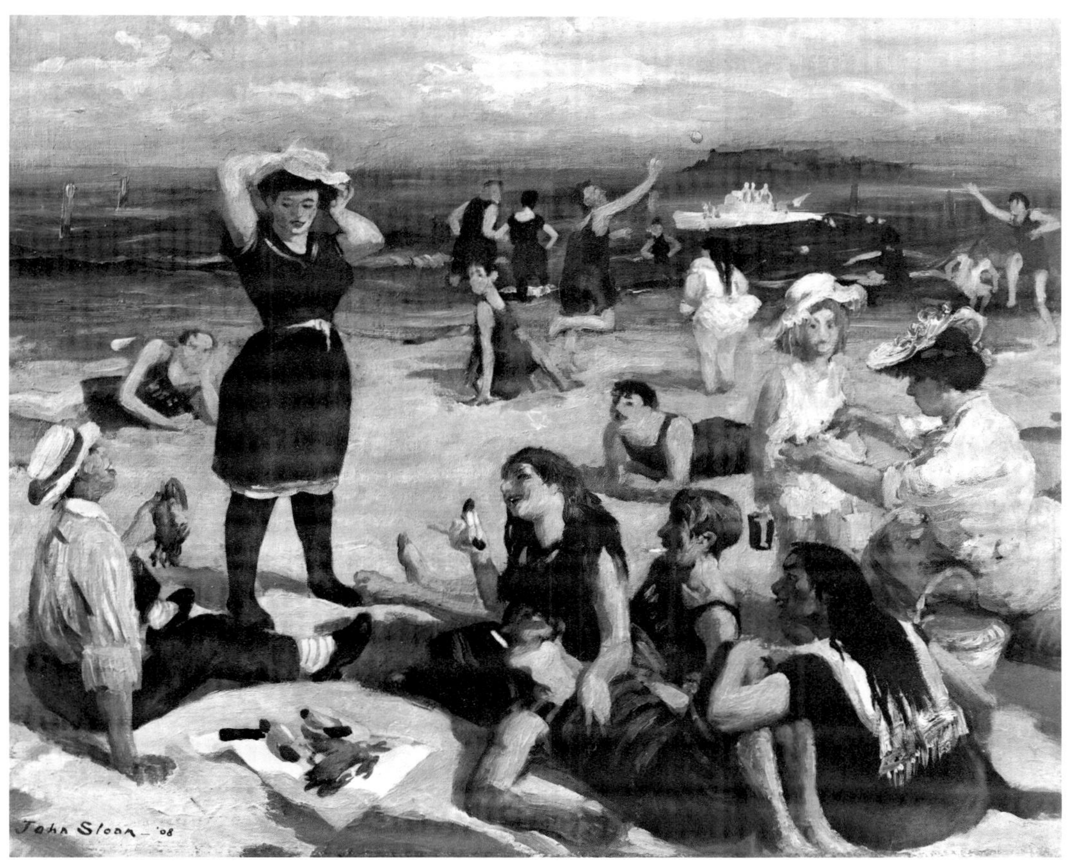

***South Beach Bathers*, 1907, 1908**
Oil on canvas
26 x 31¾ in
Lent by the Walker Art Center, Minneapolis; Gift of the T. B. Walker Foundation, Gilbert M. Walker Fund, 1948

"This Staten Island resort had few visitors compared to Coney Island, and gave better opportunity for observation of individual behavior. It is amusing to recall how very chic the bathing costume of the girl standing seemed at the time."

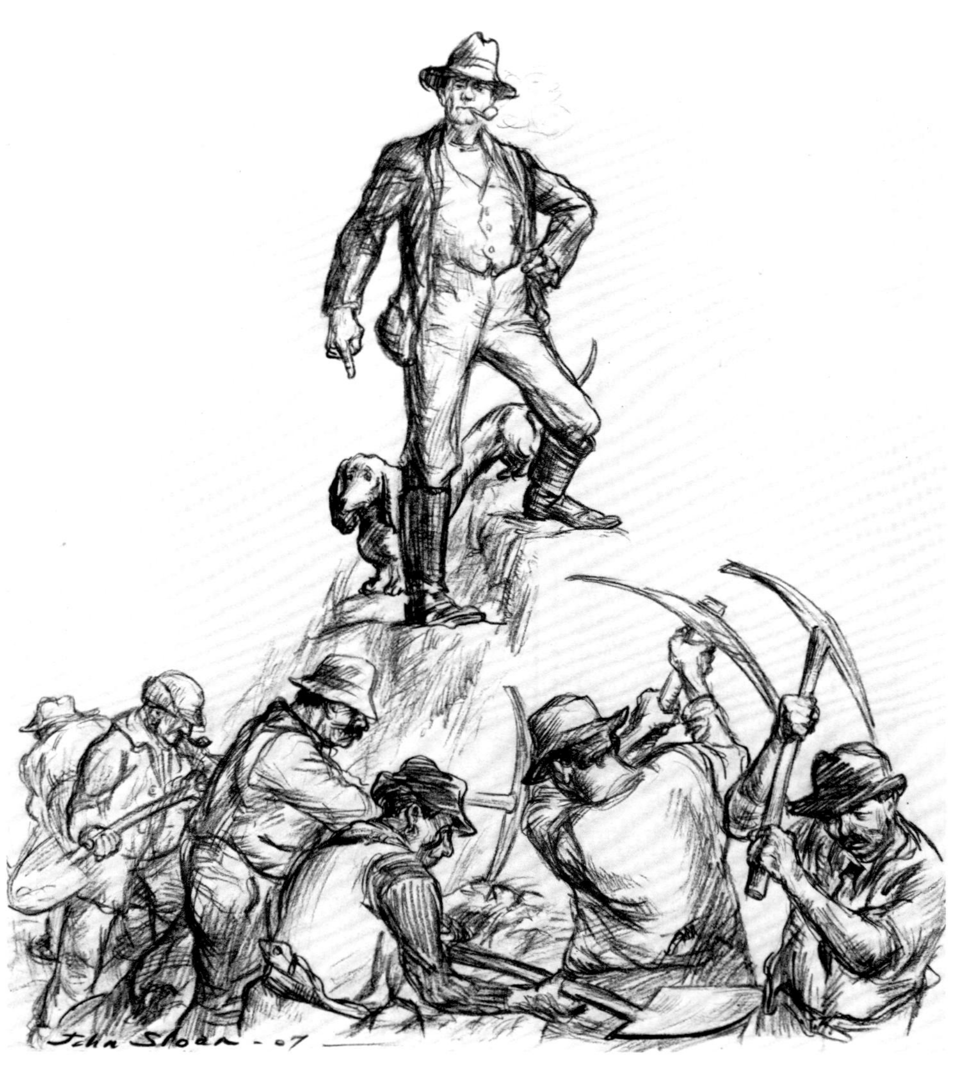

He drove his cohort of the sons of mighty Rome, 1907
Crayon on paper board
22⅞ x 19 15/16 in
Published in F. W. Brown, "Mulligan and Caspar," *Century*, August 1908, p. 578
Lent by the National Museum of American Art, Smithsonian Institution

In this Irish-humor story Mulligan, a tall Irish immigrant, was foreman of a group of Italians working on the railroad. Mulligan's pet dachshund, Caspar, alerted him when a jealous crew tried to interfere with the work. Caspar saved the day.

Throbbing Fountain, Night, 1908
Oil on canvas
32 x 26 in
Courtesy of the Kraushaar Galleries, New York

Sloan had painted the pulsating fountain in Madison Square in 1907 during the day, and in the summer of 1908 he decided to try it at night with the Metropolitan Building in the background. Many of Sloan's New York genre scenes were evening or interior subjects.

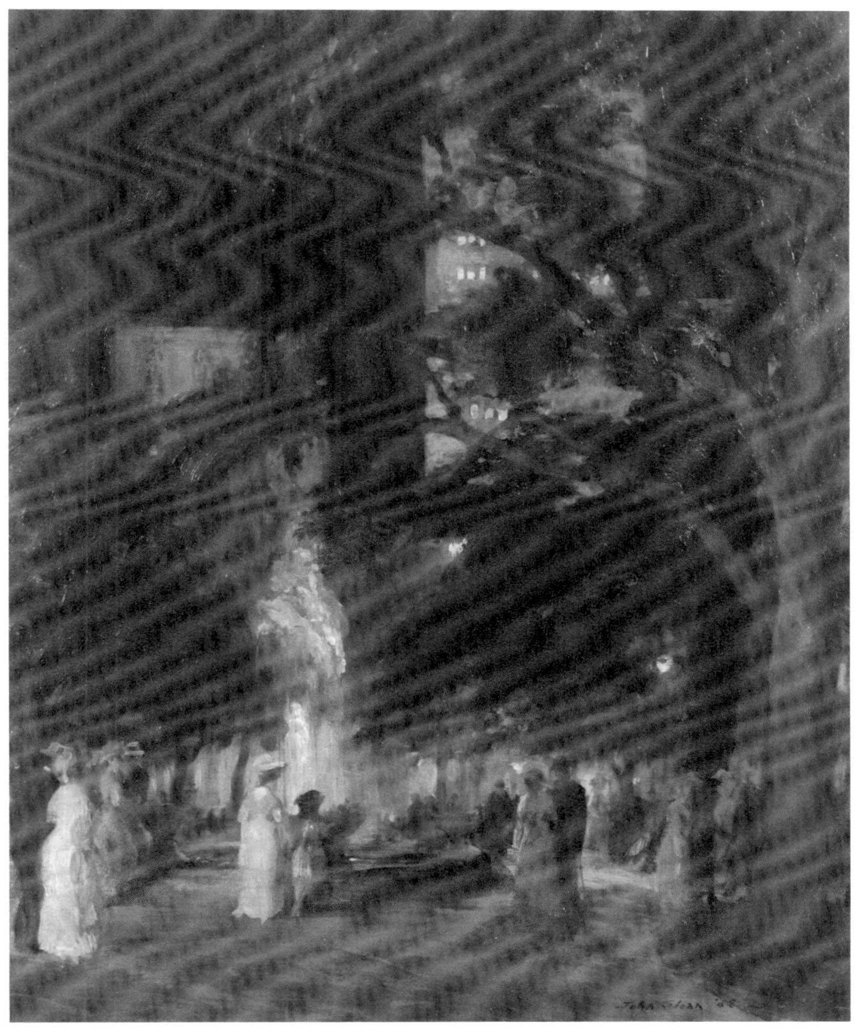

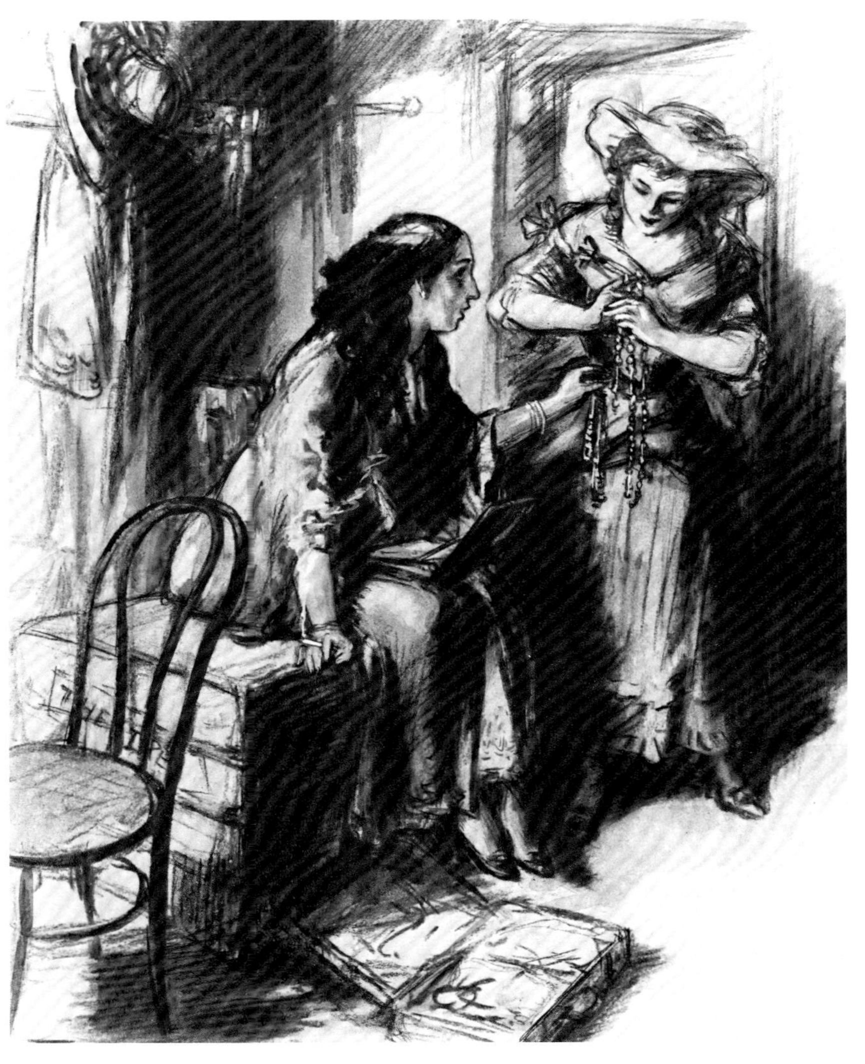

***And these were bought in Persia, my dear!*, 1908**
Crayon on illustration board
15½ x 12½ in
Published in Anonymous [Gelett Burgess], "The Making of an Actress," *Collier's*, June 13, 1908, p. 16
Lent by Mr. and Mrs. Ralph E. Hansmann

An actress recounts her experiences as a young woman pursuing an acting career. Here, the leading lady, dressed in a kimono and smoking a cigarette, sits on a truck backstage showing the young actress a necklace of beads and misses her cue to go on stage.

The Stage Wait: Ain't that Betsy the most hifalutin goose that ever cackled, 1908
Crayon, wash, watercolor, and gouache on paper
13¼ x 9⅜ in
Not published. Probably done for Anonymous [Gelett Burgess], "The Making of an Actress," *Collier's,* June 13, 1908
Lent by the McNay Art Museum, San Antonio, Texas; Gift of Alice N. Hanszen

Though this drawing was not published, the incident of the "stage wait" takes place in part two of the story written by humorist Gelett Burgess.

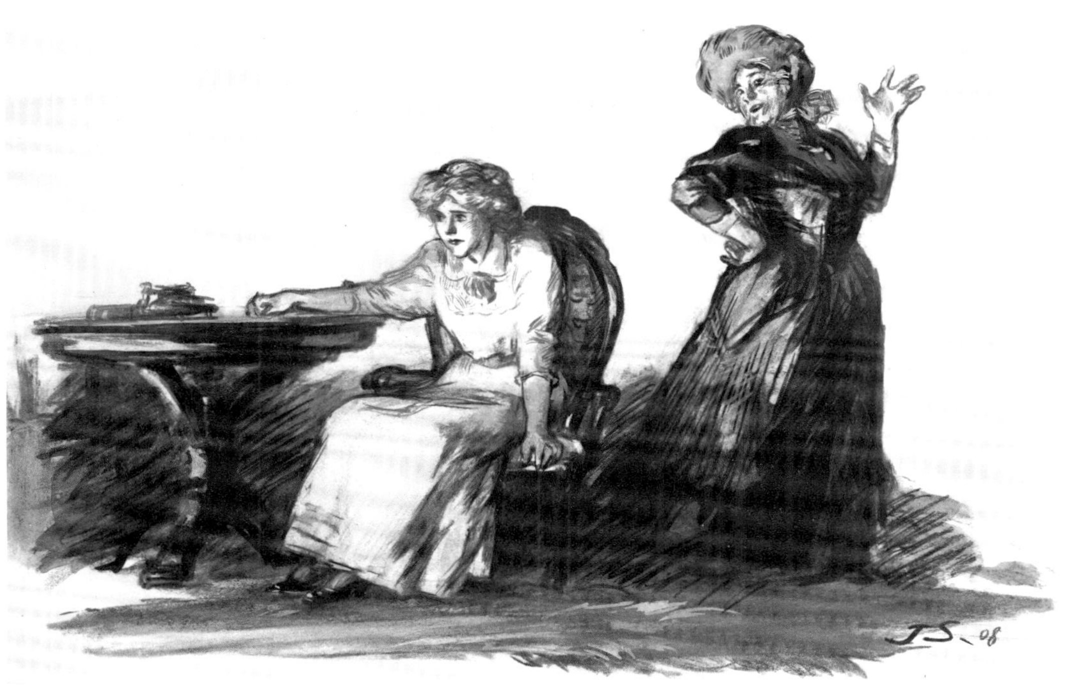

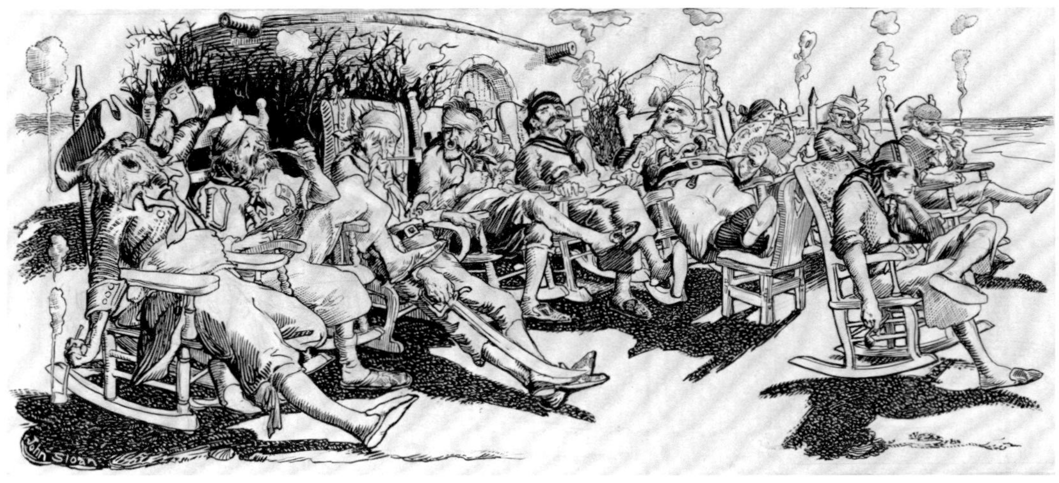

Now beginneth the playful and tragic romance in four fits of the ten fatigued pirates, who, seated in missionary furniture, lament the murderous monotony of their life, 1908

Ink and gouache on bristol board
12¼ x 23 in
Published in Ralph Bergengren, "Mehitabel," *Collier's*, November 21, 1908, p. 17
Lent by the Delaware Art Museum, Gift of Helen Farr Sloan, 1978

44

Ten bored pirates sit in rocking chairs (booty stolen from their last adventure) until they decide to kidnap a New England schoolmarm, Mehitabel Perkins, to teach them to read to ease the monotony of their life. Will Bradley, *Collier's* art editor, commissioned the drawings done in a woodcut style.

Chinese Restaurant, 1909
Oil on canvas
26 x 32 in
Lent by the Memorial Art Gallery of the University of Rochester, Marion Stratton Gould Fund

*I*t was a month after Sloan wrote in his diary, "...went to the Chinese restaurant and was glad I did for I saw a strikingly gotten up girl with dashing red feathers in her hat playing with the restaurant's fat cat," that he began the painting from memory.

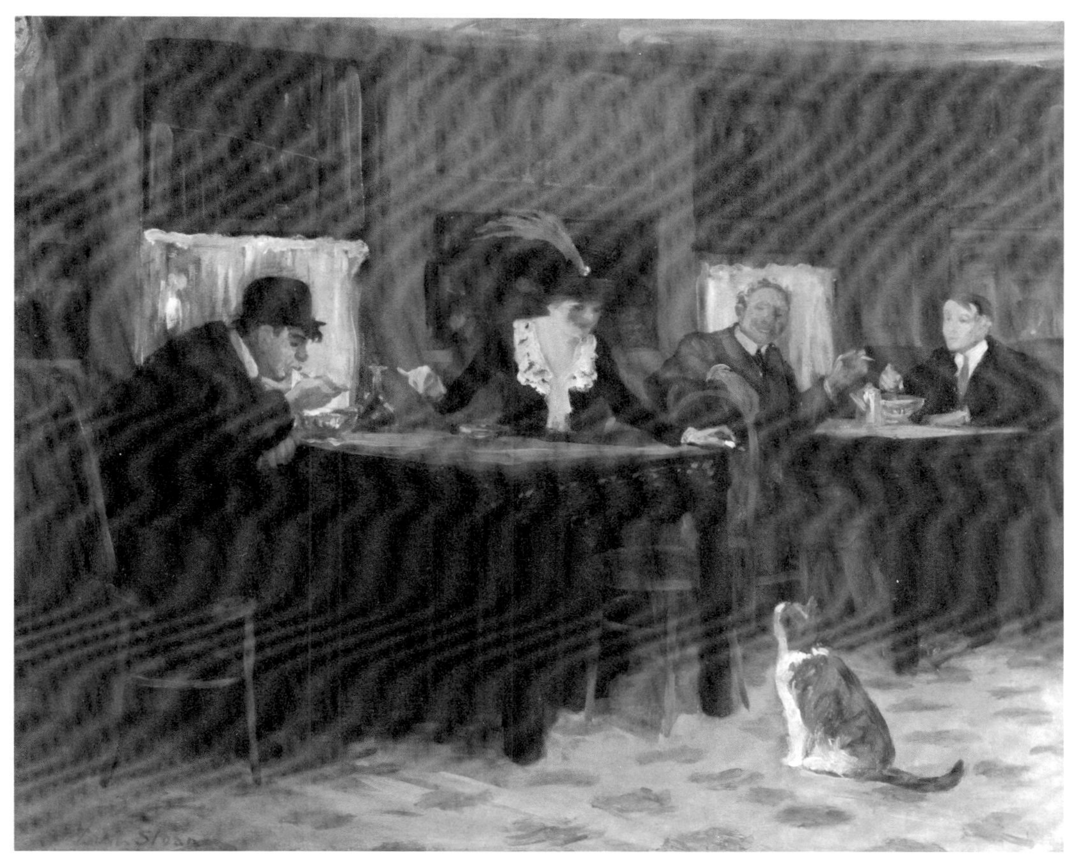

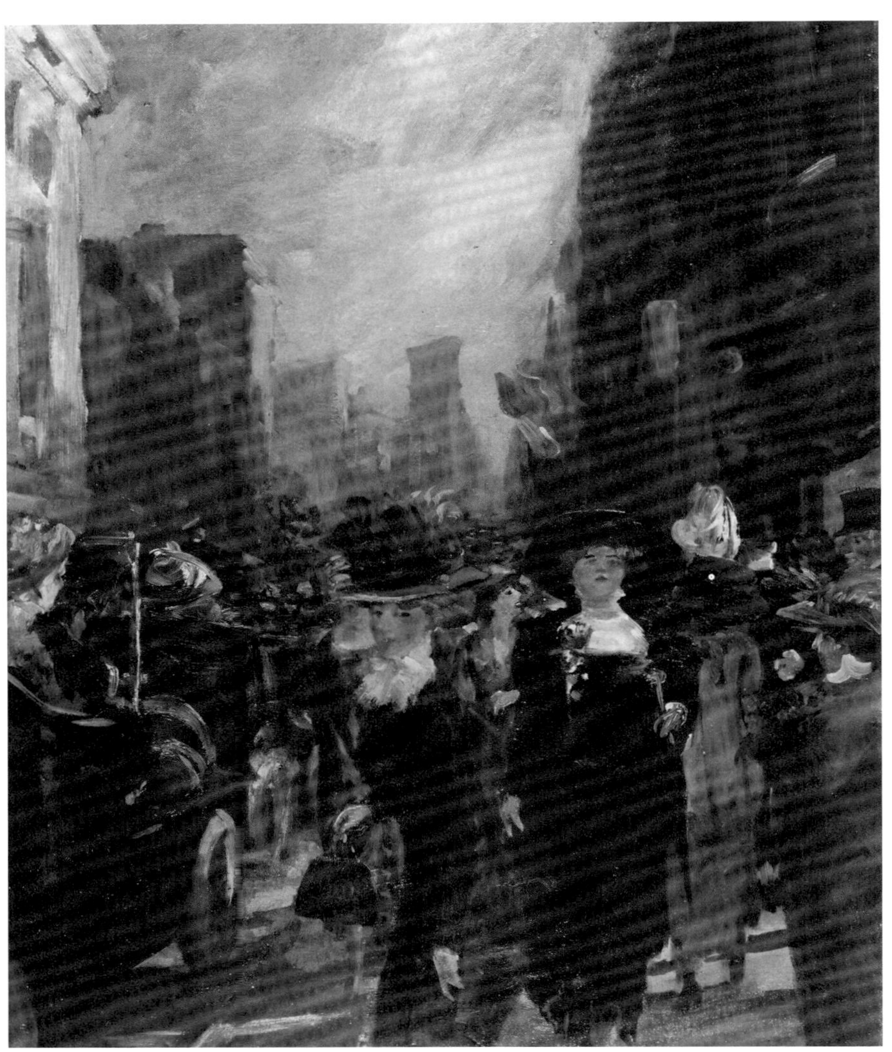

Fifth Avenue, New York, 1909, 1911
Oil on canvas
32 x 26 in
Lent anonymously

46

In 1909 Sloan began to be interested in Socialism as a remedy for the social ills he saw around him. He was determined that his political views would not color his painting, only his illustrations for publications like *The Masses,* but more than an edge of social satire appears in this work.

Three A.M., 1909
Oil on canvas
32 x 26¼ in
Lent by the Philadelphia Museum of Art,
Gift of Mrs. Cyrus McCormick, 1946

47

"These two girls I took to be sisters, one of whom was engaged in some occupation that brought her home about this hour of the morning. On her arrival the other rose from her slumbers and prepared a meal....This picture...has beauty, I'll not deny it."

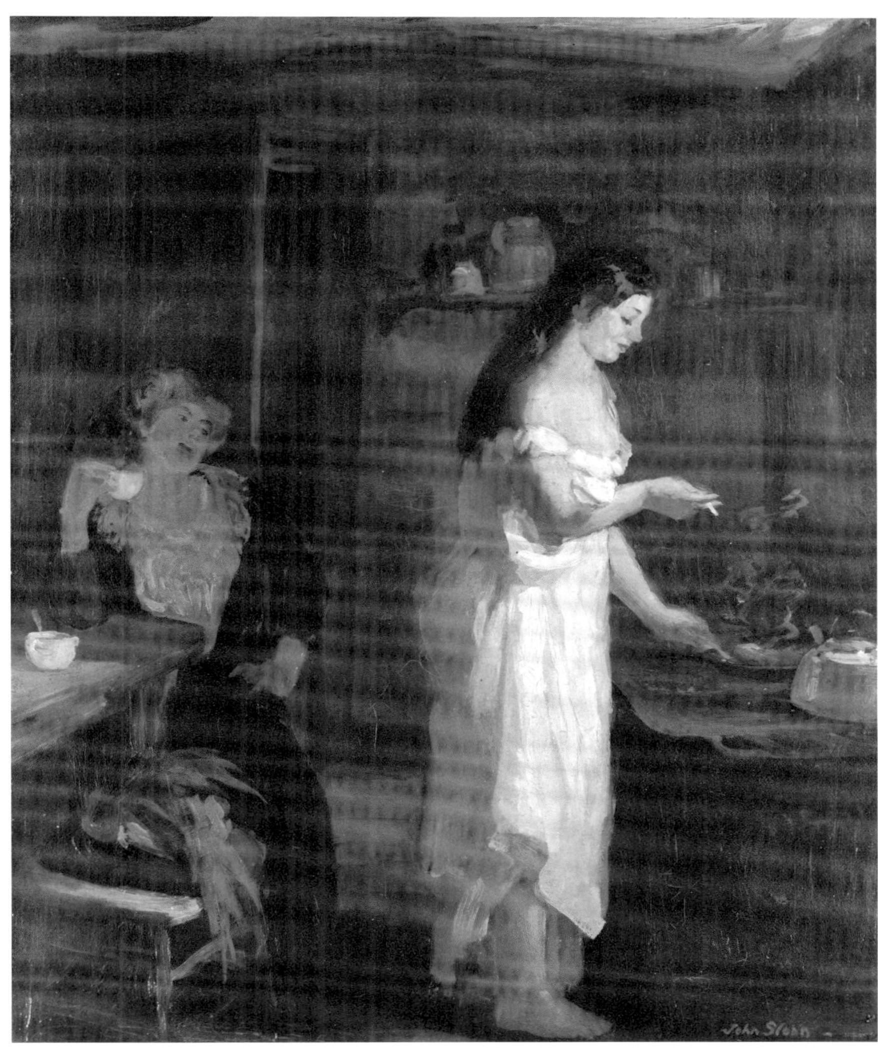

Recruiting in Union Square, 1909
Oil on canvas
26 x 32 in
Lent by the Butler Institute of American Art, Youngstown, Ohio

"**I**n the center near the fountain is a U.S. Army recruiting sign, two samples of our military are in attendance but the bums stick to the freedom of their poverty. There is a picture in this—a drawing or etching, probably"

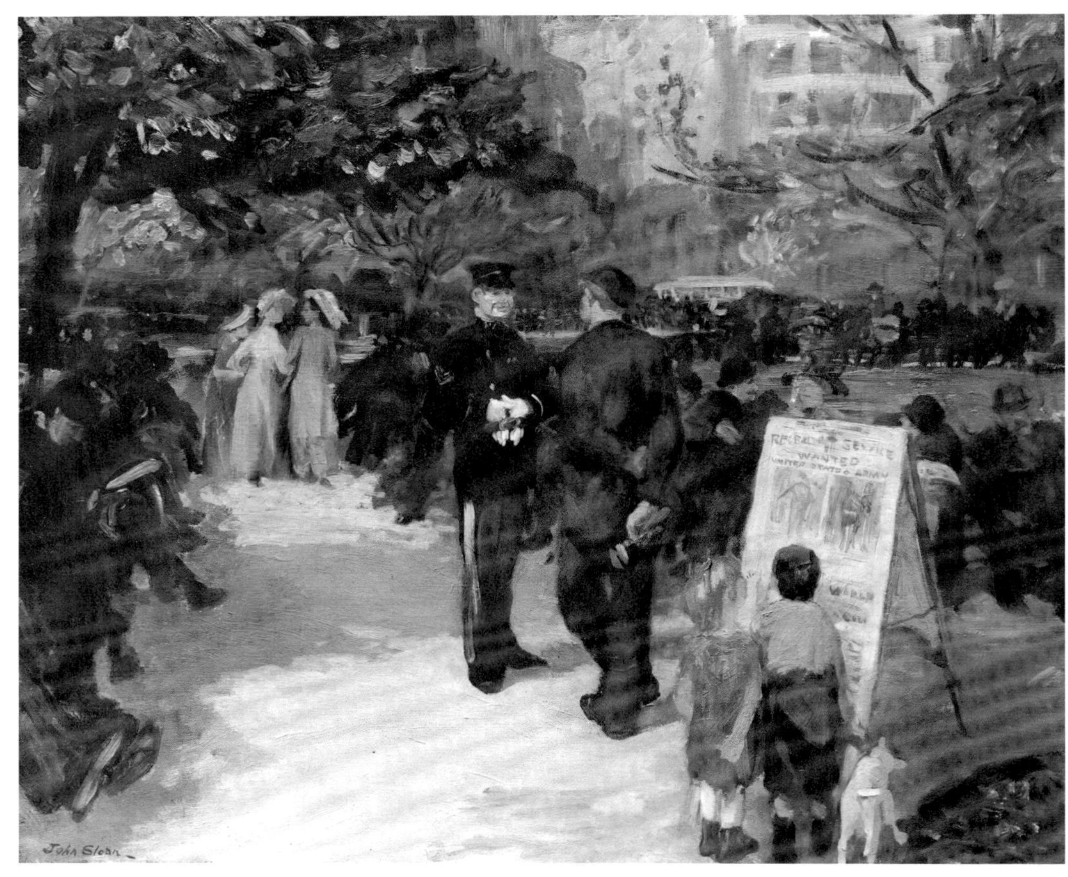

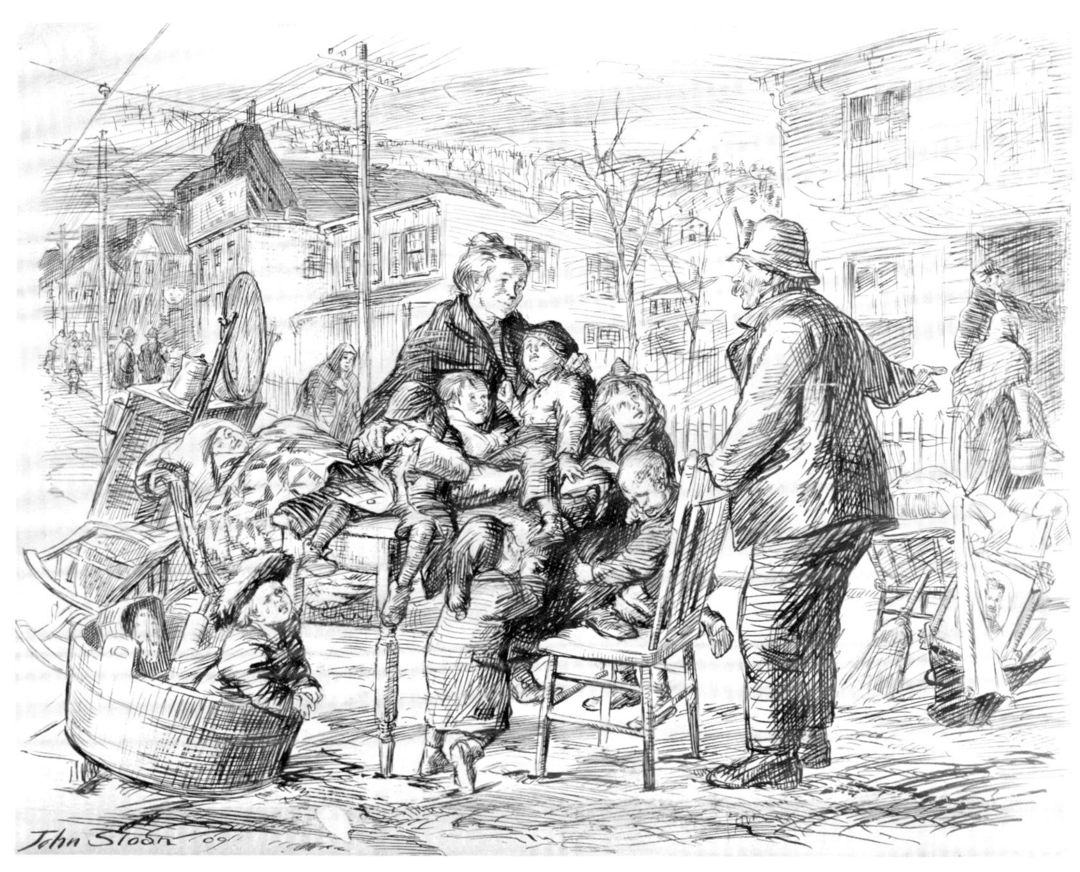

You're not so bad off. The roof's all there yet, 1909
Ink and graphite on paper
17¼ x 21½ in
Published in Caspar Day, "The Saints and Mary Toole at the Bazaar," *Century*, August 1909, p. 568
Lent by the Harvard University Art Museums (Fogg Art Museum), Gift of I. Bernard Cohen in honor of Agnes Mongan

49

When fire damaged the house of poor widow Mary Toole, her neighbors rescued the furniture and made repairs. In his diary, December 10, 1908, Sloan describes the story as "Irish humor—with a caution [from the publisher] to bring out the 'pathos.' It is a very poor effort in the literary way." He delivered four drawings for the story on January 16, 1909, and was paid $150.

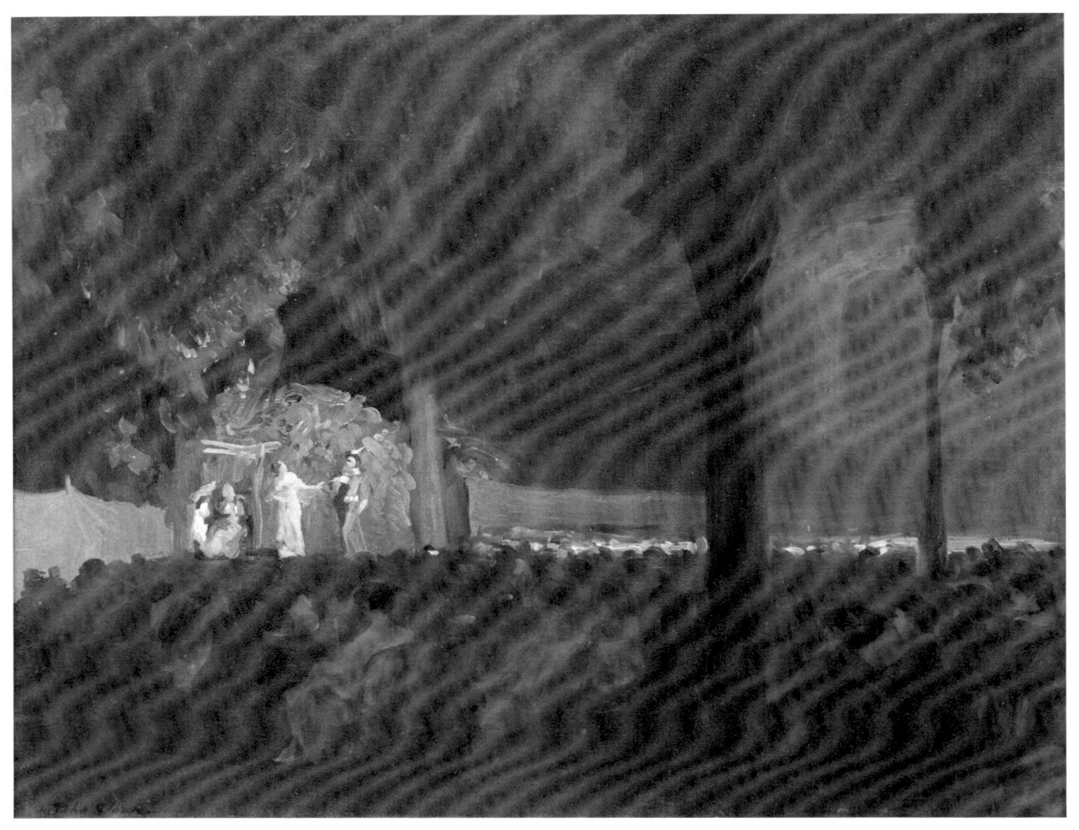

The Coburn Players, 1910
Oil on canvas
26⅛ x 32 in
Lent by the Dayton Art Institute, Museum Purchase with funds provided by the Junior League of Dayton, Ohio, Inc., and Mrs. Susanne Rike McConnaughey, 61.6

50

"This is an impression of a beautiful occasion, an outdoor performance on the campus of Columbia University. Many details are omitted—among them I note the absence of the mosquitos. These small pests attended to our ankles while the Coburns kept our minds amused."

Yeats at Petitpas, 1910
Oil on canvas
26⅜ x 32¼ in
Lent by the Corcoran Gallery of Art,
Museum Purchase, 1932

The figures represented are, from left to right: Van Wyck Brooks, biographer and historian; John Butler Yeats, painter and father of the poet; Alan Seeger, poet; Dolly Sloan; Celestine Petitpas, innkeeper; Robert Sneddon, writer; Mrs. Charles Johnston; Eulabee Dix, model and miniature painter; Fred King, an editor of the *Literary Digest*; and Sloan.

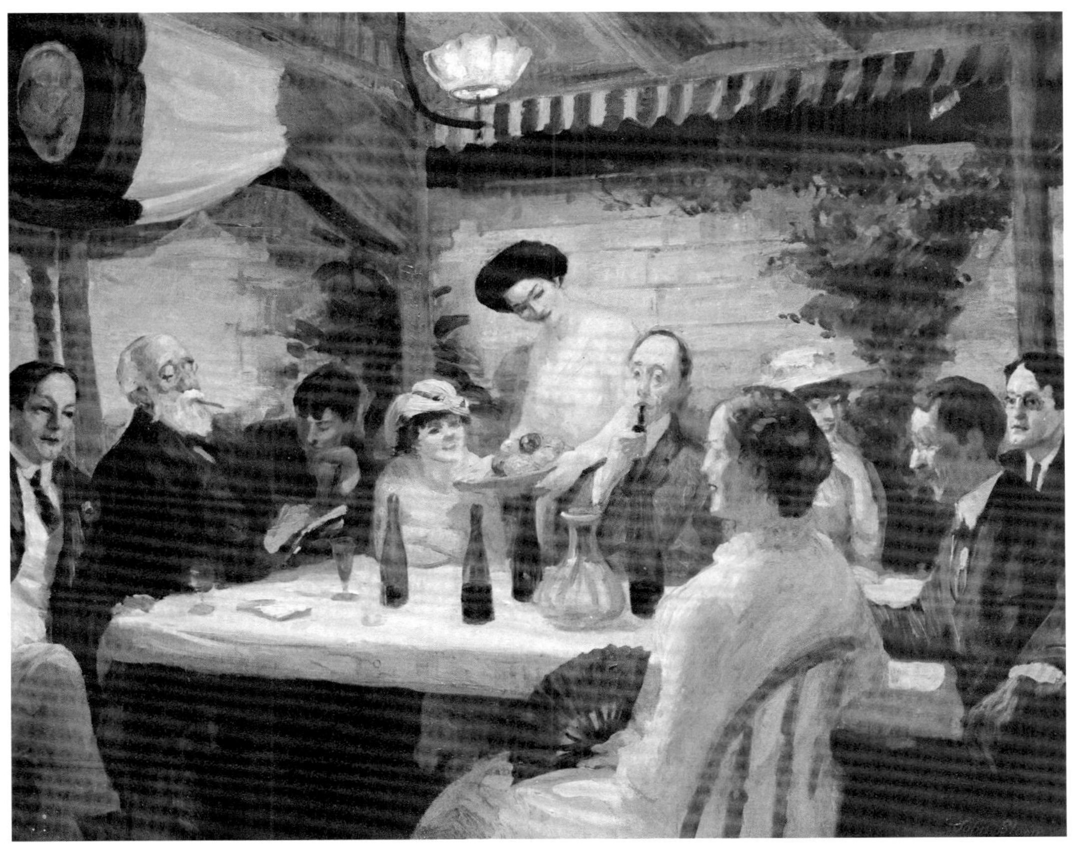

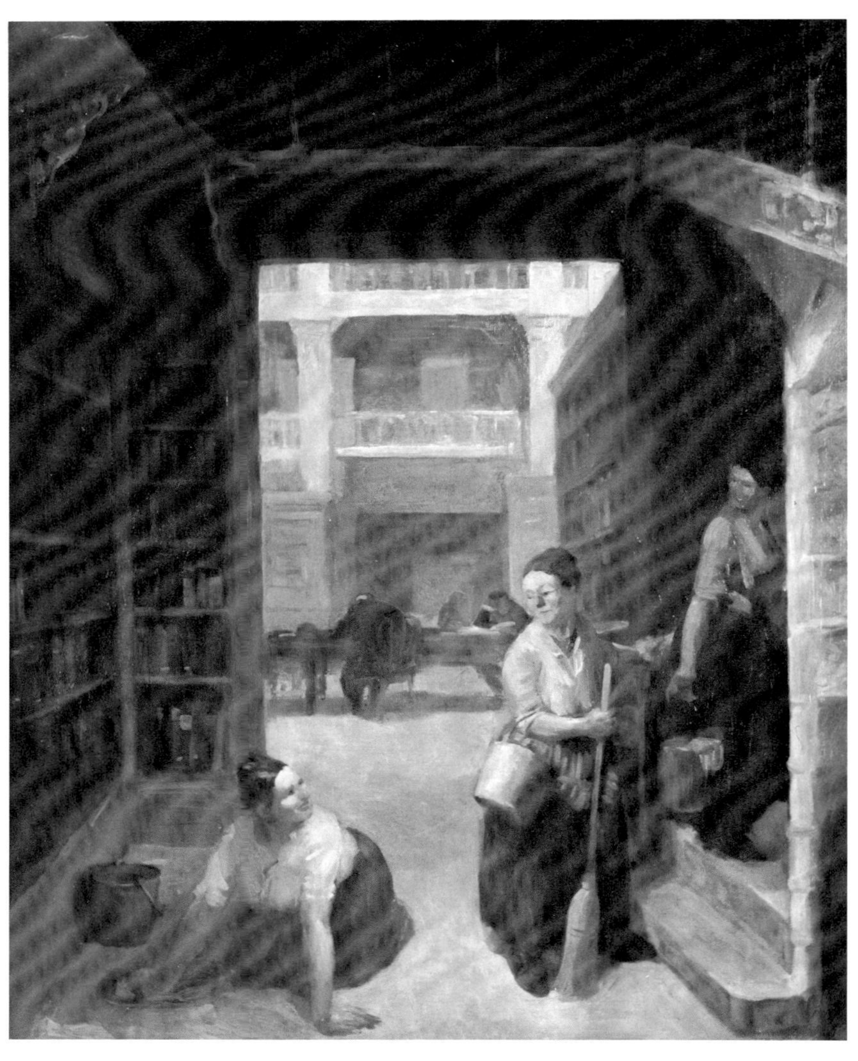

Scrubwomen, Astor Library, 1910–11
Oil on canvas
32 x 26 in
Lent by the Munson-Williams-Proctor Institute

The lively and chattering scrubwomen violating the imposing silence and dignity of the library at 425 Lafayette Street (now the Public Theater) is characteristic of Sloan's delicately barbed wit, which frequently appears in his genre paintings.

Night Windows, 1910
Etching
5¼ x 7 in
Lent by the Delaware Art Museum, Gift of Helen Farr Sloan, 1963

"**N**ight, the roofs back of us—a girl in deshabille at a window and a man on the roof smoking his pipe and taking in the charms while at a window below him his wife is busy hanging out his washed linen."

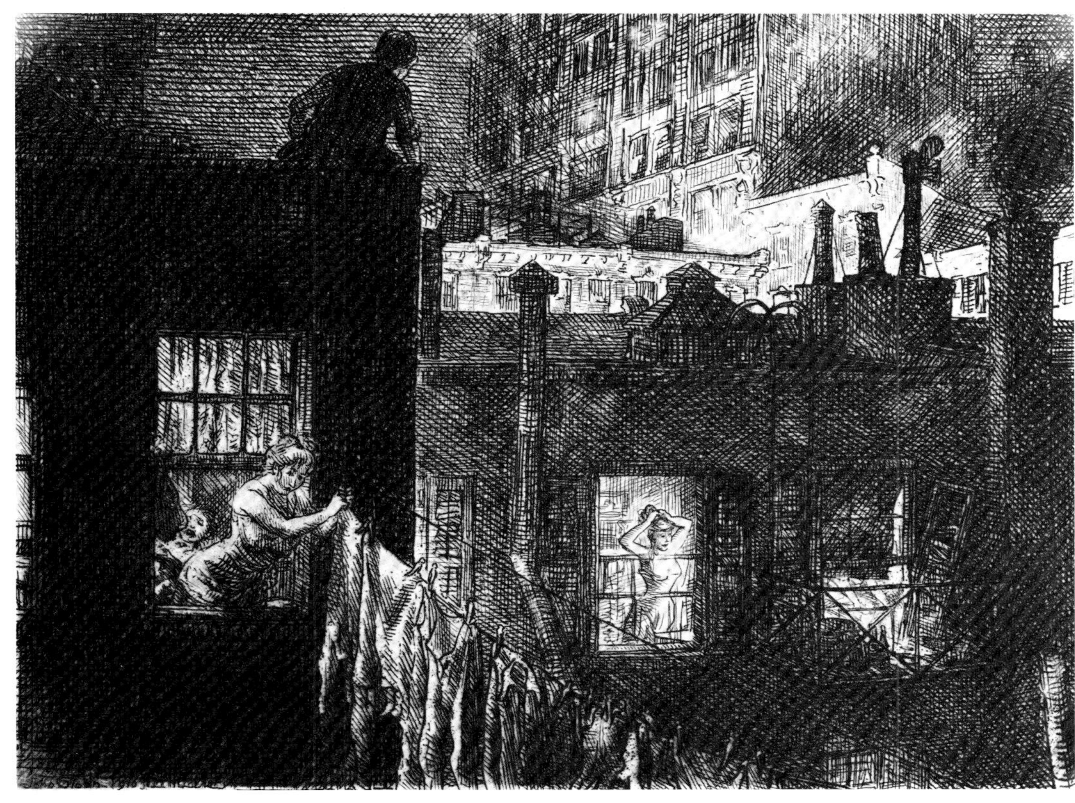

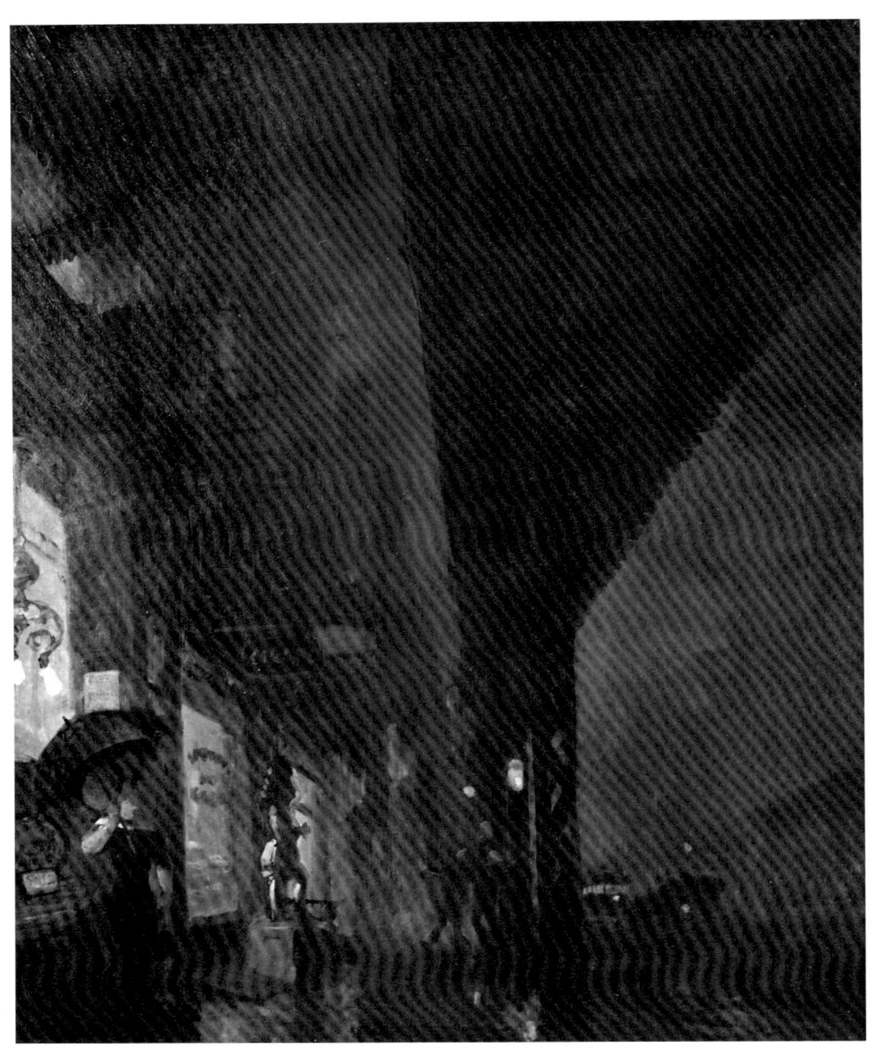

***Wet Night on the Bowery*, 1911**
Oil on canvas
27 x 22 in
Lent anonymously

In June 1911, Sloan moved from West 23rd Street to East 22nd Street, and his subject-searching walks concentrated on the East Side. This unusually dramatic painting shows the Third Avenue Elevated tracks running directly overhead and disappearing into the mist.

The ex-pirate shot so rapidly through the tap-room that Experience (invisible but determined) had hard work to keep up with him, 1911
Ink on scratchboard
10 x 13½ in
Published in Ralph Bergengren, "Delilah," *Collier's,* April 8, 1911, p. 30
Lent by Jim and Judi Kaiser

The pirate named Pigge sneaks away from his compatriots and becomes smitten with love for the widow Mrs. Martha Egge, owner of a respectable New England tavern. He offers to do chores for her, such as killing a chicken that runs through the taproom. Sloan was paid $225 for his four drawings; one of the pirates in the series is modeled after his friend Robert Henri.

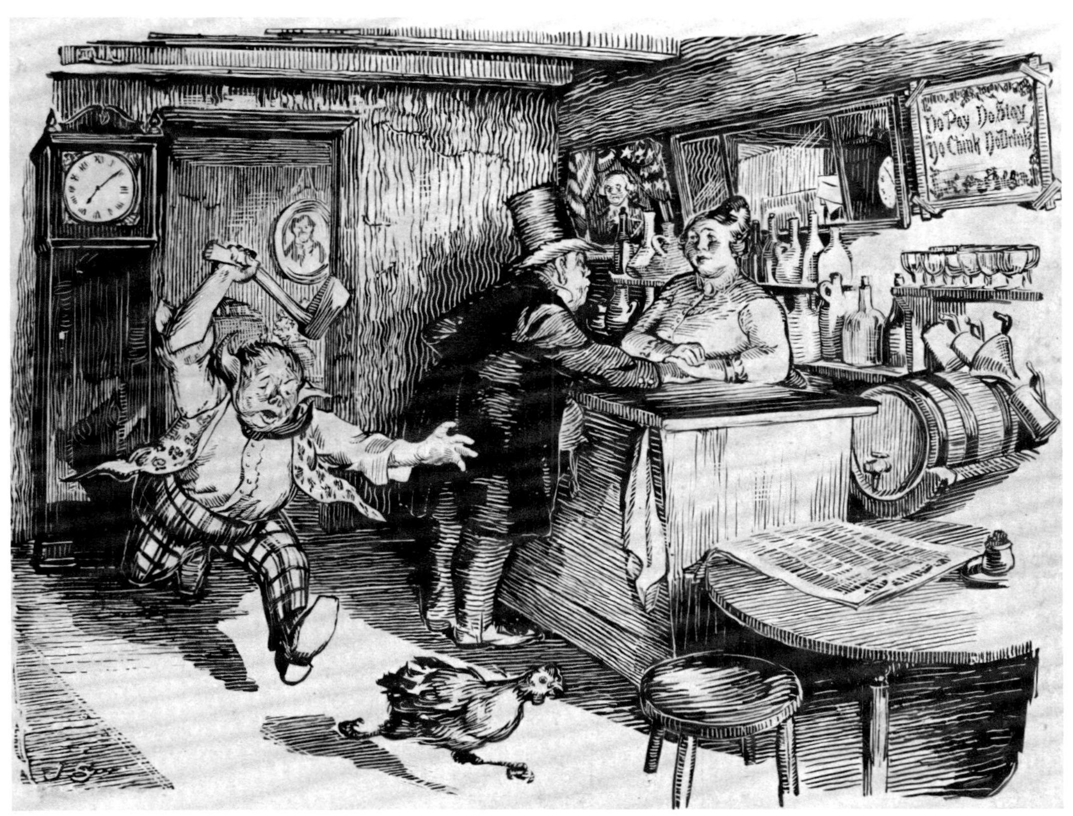

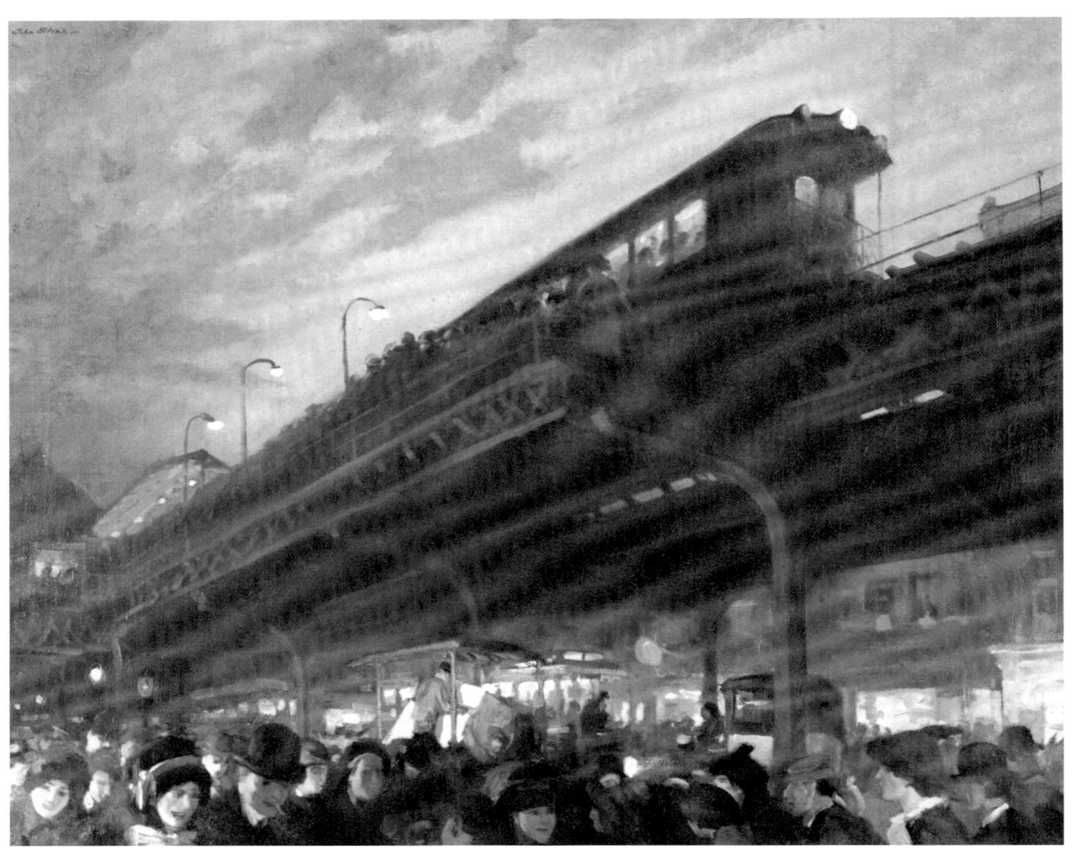

Six O'Clock, Winter, 1912
Oil on canvas
26 x 31 in
Lent by the Phillips Collection, Washington, D.C.

Completely different in mood from the forlorn, almost menacing darkness of *Wet Night on the Bowery,* Sloan shows the Third Avenue "El" near 18th Street as a warm and comforting bearer of homeward-bound workers on a cold February evening.

***McSorley's Back Room*, 1912**
Oil on canvas
26 x 32 in
Lent by the Hood Museum of Art, Dartmouth College, Hanover, New Hampshire. Purchased through the Julia L. Whittier Fund.

Sloan never met John McSorley, who founded the ale house "McSorley's Old House at Home" on 7th Street near Cooper Union in the 1850s, but his son told him that the old man used to sit in the sun in his back room, holding court, and Sloan painted this tribute from his imagination.

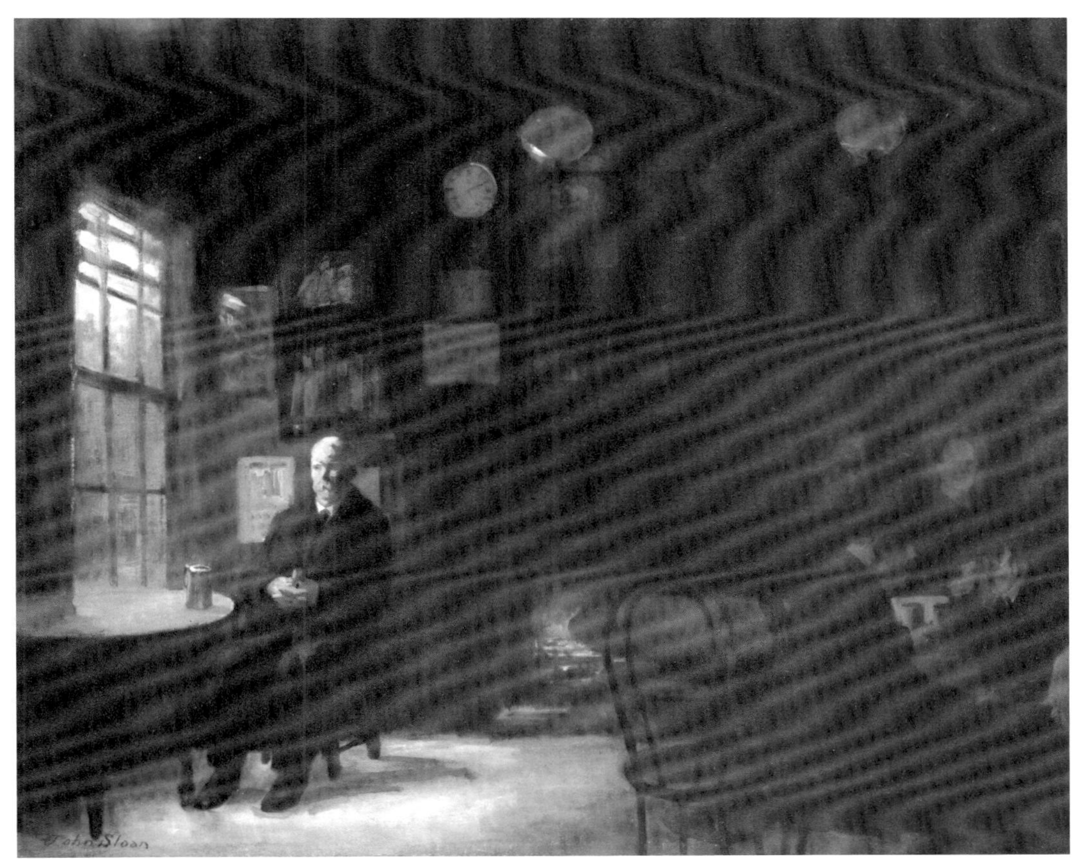

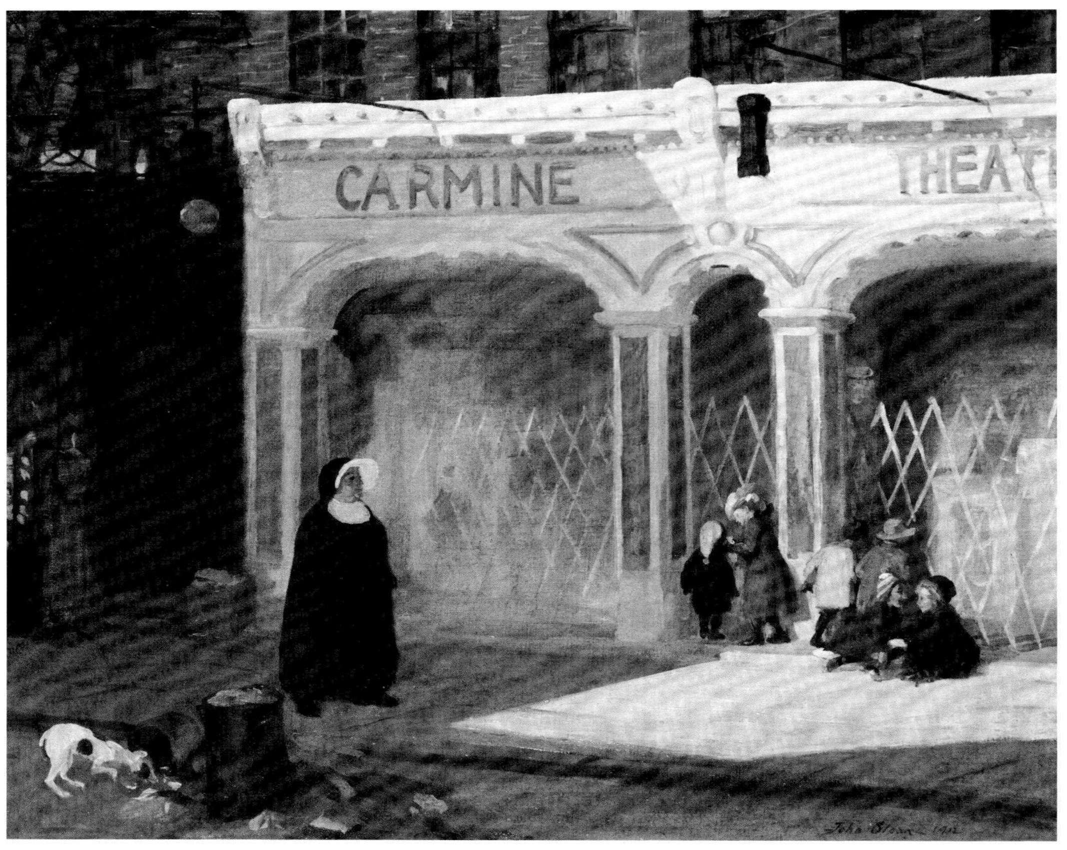

Carmine Theatre, 1912
Oil on canvas
26⅛ x 32 in
Lent by the Hirshhorn Museum and Sculpture Garden, Smithsonian Institution; Gift of Joseph H. Hirshhorn Foundation, 1966

58

The Carmine Theatre was a small movie theatre at Bleecker and Carmine Streets in Greenwich Village. In 1939 Sloan wrote: "In those days it was called 'ash can art'—today it's the American Scene."

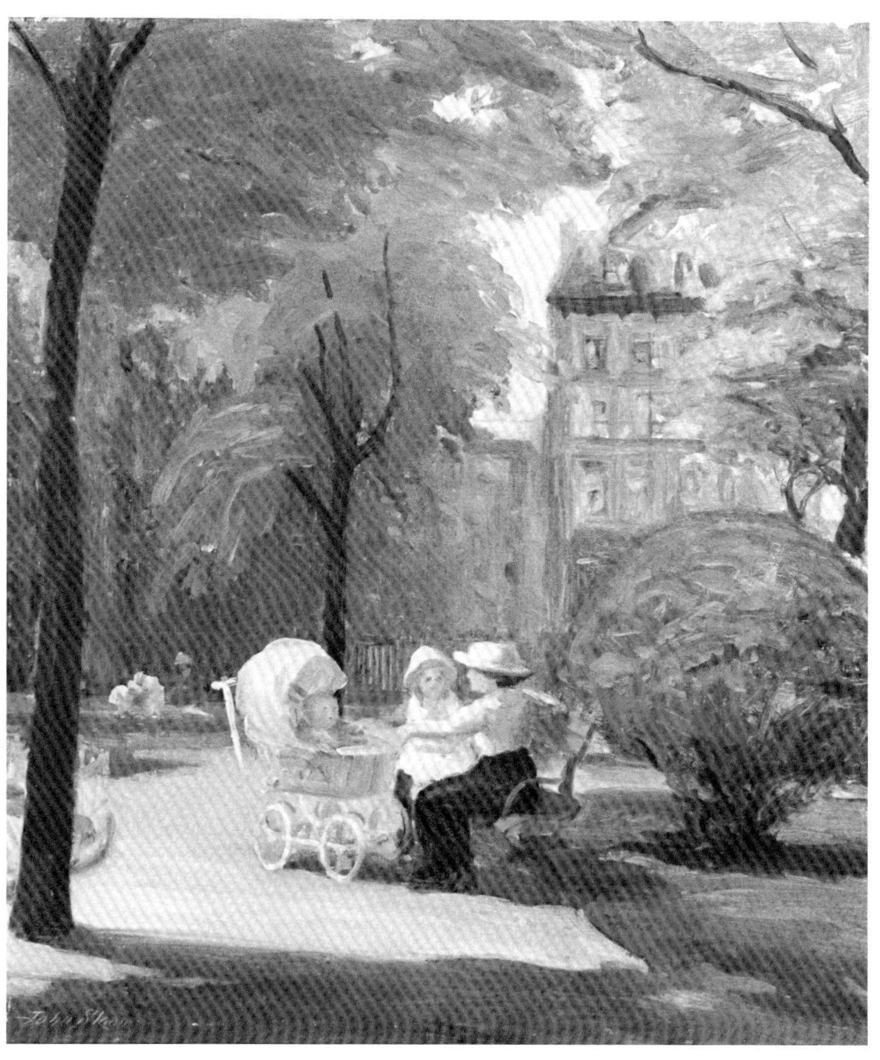

Spring, Gramercy Park, 1912
Oil on canvas
24 x 20 in
Lent by Mr. Albert Hackett

59

Wholly different in the attitude toward wealth and privilege demonstrated in *Fifth Avenue,* Sloan found nothing but peace and beauty in the exclusive and privately controlled precinct of Gramercy Park.

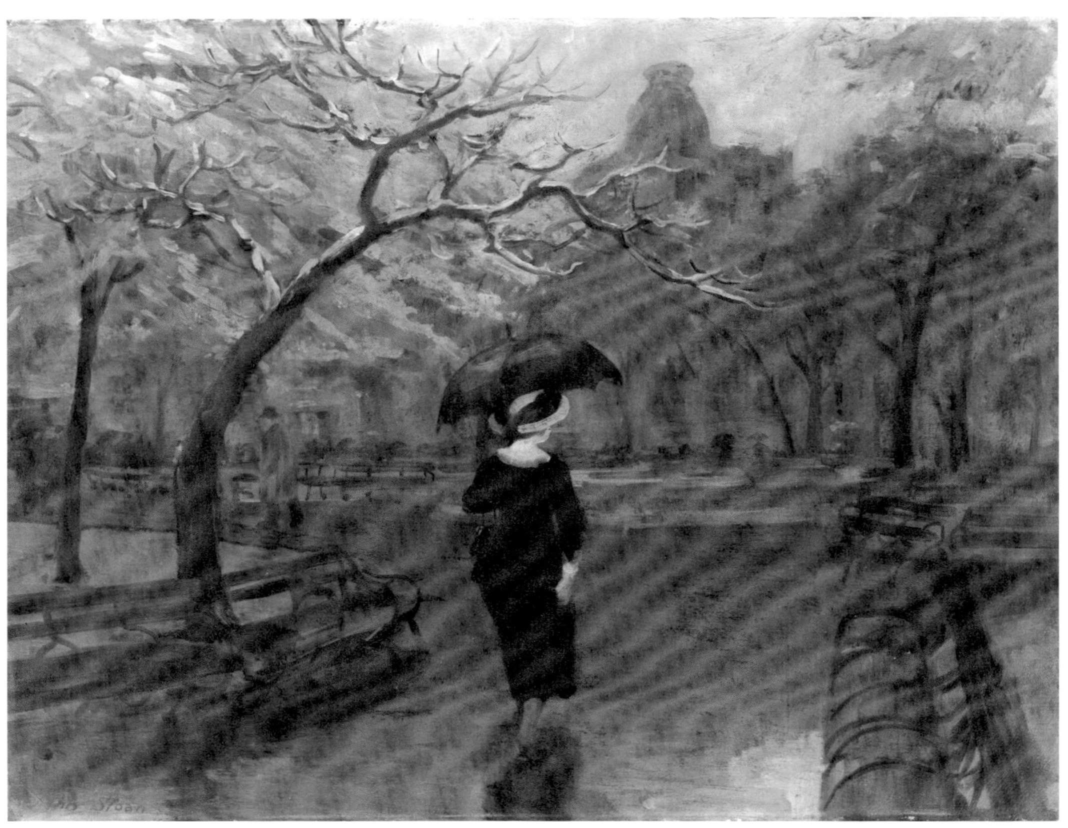

Spring Rain, 1912
Oil on canvas
20¼ x 26¼ in
Lent by the Delaware Art Museum, Gift of the John Sloan Memorial Foundation, 1986

In 1909 Sloan began to use a method of premixing his colors according to a logical system developed by the artist H. G. Maratta. The colors could be related to the intervals of the musical scale. Sloan said this painting was in a dominant seventh chord.

A *Window on the Street, 1912*
Oil on canvas
26 x 32 in
Lent by the Bowdoin College Museum of Art, Brunswick, Maine

"The color theme of this canvas is, I think, in close harmony with the subject. The sullen wistfulness of the woman whose housekeeping was limited to one room. Dominant red-purple cushion and smothered red brickwork."

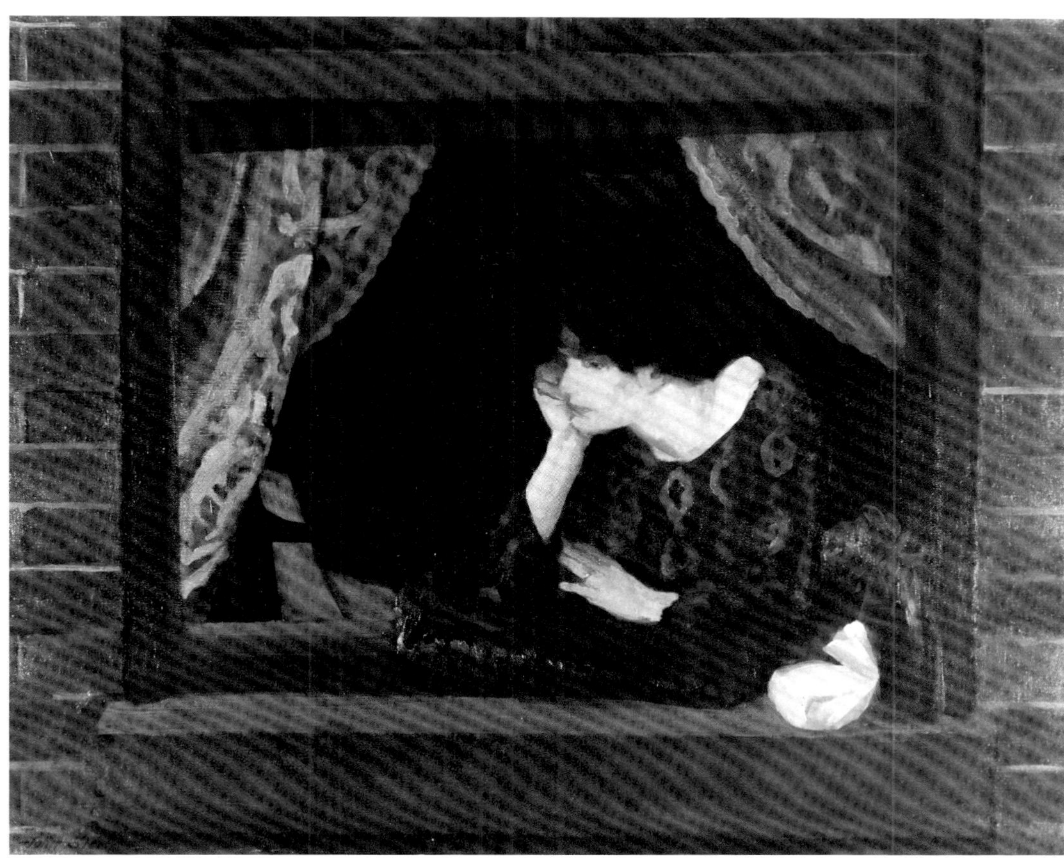

Sunday Afternoon in Union Square, 1912
Oil on canvas
26¼ x 32¼ in
Lent by the Bowdoin College Museum of Art, Brunswick, Maine

The two fashionably dressed women taking a Sunday stroll are clearly successful in their intention to draw stares. The narrative element in this painting places it closer to Sloan's illustrations than to many of his other paintings which are observed events.

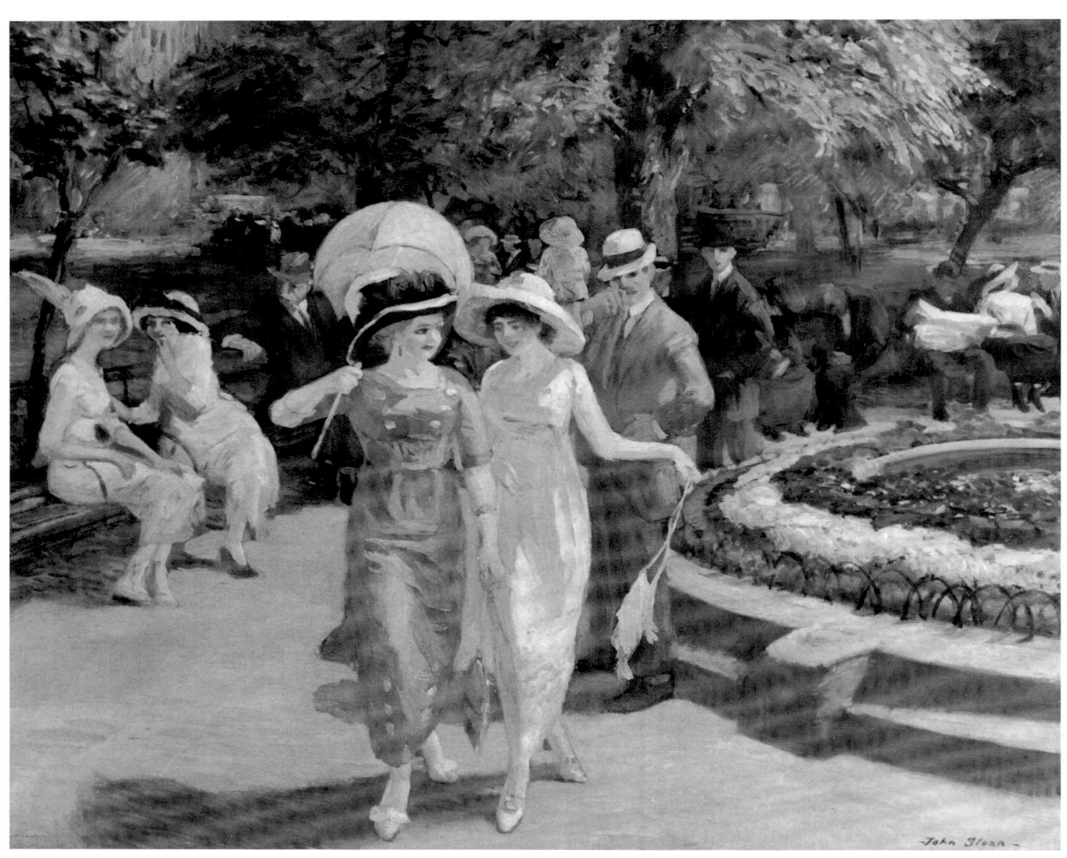

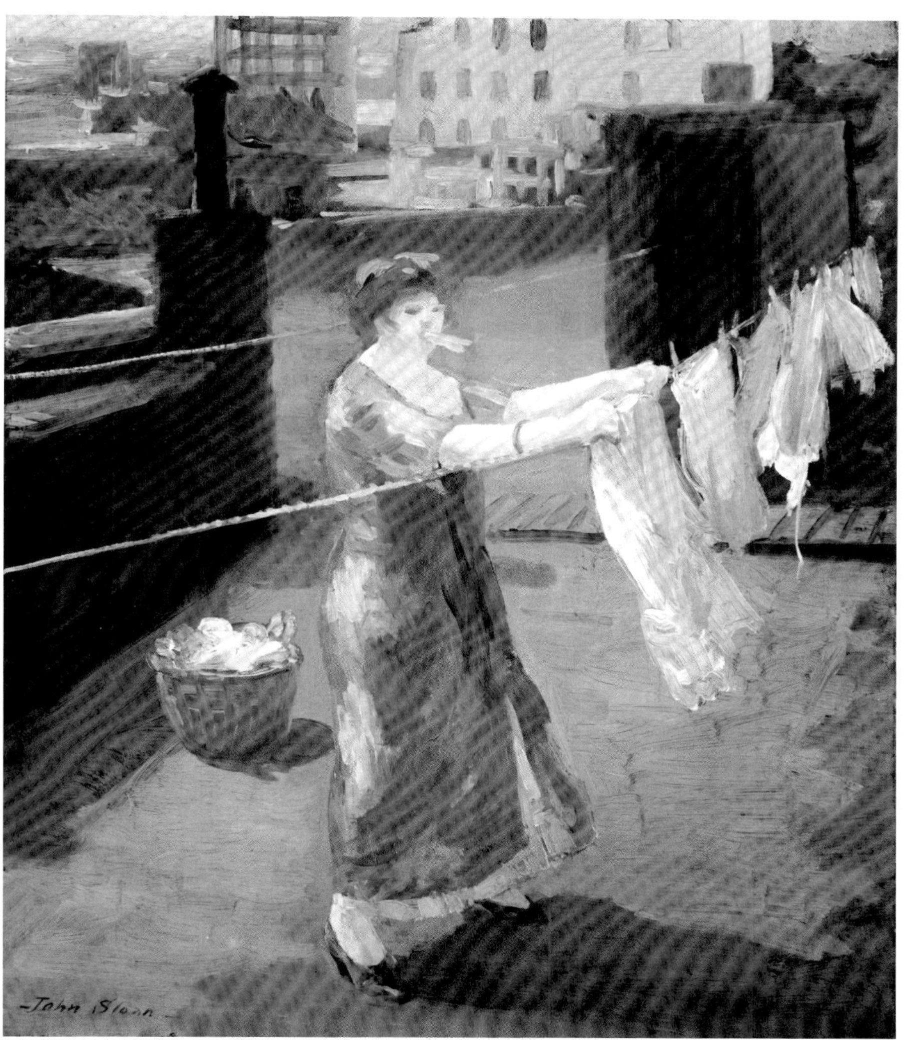

***Red Kimono on the Roof*, 1912**
Oil on canvas
24 x 20 in
Lent by the Indianapolis Museum of Art

In 1912 Sloan was able to take a studio separate from his living quarters for the first time. It was on the eleventh floor of 35 6th Avenue at West 4th Street, and he was able to look down on the rooftop life of the shorter buildings around him.

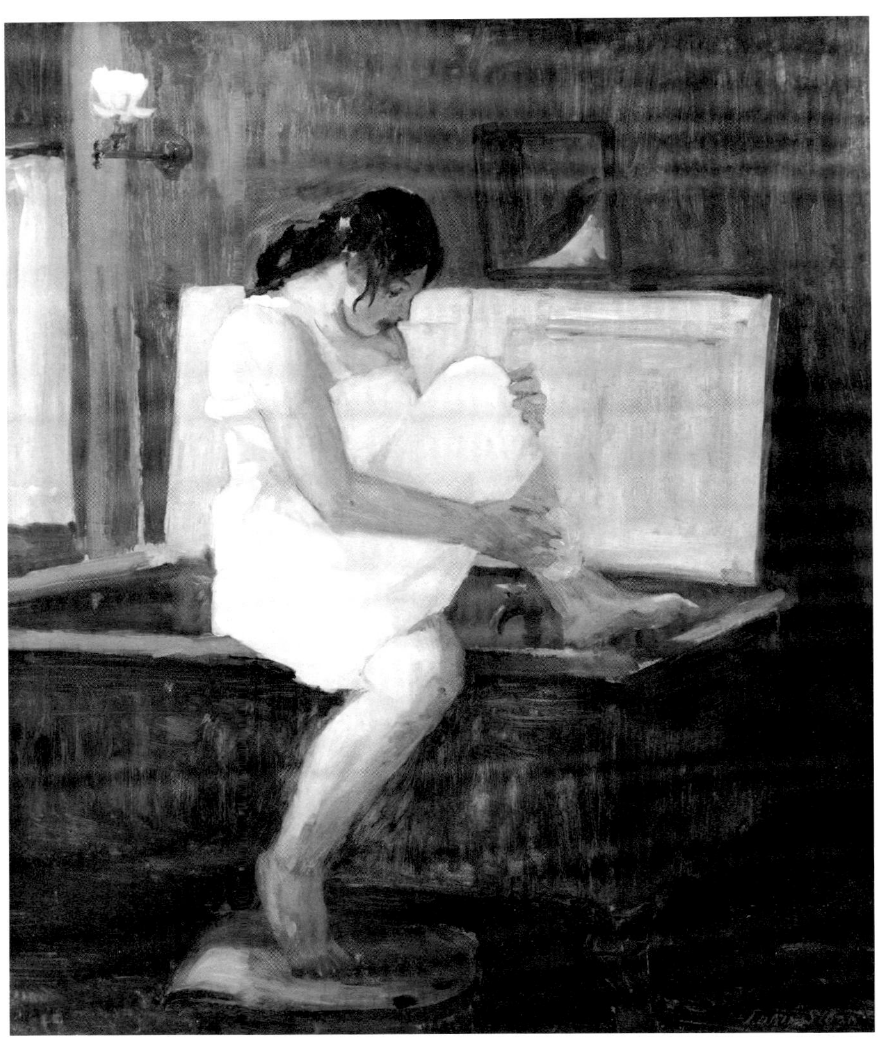

Kitchen and Bath, 1912
Oil on composition board
24 x 20 in
Lent by the Whitney Museum of American Art, New York; Gift of Mr. and Mrs. Albert Hackett, 60.44

Sloan's new and larger studio made it possible for him to begin to work from the figure seriously, which he was to continue for the rest of his career. Despite its resemblance to Sloan's through-the-window vignettes, this was actually painted from a model.

No caption (Hooray for Mother), 1912
Crayon, ink, and gouache on paper
8 x 10 in (sight)
Published in Mary Alden Hopkins, "Women March," *Collier's*, May 18, 1912, p. 13
Lent by Gary M. and Brenda H. Ruttenberg

On the stone balustrade of the Public Library terrace, a distinguished-looking father, wearing eyeglass ribbon, stands with his three children watching for their mother marching for the vote. "See, baby, there's mother! Look, baby, Look! Hooray for mother!"

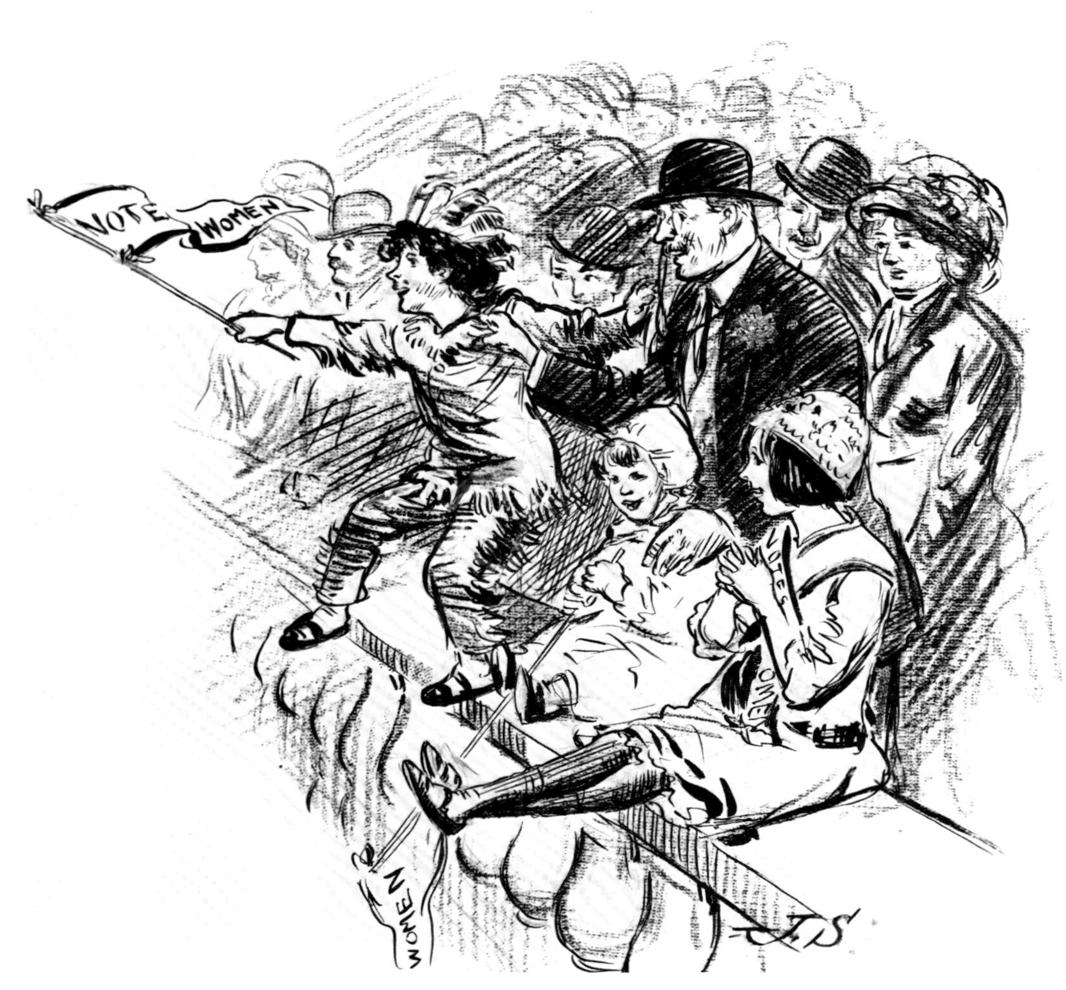

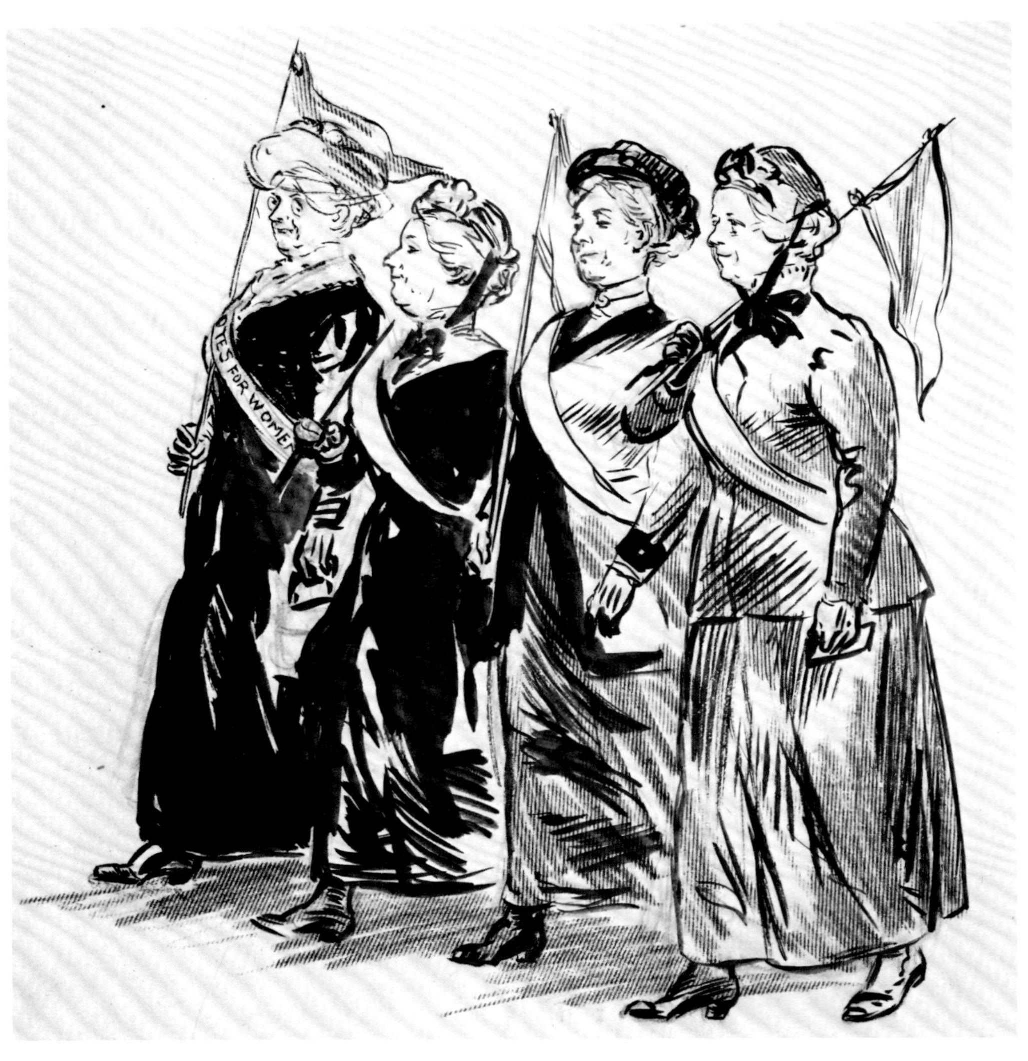

No caption (Four women marching), 1912
Crayon, ink, and graphite on paper
8½ x 11 in
Published in Mary Alden Hopkins, "Women March," *Collier's*, May 18, 1912, p. 31
Lent by The University of Michigan Museum of Art, Museum Purchase, 1964/2.154

On May 4, 1912, 10,000 men and women marched in support of women's suffrage in New York City up Fifth Avenue from Washington Square to Carnegie Hall. Though Sloan no doubt attended this march, he did not mention it in his diary.

New York Harbor, 1912
Charcoal and crayon on paper
15 x 12 in
Published in Honoré Willsie, "What is an American?", *Collier's*, November 9, 1912, p. 13
Lent anonymously

This scene of the New York City skyline with a steamship liner entering the harbor was a headpiece for an article that discussed the influx of southern and Eastern European immigrants in America and their impact on lifestyle and workplace.

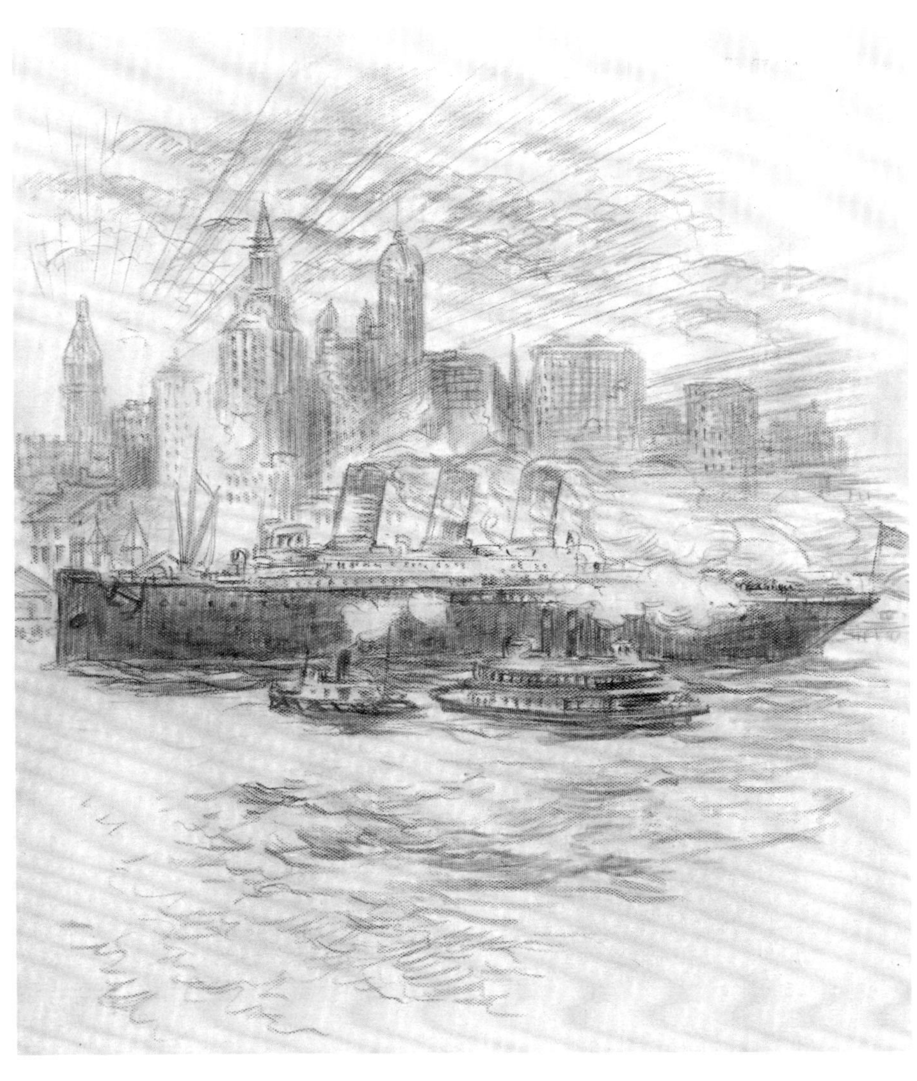

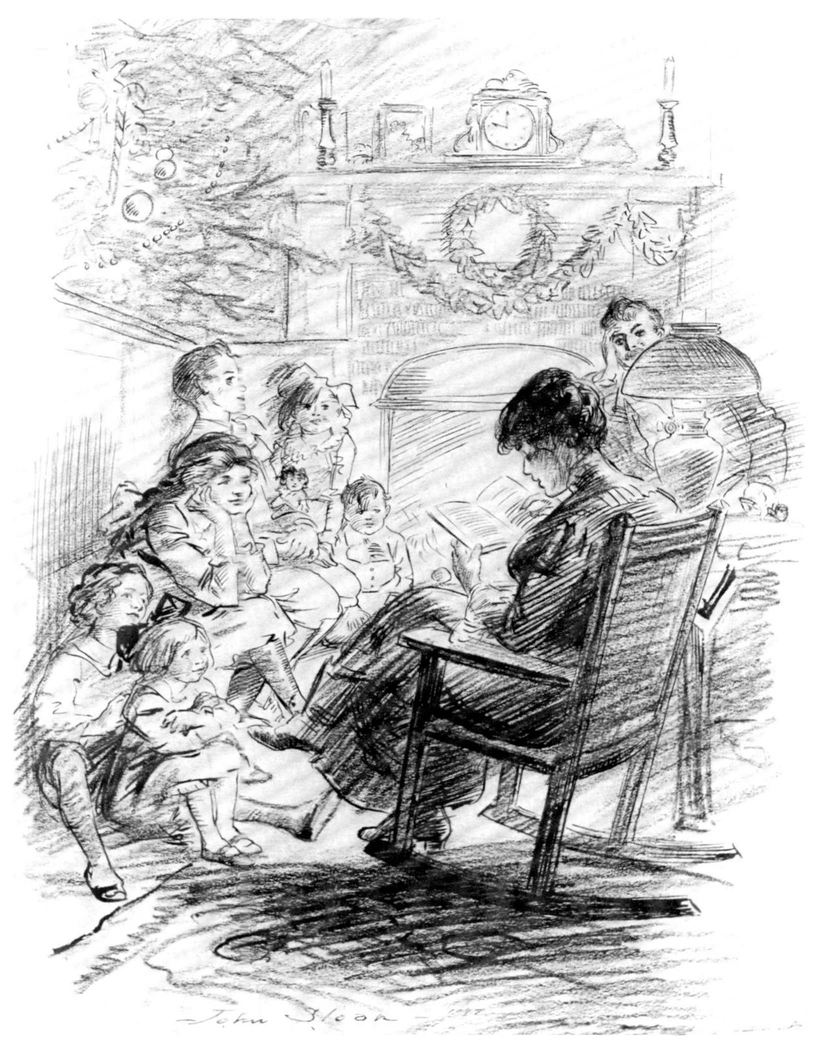

Those pictures old, but ever new, 1912
Crayon and ink on paper
17 x 13 in
Published in T. A. Daly, *Madrigali* (Philadelphia: David McKay, 1912), p. 168
Lent by Mr. and Mrs. Leonard Daly

*I*n 1912 Sloan made eleven drawings and an etching for T. A. Daly's book *Madrigali*. This drawing for the poem "The Christmas Reading" tells of reading Dickens's "Christmas Carol" to children.

Swinging in the Square, 1912
Etching
4 x 5½ in
Lent by the Delaware Art Museum, Gift of Helen Farr Sloan, 1963

"Stuyvesant Square. The peak of the swing, like the cover for *The Masses [At the Top of the Swing,* no. 73], but with deeper meaning. I felt that most women reached the best age then." "Growth toward real womanhood is often checked at about this age."

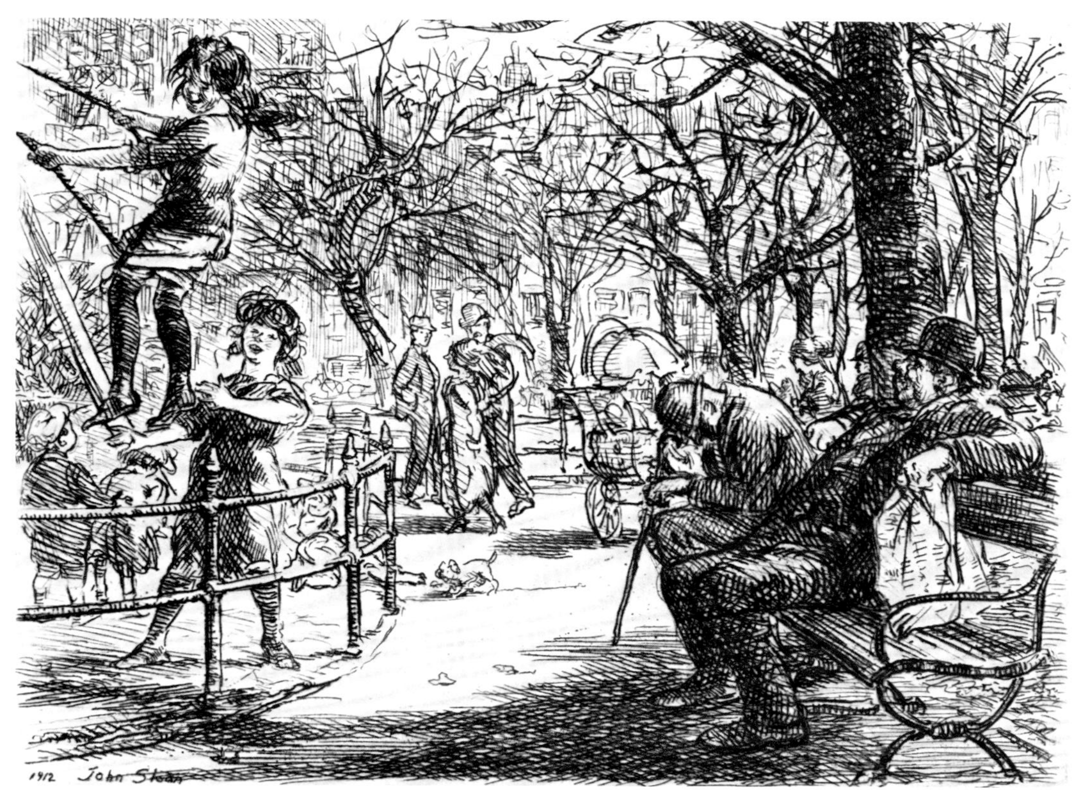

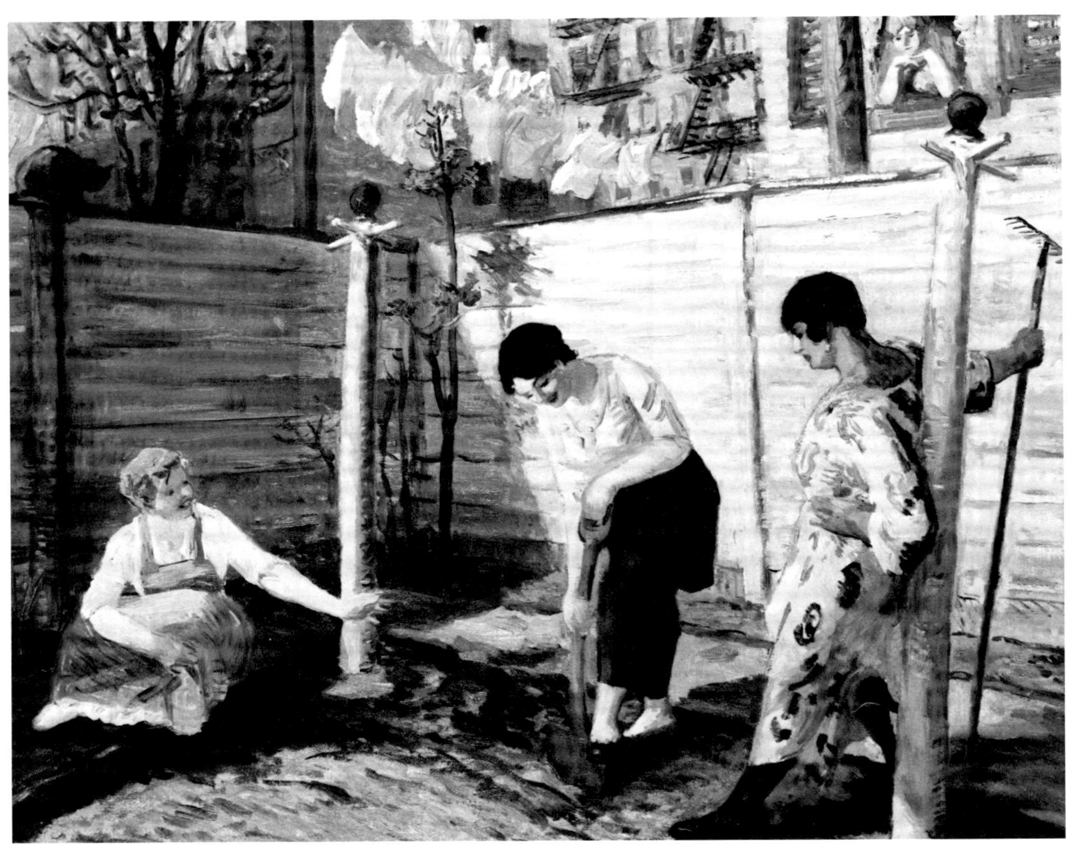

Spring Planting, Greenwich Village, 1913
Oil on canvas
26 x 32 in
Lent by the Columbus Museum of Art, Ohio; Museum Purchase, Howald Fund II, 1980

In 1913 Sloan moved his residence to the West Village where "our living quarters on West Fourth Street overlooked Greenwich Village back yards. The picture fixes a lovely spring day and a group of merry boarders in the next door yard fired with the momentary energy to till the soil."

Movies, 1913
Oil on canvas
19⅞ x 24 in
Lent by the Toledo Museum of Art,
Museum Purchase Fund

Sloan's file card for this painting identifies the subject as being on Carmine Street, and it would appear to be the same building as shown in *Carmine Theatre* (no. 58), painted a year earlier.

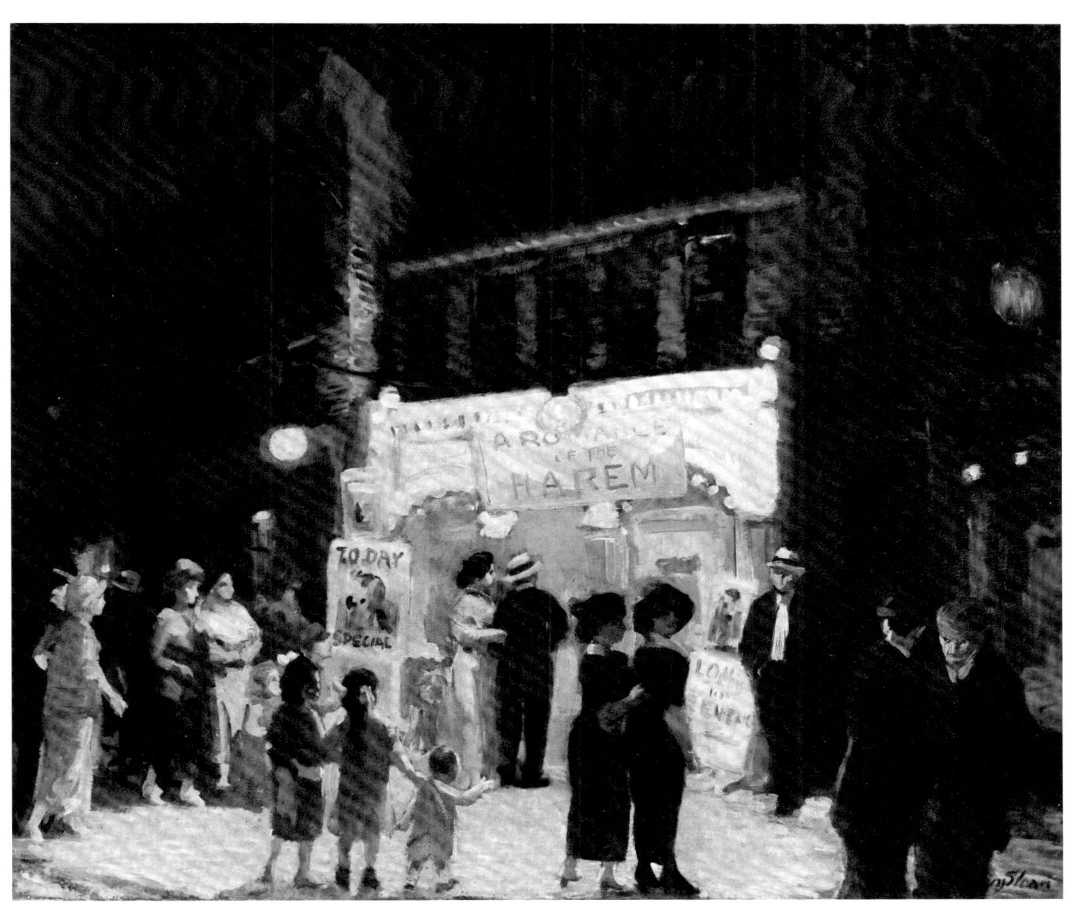

Rain, Roof Tops, West 4th Street, 1913
Oil on canvas
20 x 24 in
Lent by the Hirshhorn Museum and Sculpture Garden, Smithsonian Institution; Gift of the Joseph H. Hirshhorn Foundation, 1966

Practically all of Sloan's New York City genre subjects were painted from memory or, occasionally, sketches, but between 1906 and 1910 he painted some fifty small landscapes from nature, which gave him practice for this scene from his studio window.

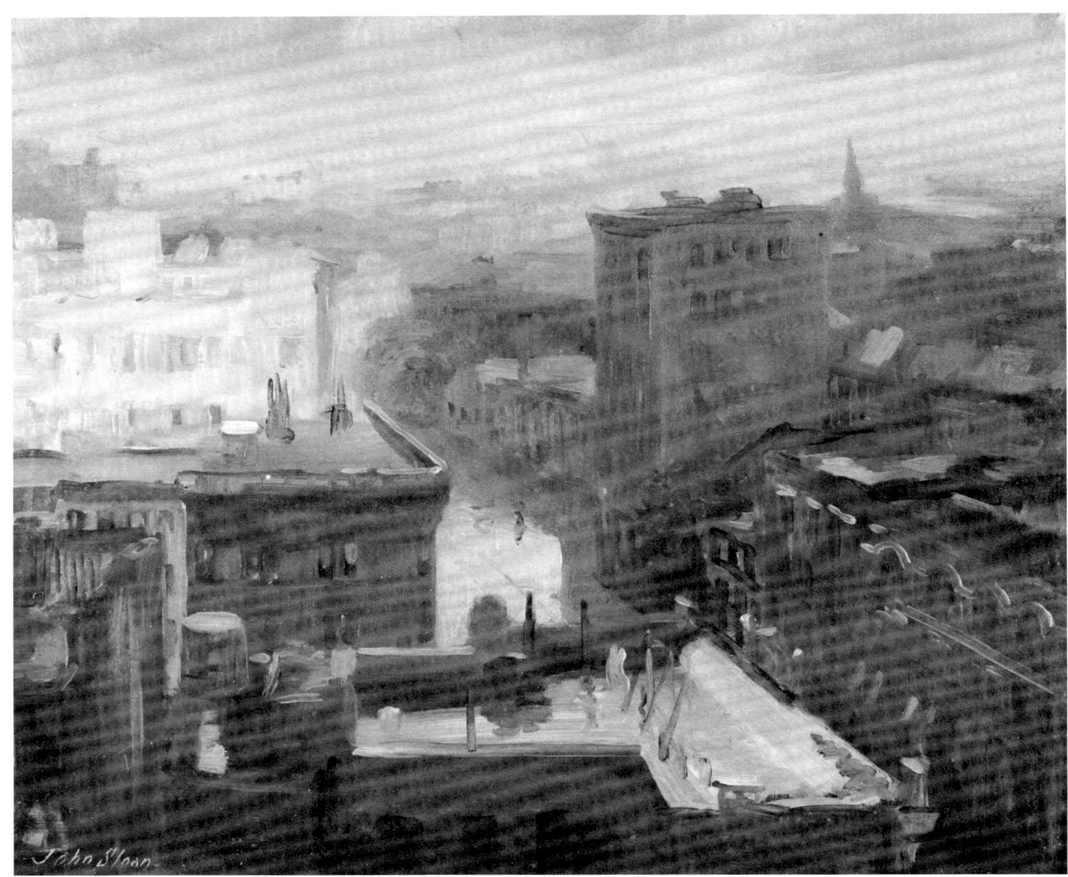

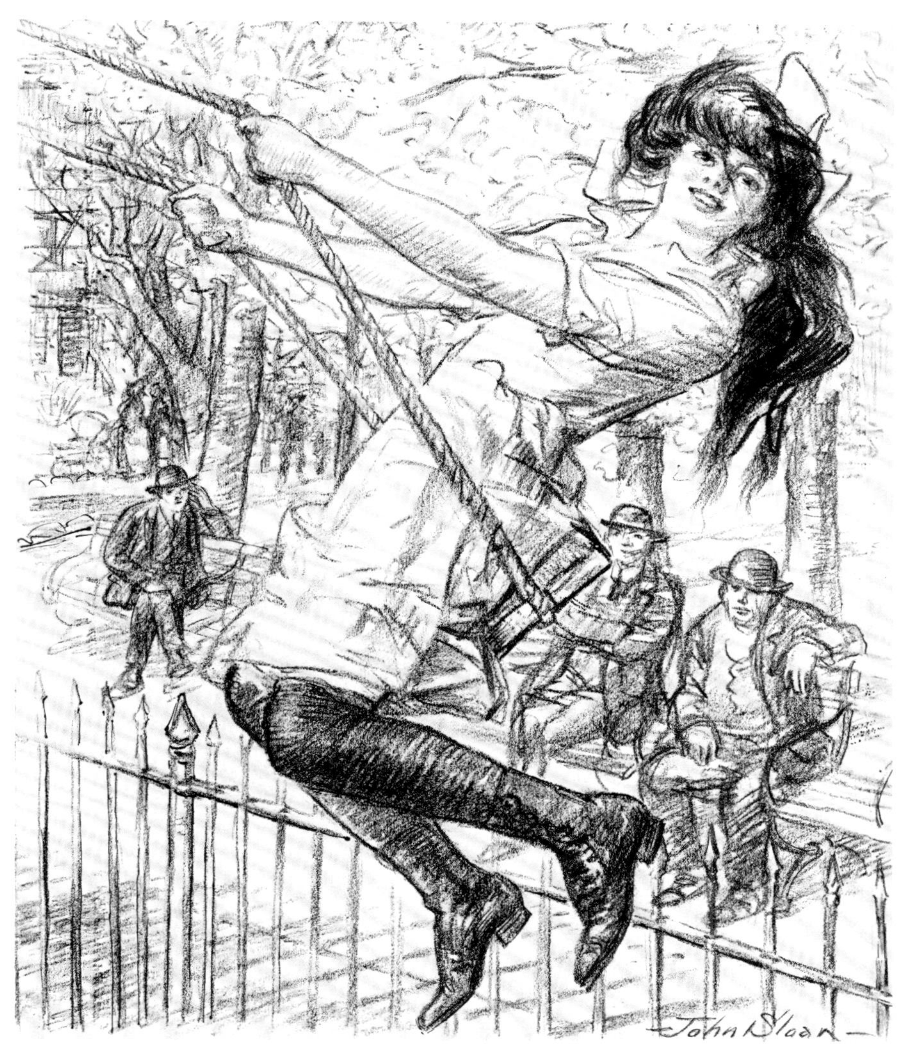

At the Top of the Swing, 1913
Chalk and ink on board
15¾ x 13⅛ in
Published in *The Masses,* May 1913, cover
Lent by Yale University Art Gallery, Gift of Dr. Charles E. Farr

In his diary for June 26, 1906, Sloan recorded: "Walked down to the East Side this afternoon, enjoyed watching the girls swinging in the Square, Avenue A and 8th Street East. A fat man watching seated on a bench interested in the more mature figures." This incident seems to have inspired the cover for *The Masses,* as well as an etching done in 1912.

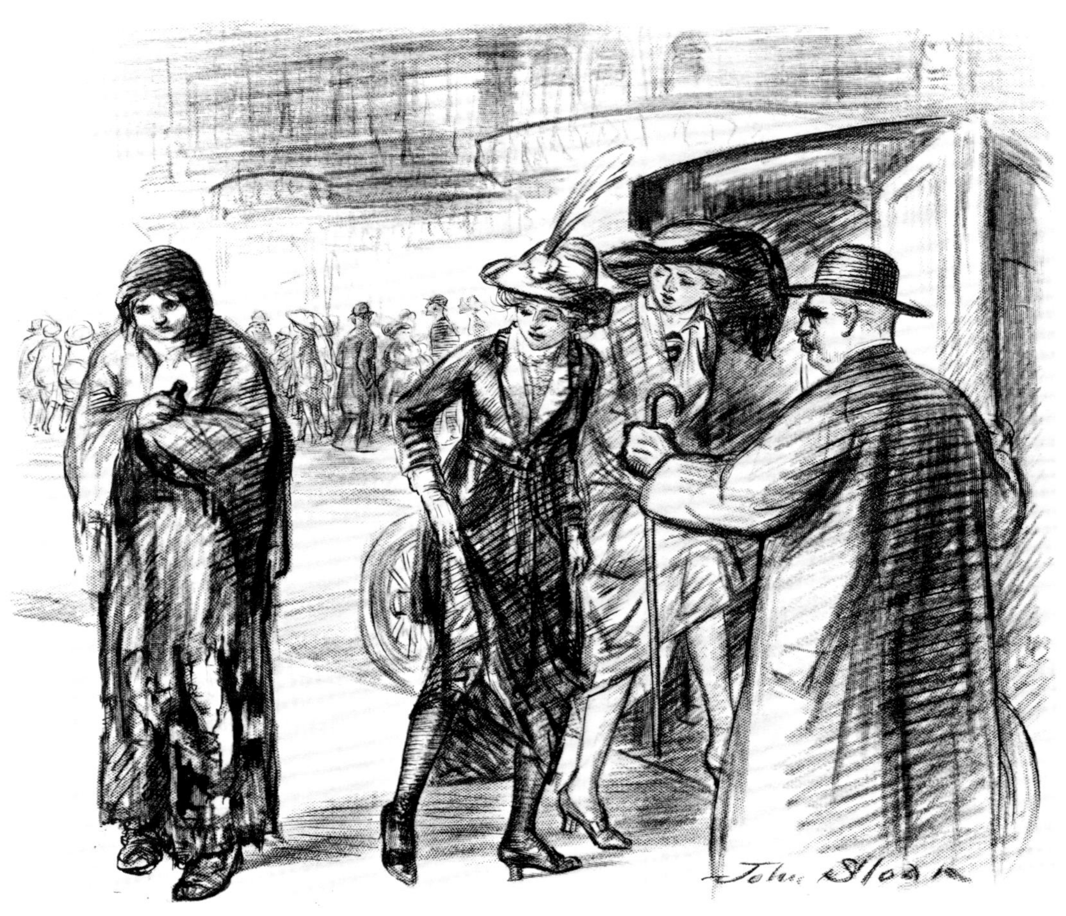

Circumstances alter cases: "Positively disgusting! It's an outrage to public decency to allow such exposure on the streets!" 1913
Crayon and ink on paper
12¼ x 14⅛ in
Published in *The Masses,* May 1913, p. 17
Lent by the Delaware Art Museum, Gift of Helen Farr Sloan, 1984

74

Sloan contributed sixty drawings to *The Masses,* a liberal magazine modeled after European satirical publications such as *Simplicissimus* and *L'Assiette au Beurre*. He was sensitive to the plight of the poor and here contrasts the fashionably dressed women with the downtrodden.

Education, 1913
Crayon and ink on paper
19 x 12½ in
Published in *The Masses*, June 1913, p. 17
Lent by the Delaware Art Museum, Gift of Helen Farr Sloan, 1987

As art editor from 1912 to 1914, Sloan redesigned *The Masses*, introducing a clean, uncluttered layout and bold, simplified typography. The drawings, usually in ink or crayon, were printed by the linecut process and have a strong visual impact.

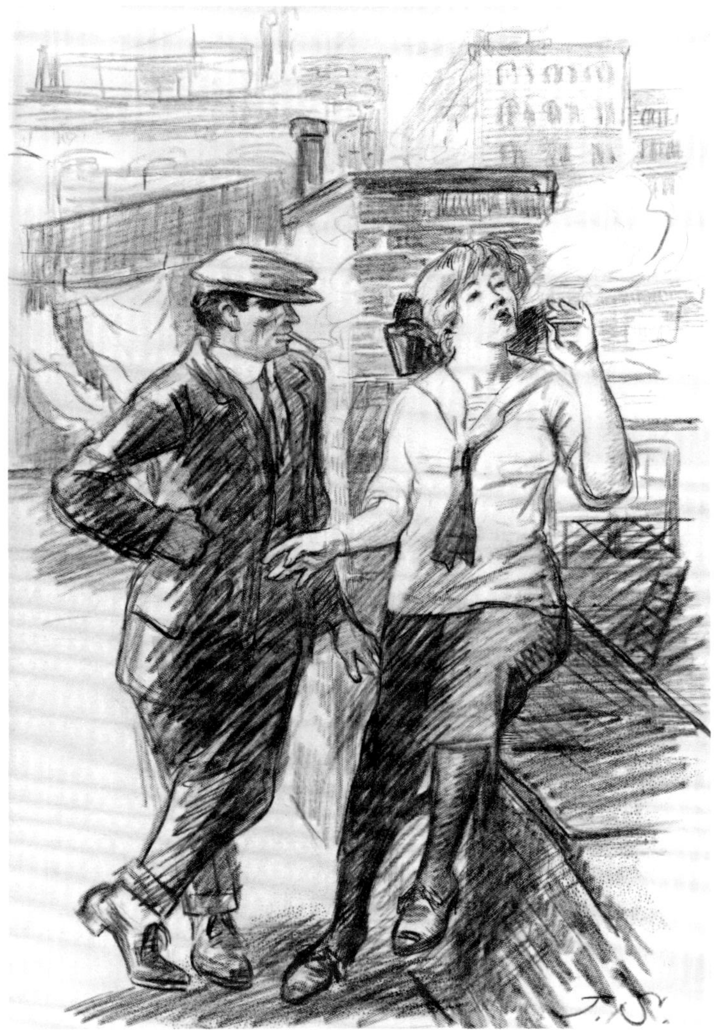

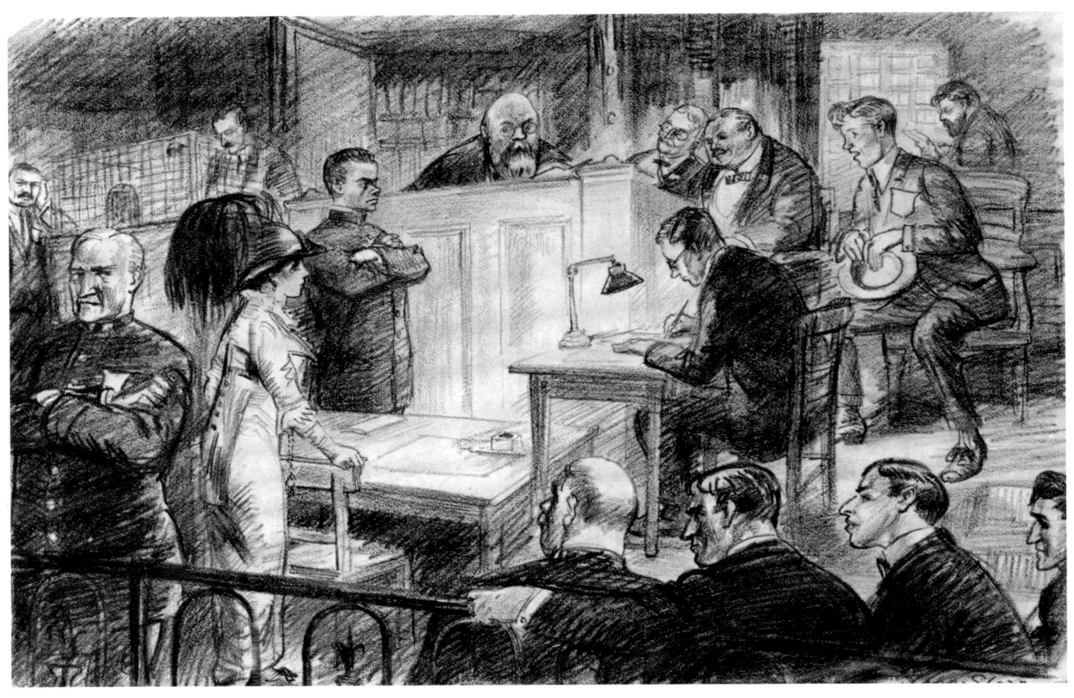

The Women's Night Court: Before Her Makers and Her Judge, 1913
Crayon on paper
16½ x 25 in
Published in *The Masses,* August 1913, pp. 10–11
Lent by the Whitney Museum of American Art, New York; Purchase, 36.38

Sloan sometimes visited the women's night court at Jefferson Market on Sixth Avenue to sketch the proceedings. The subject of this drawing relates to a play by Frank T. Shay about prostitutes and the unfair court system published in the same issue.

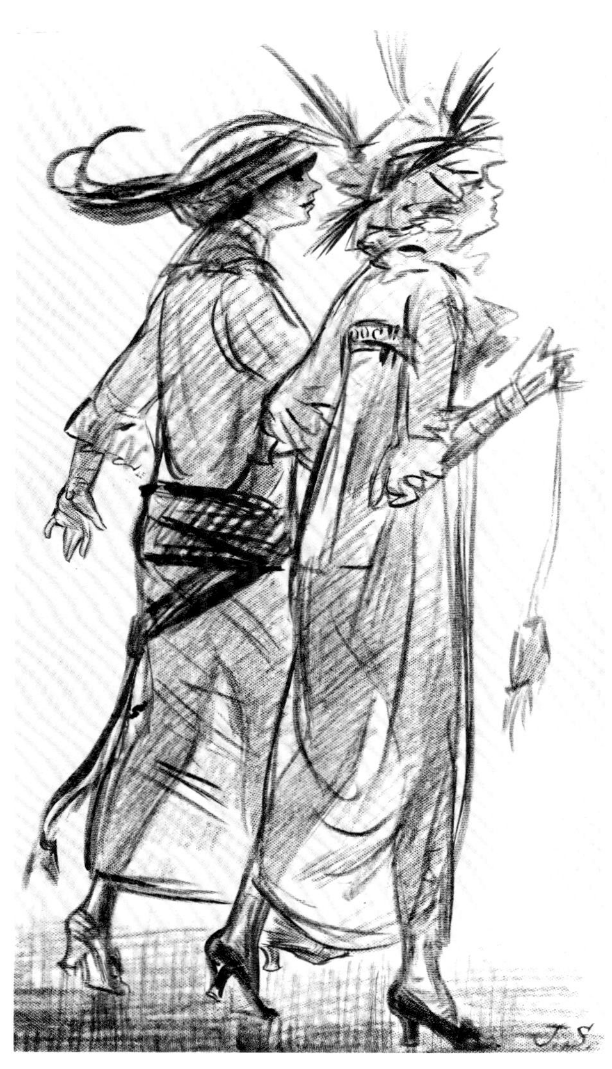

The net result as seen on Broadway, 1913
Crayon and ink on paper
17 x 9½ in
Published in *The Masses*, August 1913, p. 17
Lent by the Delaware Art Museum, Gift of Helen Farr Sloan, 1987

Artists for *The Masses* enjoyed poking fun at the fashion of the day, as well as pointing out social injustice. The complete caption for this drawing is: "The net result as seen on Broadway; items from a department store's newspaper advertisement—net undervests... $1.50, net combinations...$3.50, net petticoats...$4.00, net dresses...$30.00."

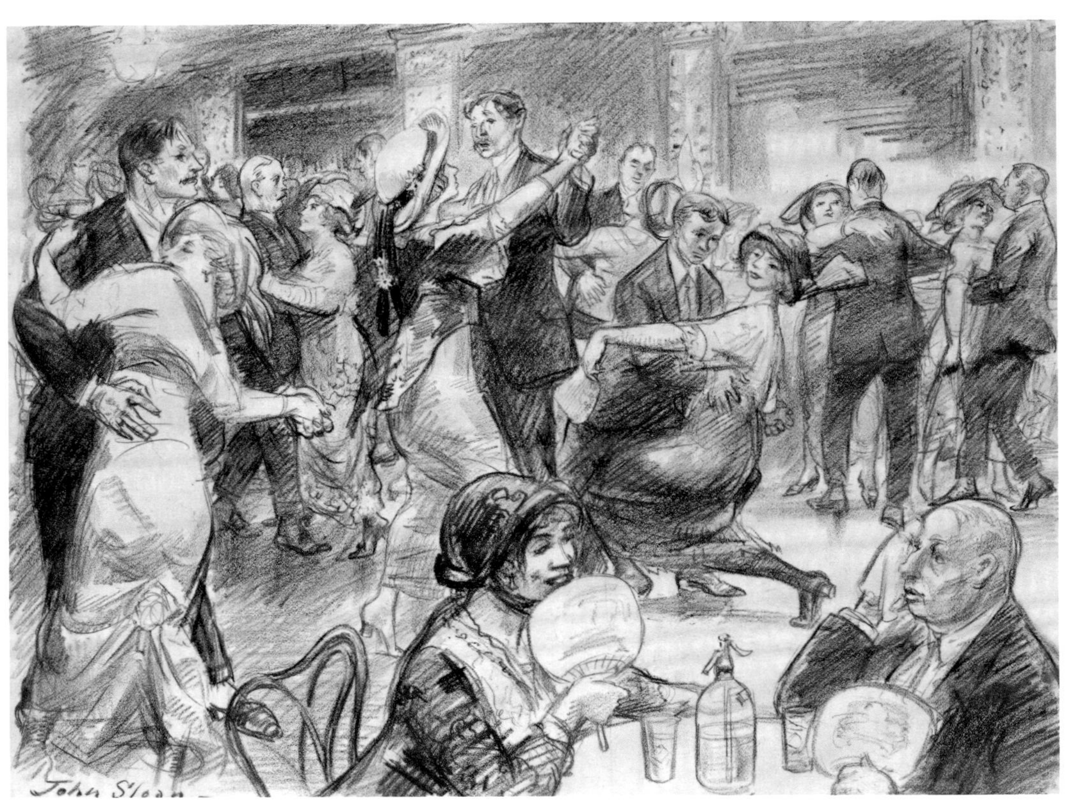

The Hot Spell in New York, 1913
Crayon on paper
19⅝ x 25⅝ in
Published in *Harper's Weekly*, September 6, 1913, pp. 16–17
Lent by Georgia Museum of Art, The University of Georgia, University Purchase

Sloan made twenty-four drawings for *Harper's Weekly. The Hot Spell in New York* was reproduced as a double-page spread and shows Robert and Marjorie Henri dancing at the left. The turkey trot and tango were popular dances of the day.

Professor, will you play "The Rosary"?, 1913
Charcoal and ink on paper
19⅝ x 17⅝ in
Published in *Harper's Weekly*, September 13, 1913, cover
Lent by the Addison Gallery of American Art, Phillips Academy, Andover, Massachusetts

Sloan made two cover designs for *Harper's Weekly*. The caption refers to a popular song of the period: "The hours I spend with you, dear heart/ Are like a string of pearls to me/ I tell them over one by one/ My rosary—my rosary."

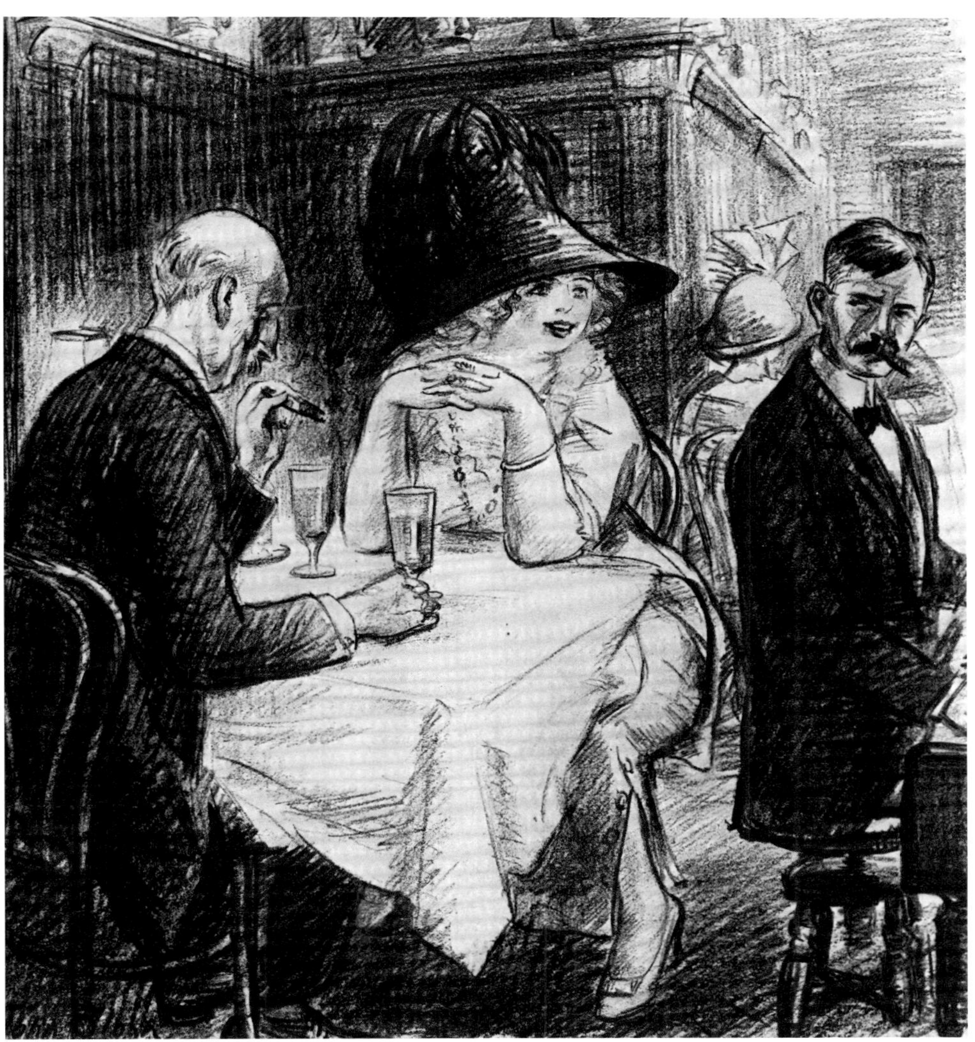

A *mug of ale at* McSorley's, 1913
Crayon on paper
17 x 21 in (sight)
Published in *Harper's Weekly,* October 25, 1913, pp. 16–17
Lent by the Harvard University Art Museums (Fogg Art Museum), Bequest of Meta and Paul J. Sachs

This drawing follows the article "McSorley's Saloon," in which Hutchins Hapgood observed: "Rembrandt would have delighted in McSorley's and I think that Velasquez would have found his account there, too, as our own John Sloan does." In 1928 Sloan painted a similar subject, *McSorley's Cats*.

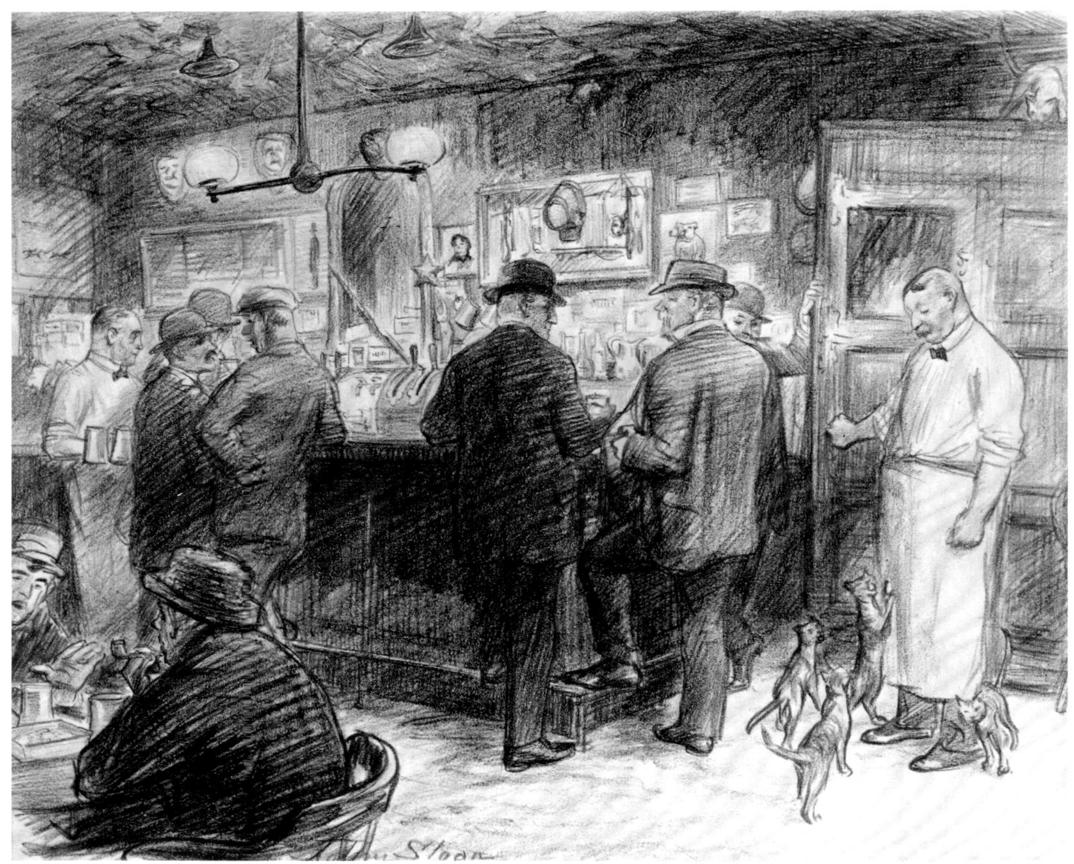

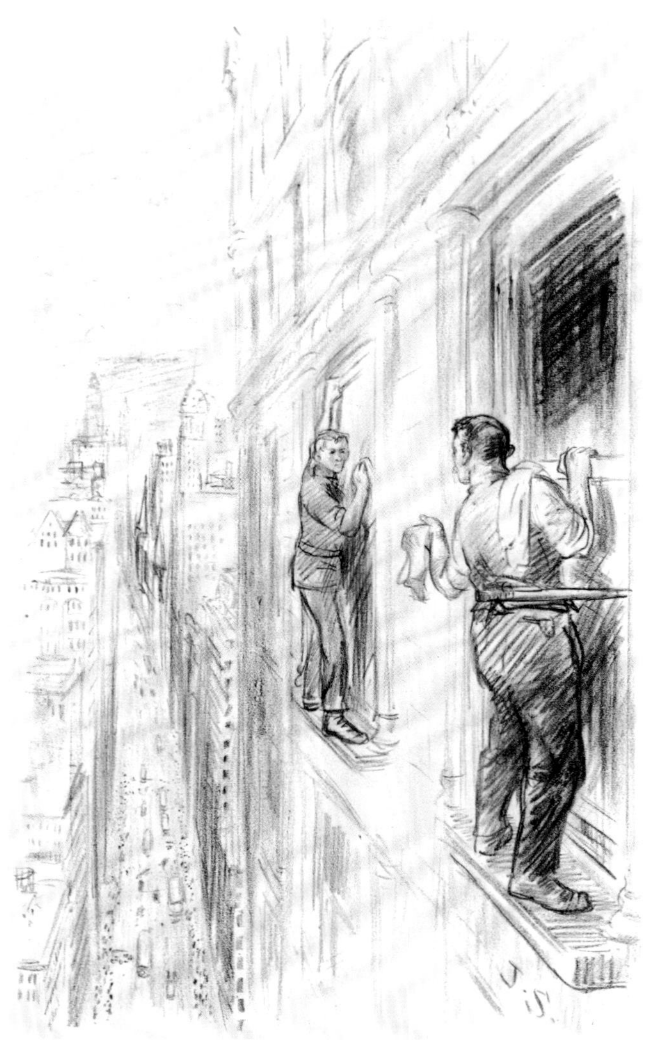

Window Washers (also called _The Window Cleaners_), _1913_
Crayon on paper
20¾ x 12¾ in
Published in *Harper's Weekly,* December 27, 1913, p. 2
Lent by the Sheldon Memorial Art Gallery, University of Nebraska, James E. M. and Helen Thomson Collection

Under Norman Hapgood's editorship, *Harper's Weekly* presented a more liberal editorial policy. This drawing refers to the issue of worker safety with the following caption: "Sure! Yuh wanta git insures—the comp'ny pays yer funeral if yer killed, and if yer injured fer life yuh git ten t'tousand dollars!"

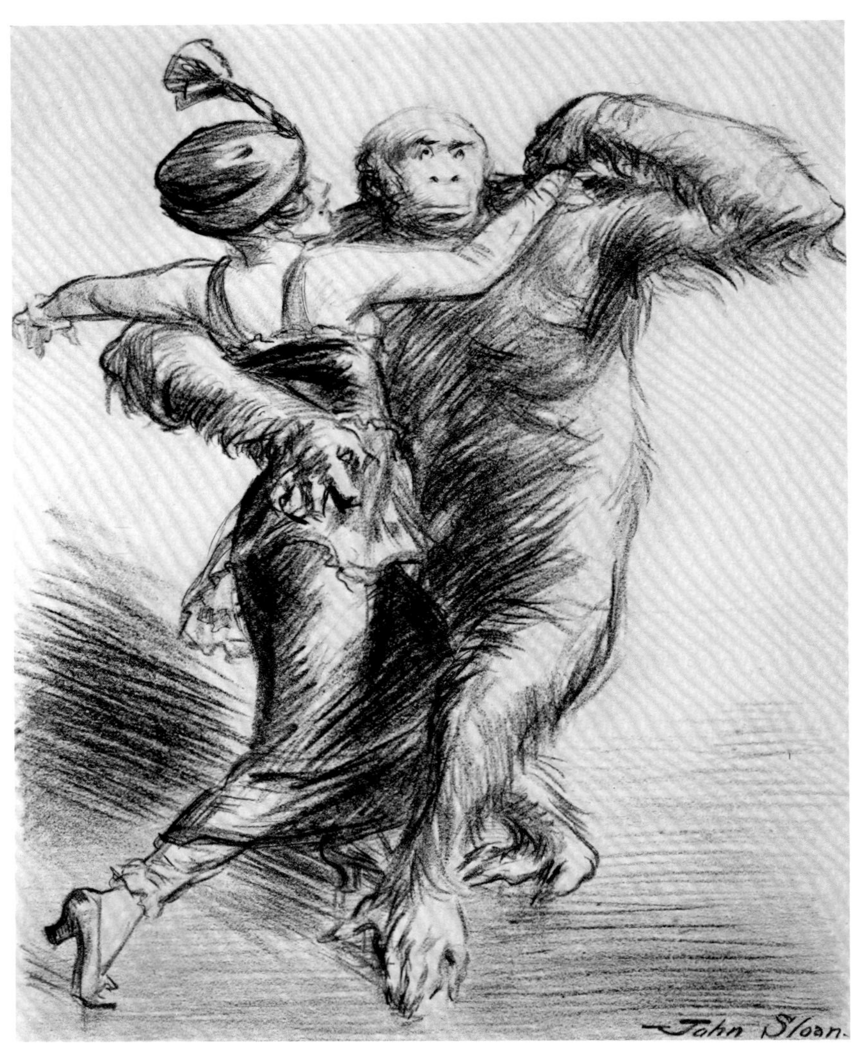

***Orango-Tango*, c. 1914**
Crayon on paper
17½ x 14 in
Published in *The Masses*, February 1914, p. 4
Lent by Mrs. Edwin H. Herzog
(Not in exhibition)

Sloan's humor extended to the rage for new dance steps. The caption included the following commentary: "An Editor: 'I think that is a reactionary picture. The tango is all right.' An Artist: 'Yes, the *tango* is all right—this is the orango-tango.'"

Ludlow, Colorado, 1914
Lithographic crayon on paper
18¾ x 12½ in
Published in *The Masses*, June 1914, cover
Lent by the Hood Museum of Art, Dartmouth, College, Hanover, New Hampshire; Gift of Helen Farr Sloan through the Friends of Dartmouth Library

83

The June 1914 issue of *The Masses* reported on a fight between striking miners in Colorado and the National Guard who set fire to the tents where miners were living with their families. Many died in the fire and the ensuing battle. Sloan created this haunting image for the cover of the magazine.

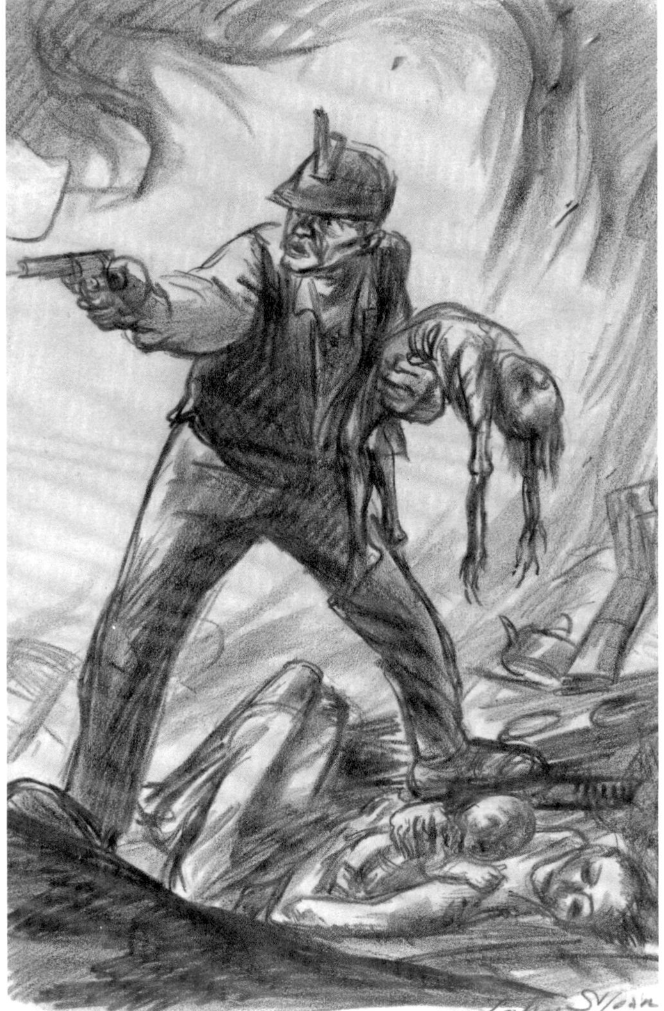

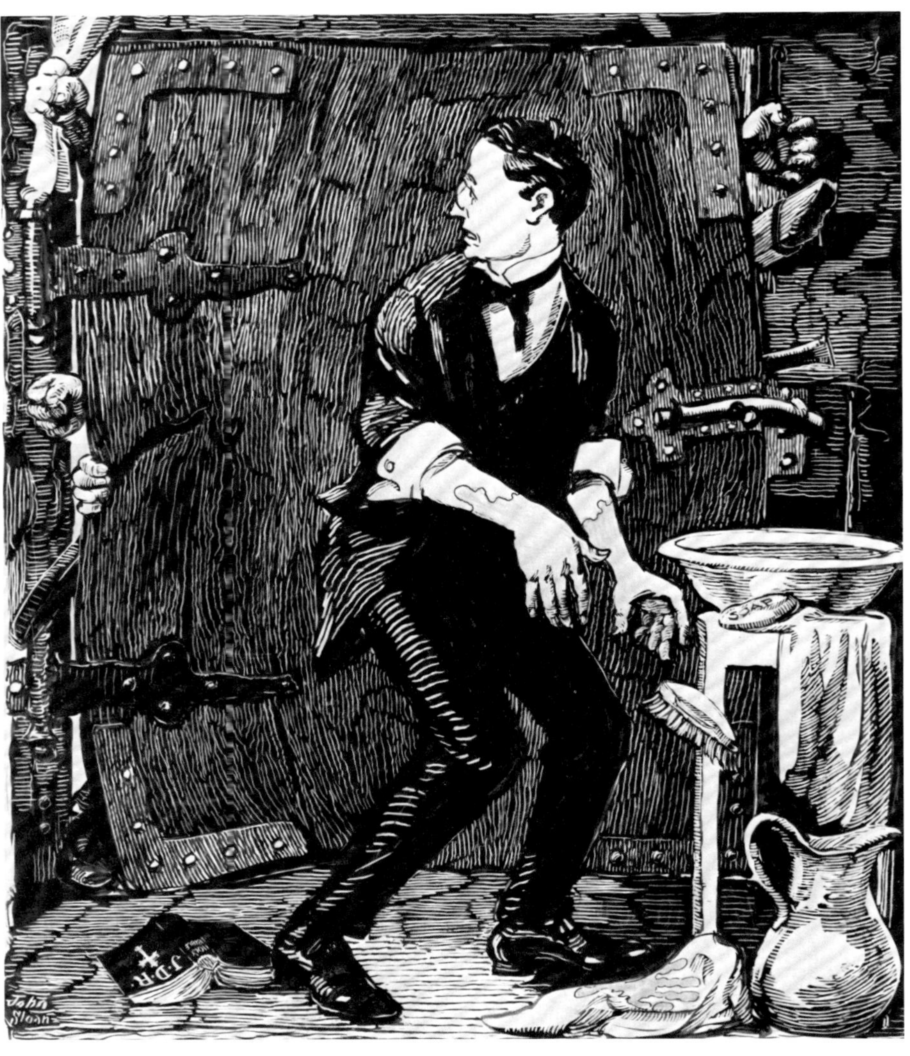

Caught red-handed, 1914
Ink and blue pencil on scratchboard
16½ x 14 in
Published in *The Masses,* July 1914, cover
Lent by the Delaware Art Museum, Gift of Helen Farr Sloan, 1986

Done in Sloan's woodcut style previously used for humorous stories, this image implicates John D. Rockefeller, owner of the Colorado mines, for his responsibility in the deaths of the miners and their families. On the cover, the hands were printed in red as if covered with blood.

Love on the Roof, 1914
Etching
6 x 4⅜ in
Lent by the Delaware Art Museum, Gift of Helen Farr Sloan, 1963

In Gertrude Vanderbilt Whitney's suit for the custody of young Gloria Vanderbilt in 1934, the defense cited Mrs. Whitney's possession of this print as one piece of evidence showing that the girl would be brought up in an immoral atmosphere if Mrs. Whitney won.

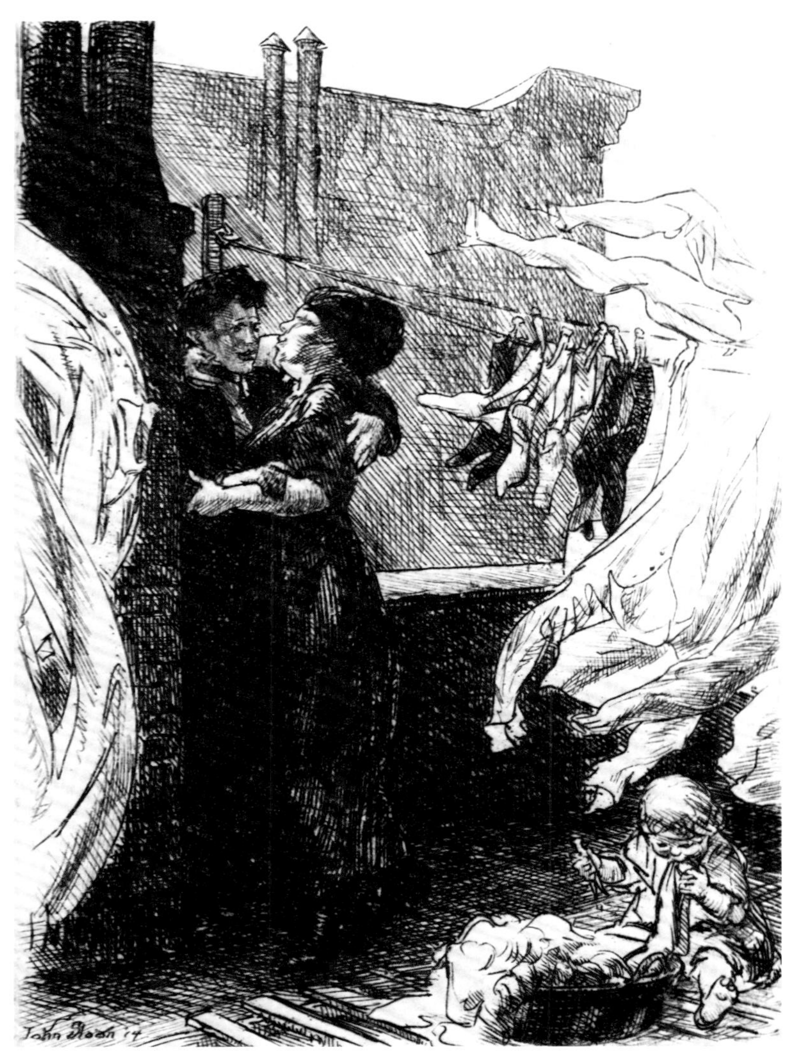

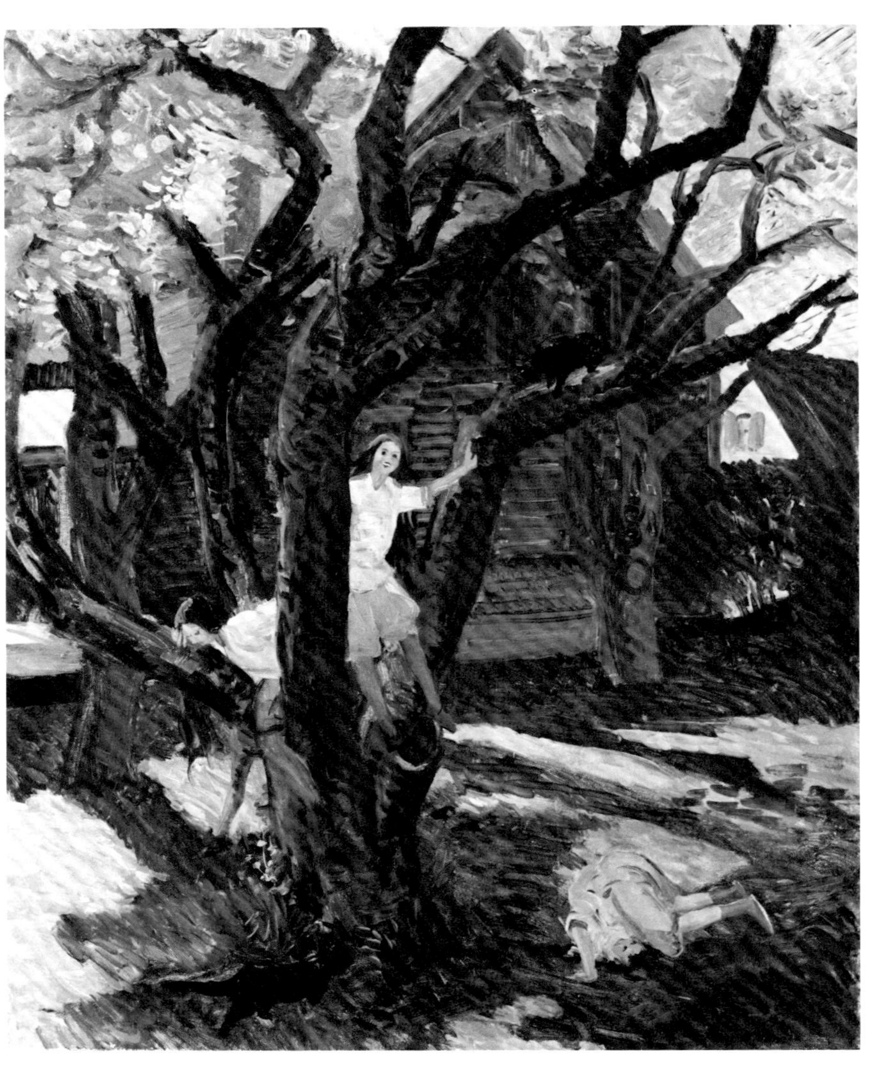

Sally, Sarah and Sadie, Peter and Paul, 1915
Oil on canvas
32 x 26 in
Courtesy of the Kraushaar Galleries, New York

Sloan was deeply affected by the work of such European Post-Impressionist painters as Van Gogh and Toulouse-Lautrec which he saw in the Armory Show of 1913, and his palette lightened and brightened. He began to draw with paint, as in this canvas done in Gloucester, Massachusetts.

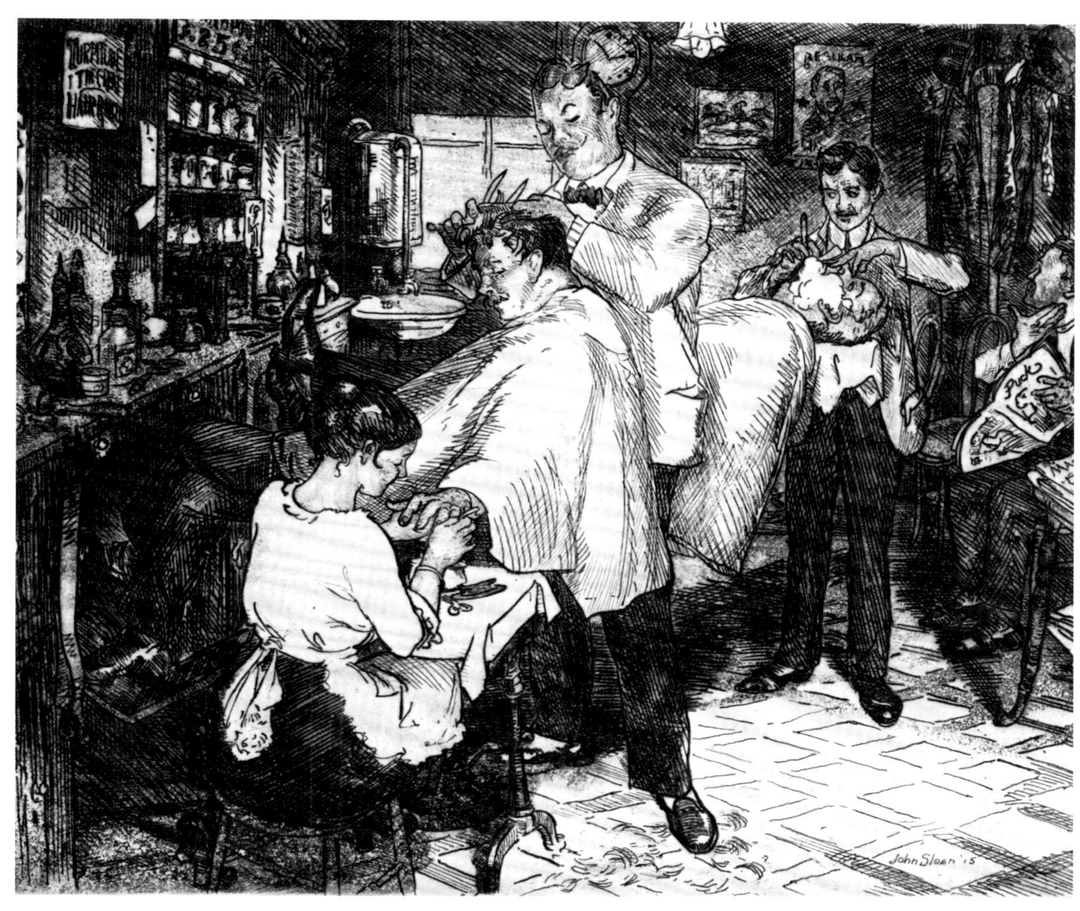

Barber Shop, 1915
Etching
16 x 12 in
Lent by the Delaware Art Museum, Gift of Helen Farr Sloan, 1963

The details in this, Sloan's first experiment with aquatint, are of interest. The waiting customer, feeling his beard, is reading *Puck*, an illustrated humor magazine of the time, and *The Masses*, of which Sloan was art editor, is in a pile beside him.

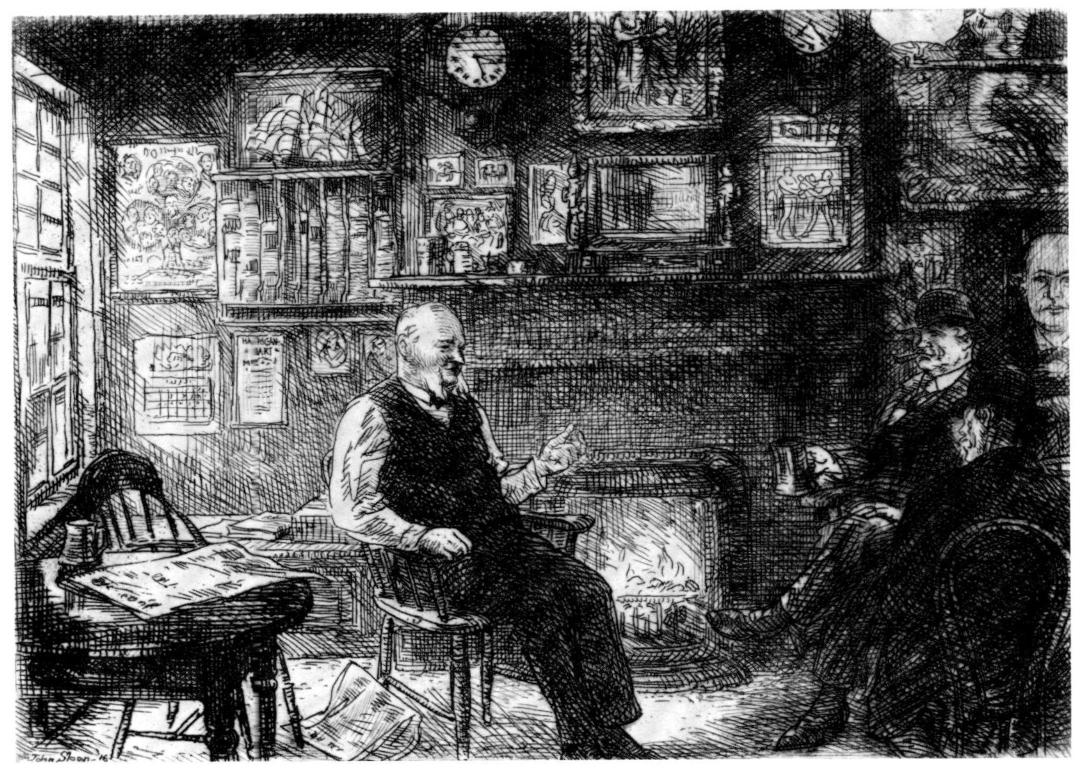

McSorley's Back Room, 1916
Etching
5¼ x 7 in
Lent by the Delaware Art Museum, Gift of Helen Farr Sloan, 1963

Sloan painted McSorley's twice in the early Teens and three times in the late 1920s in addition to making this plate. He said he had been into McSorley's about ten times in his life, which resulted in numerous sketches that aided his memory in creating the works.

Sixth Avenue, 1917
Oil on board
8⅝ x 11⅝ in
Lent by the Delaware Art Museum, Gift of Helen Farr Sloan, 1985

In late 1915 Sloan established his studio at 88 Washington Place with a view north up 6th Avenue dominated by the tower of Jefferson Market Jail. A similar view can be seen in *Jefferson Market, Sixth Avenue* (no. 90) and *Snowstorm in the Village* (no. 104).

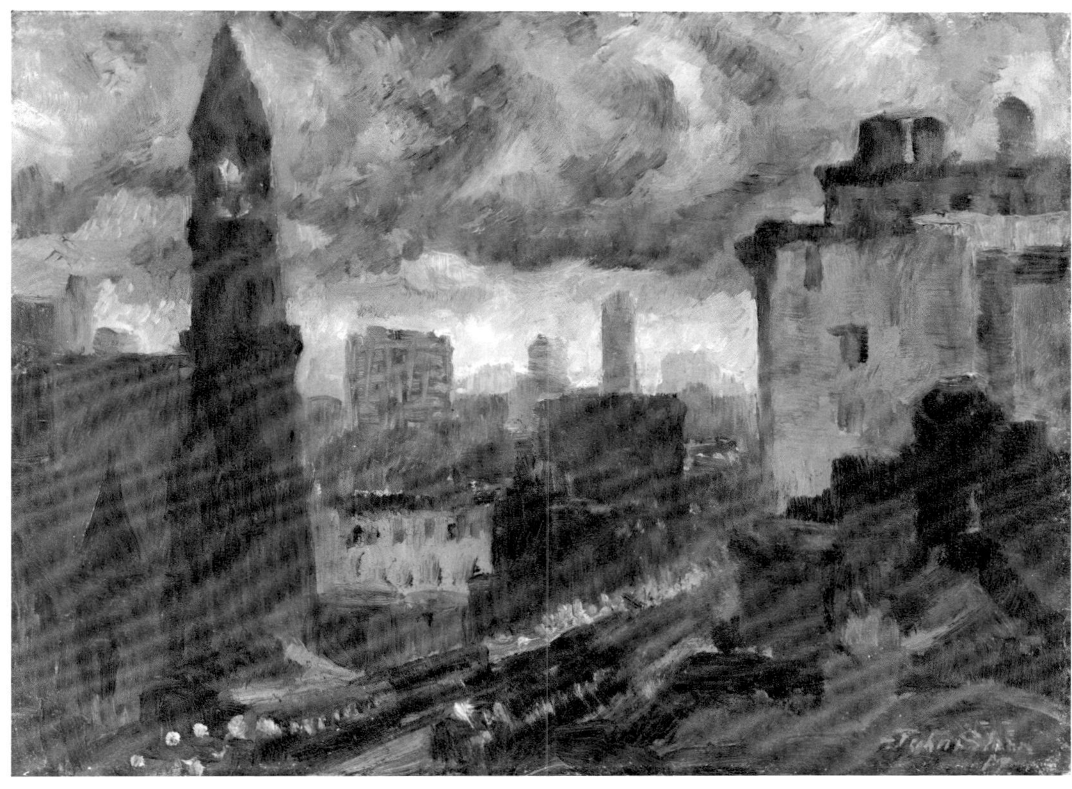

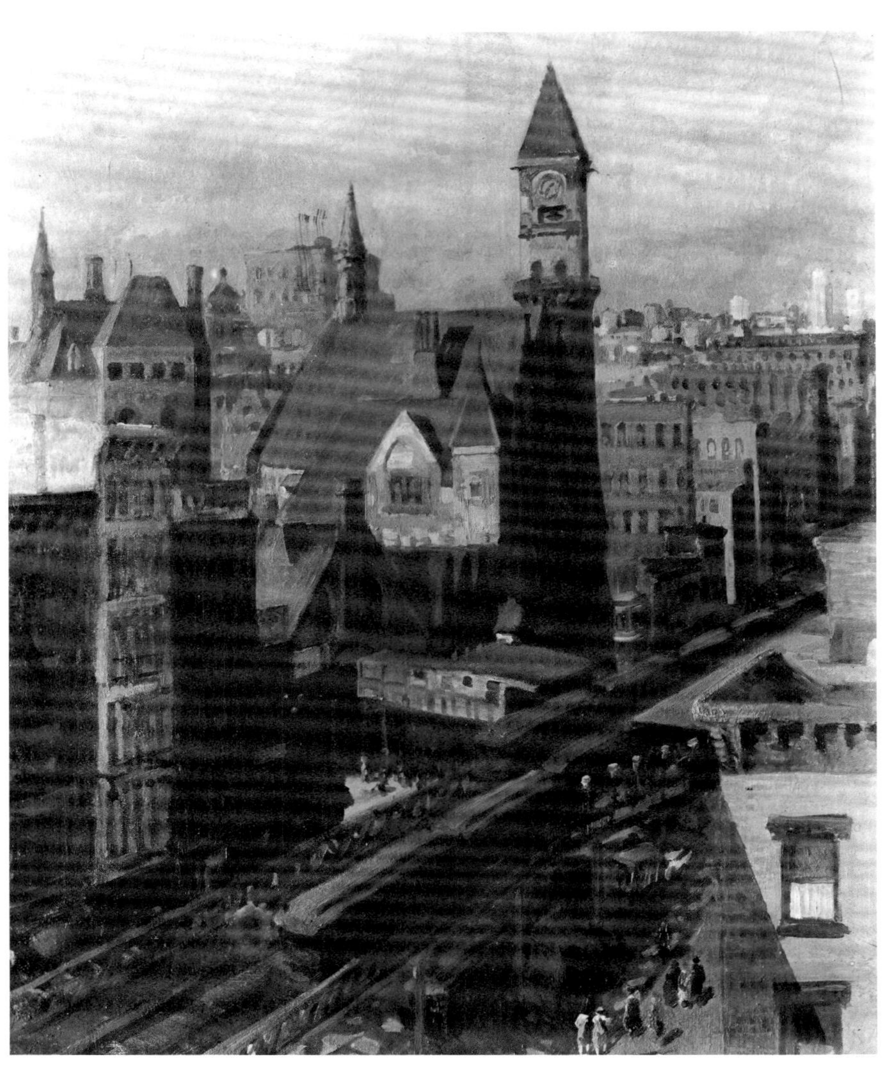

Jefferson Market, Sixth Avenue, 1917, 1922
Oil on canvas
32 x 26 in
Lent by the Pennsylvania Academy of the Fine Arts, Philadelphia, Gilpin Fund Purchase

90

Painted in 1917 with some reworking in 1922, this painting demonstrates Sloan's increasing concern with the geometrical composition of his canvases, involving a complex interplay of verticals, diagonals, and triangles that stemmed from his study of modern painting.

Hill, Main Street, Gloucester, 1917
Oil on canvas
24¾ x 11⅝ in
Lent by the Parrish Art Museum, Littlejohn Collection

"Down this picturesque dip into town rolls a blue Mercedes, a few years old but full of pep and power. The driver is Randall Davey, who painted in Gloucester several summers. The picture is rich in tone and was painted on the spot."

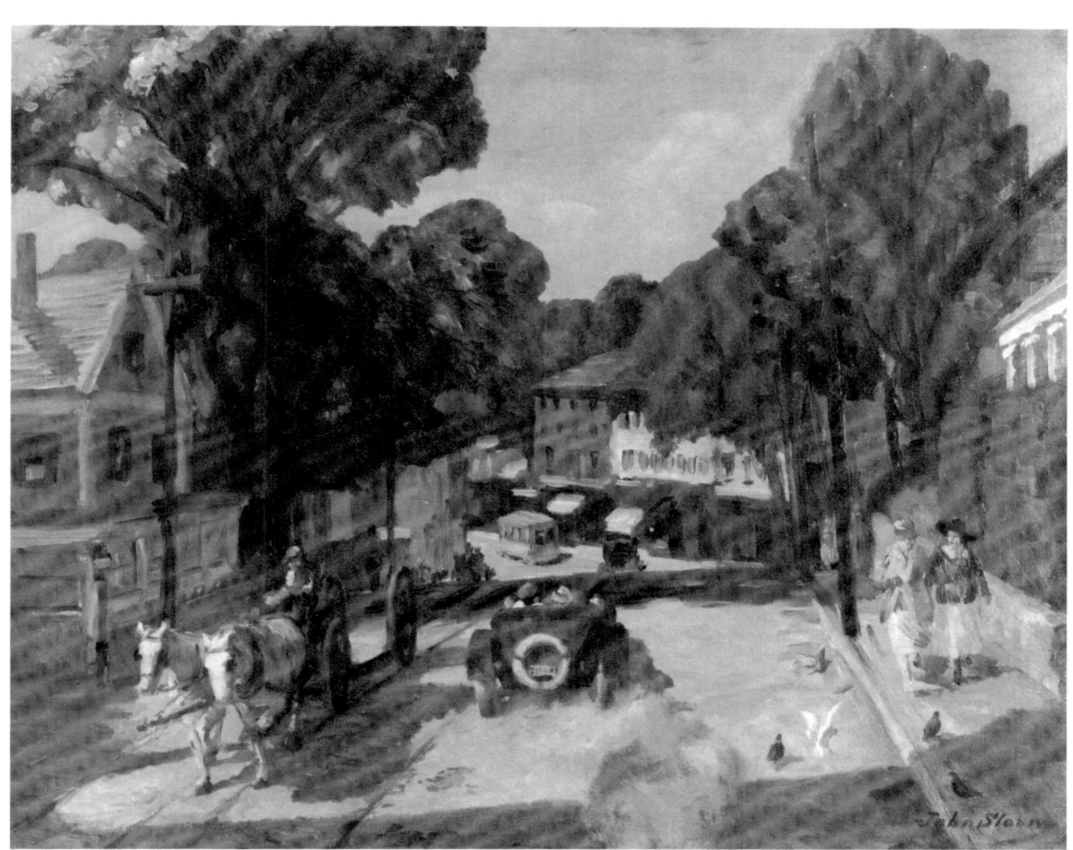

The Wayside Inn, Gloucester, 1918
Oil on canvas
26¾ x 20¼ in
Lent by the Milwaukee Art Museum, Gift of Mr. and Mrs. Donald B. Abert, 1974

The trolley coming into Gloucester from the fishing village of Rocky Neck and the summer visitors strolling on the sidewalk appear in a number of Sloan's genre scenes of small-town life.

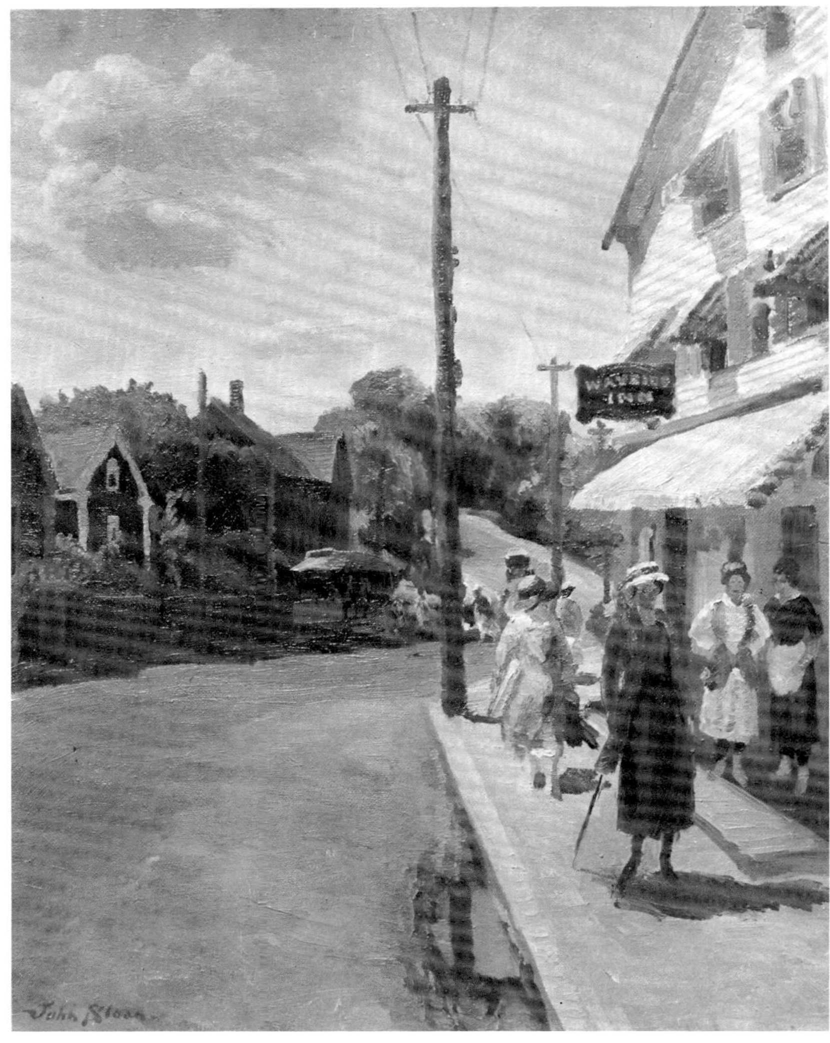

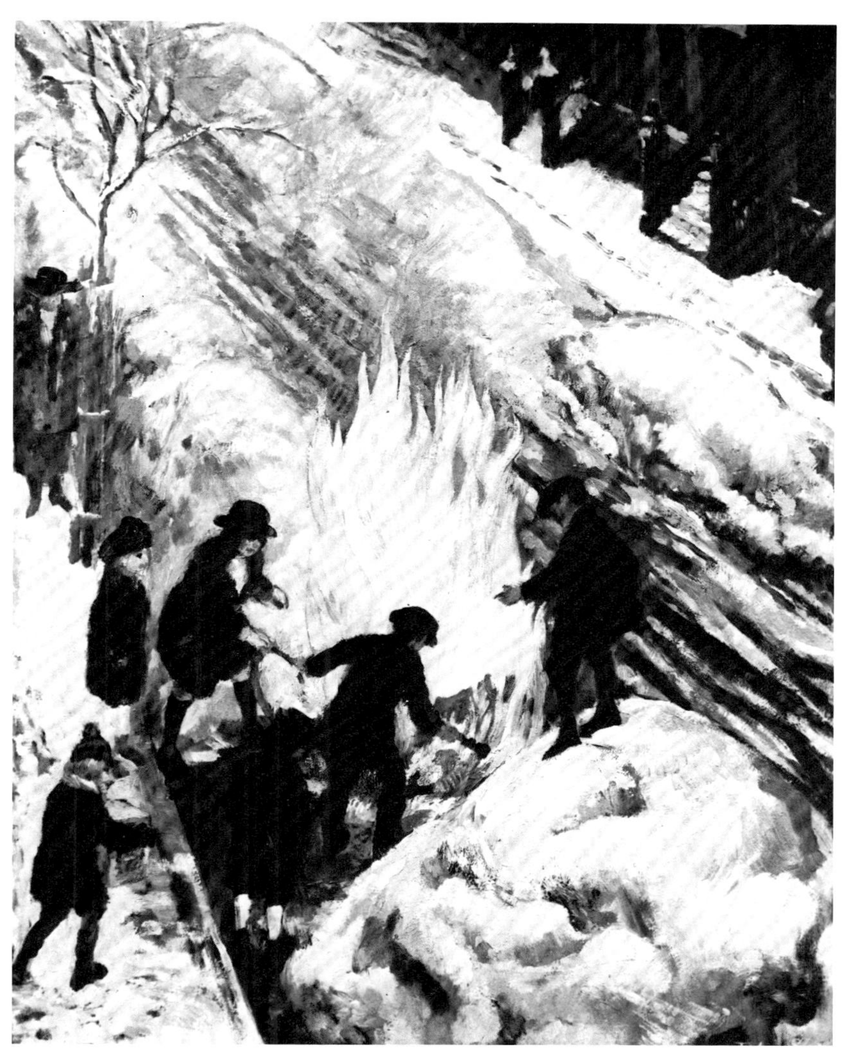

Bonfire in the Snow, 1918
Oil on canvas
24 x 19¾ in
Lent by the Montclair Art Museum, Montclair, New Jersey.

93

The animal spirits of children and young people were a constant source of joy for Sloan and were depicted in many of his prints, drawings, and paintings.

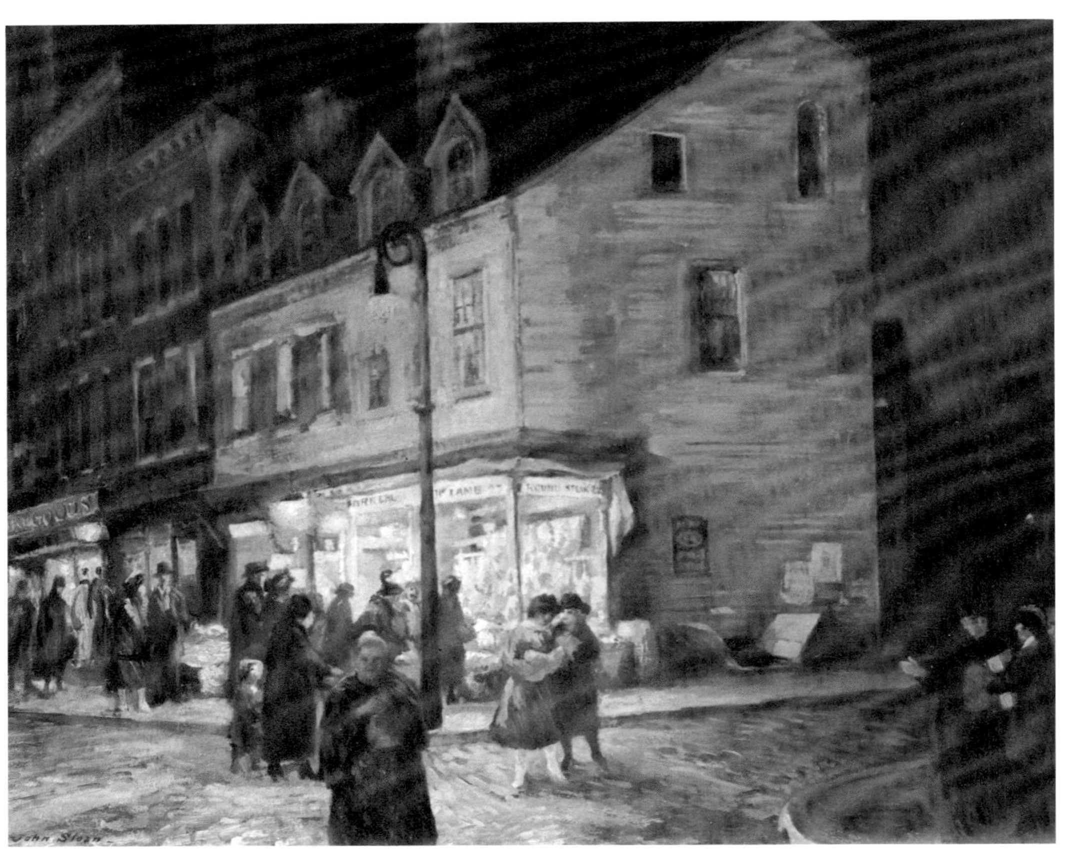

Bleecker Street, Saturday Night, 1918
Oil on canvas
26¼ x 32⅛ in
Lent by the IBM Corporation, Armonk, New York

"**T**his old thoroughfare in the Greenwich Village section was once a fashionable residence street...The amputated building shown had been recently curtailed in cutting through the new 7th Ave. downtown. A cheerful, happy street, there's many another bleaker."

Going Through the Hired Man's Trunk, 1920
Ink and crayon on paper
10½ x 11½ in
Published in Edgar Lee Masters, *Mitch Miller* (New York: Macmillan Co., 1920), p. 62
Lent by the Delaware Art Museum, Gift of Helen Farr Sloan, 1986

Edgar Lee Masters, famous for his *Spoon River Anthology*, tells the story of two young boys, Mitch Miller and Skeeters Kirby, growing up in a small midwestern town. "There wasn't a soul at home but Willie Wallace, the hired man. He was shavin' himself, goin' to see his girl, and he let us play on his Jews harp and smell the cigars he had in his trunk, which he had perfumed with cinnamon or somethin'."

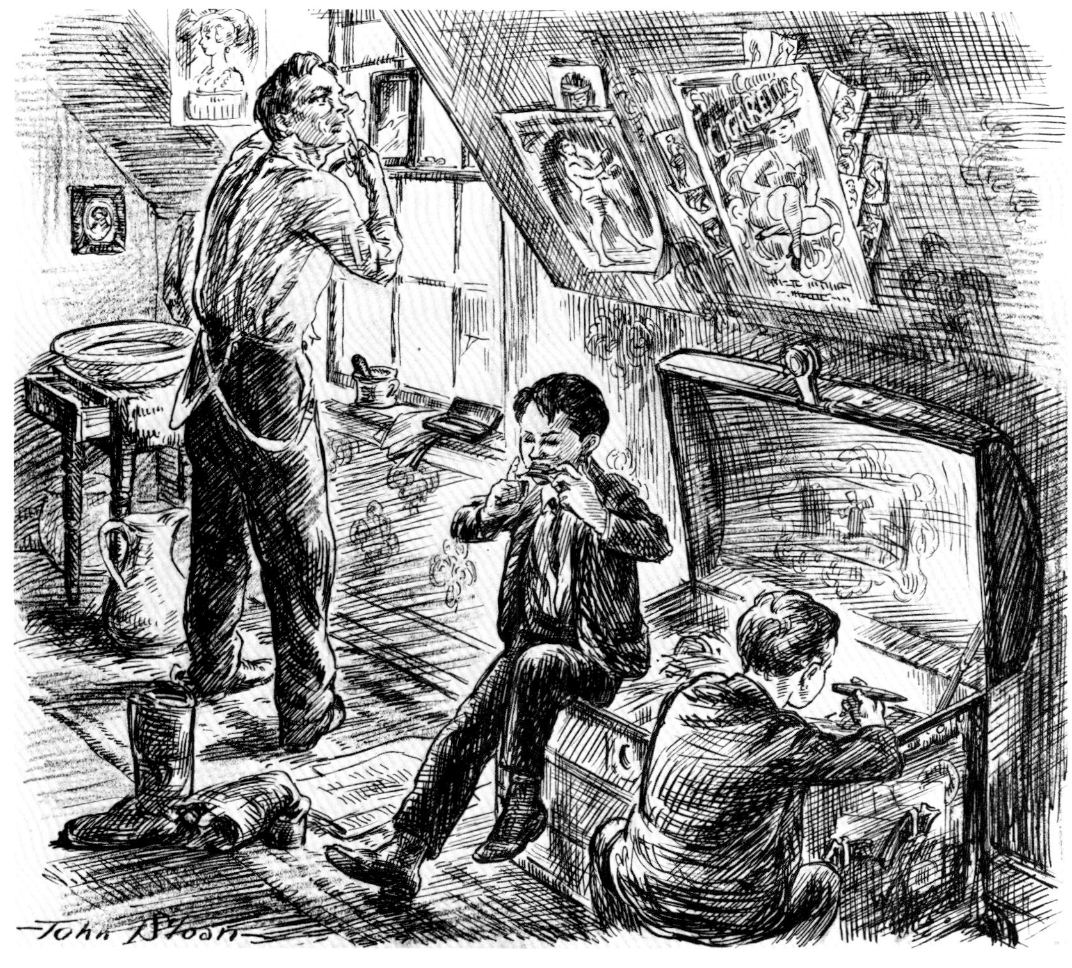

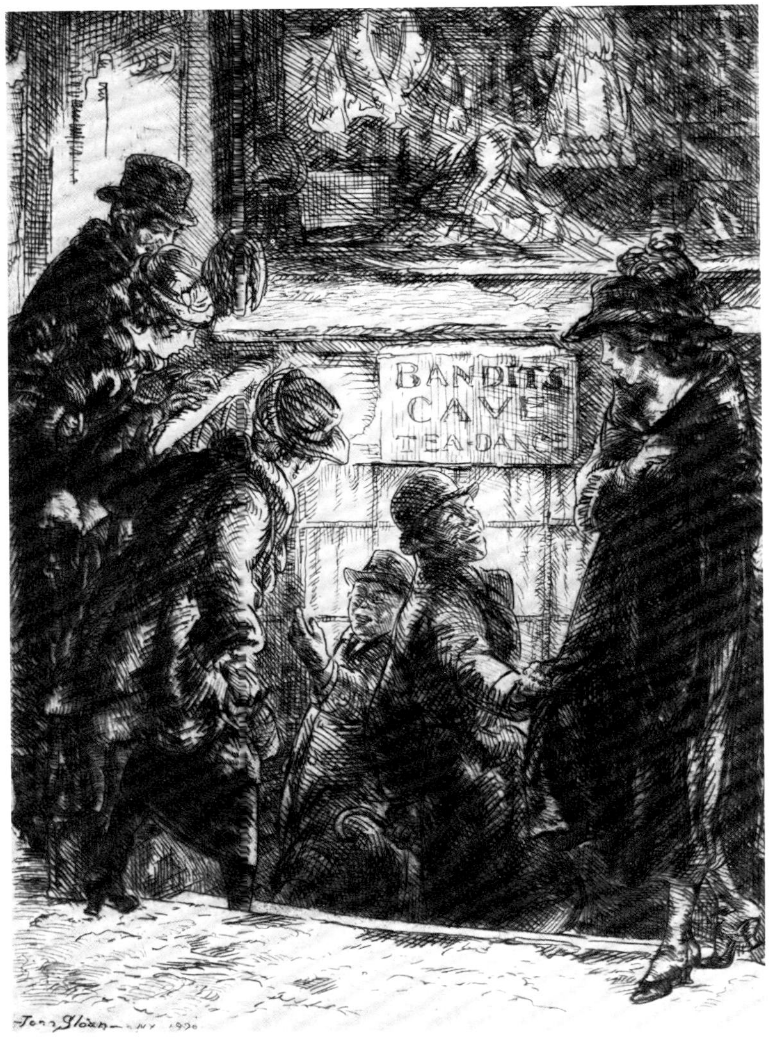

Bandit's Cave, 1920
Etching
7 x 5 in
Lent by the Delaware Art Museum, Gift of Helen Farr Sloan, 1963

Sloan felt very strongly that Prohibition, which caused the disappearance of the neighborhood saloon and the rise of illegal but condoned speakeasies, ruined the neighborhood feeling of New York and contributed to his decline of interest in painting it.

The City from Greenwich Village, 1922
Oil on canvas
26 x 33¾ in
Lent by the National Gallery of Art, Washington; Gift of Helen Farr Sloan, 1970.1.1

In its complexity, *The City from Greenwich Village* was the culmination of Sloan's city paintings. His interest in the subject had been waning for some time, however. He wrote: "Automobiles fill the streets and Prohibition turned the night life of the city into a nightmare of clubs and commercial entertainment. The city was spoiled for me."

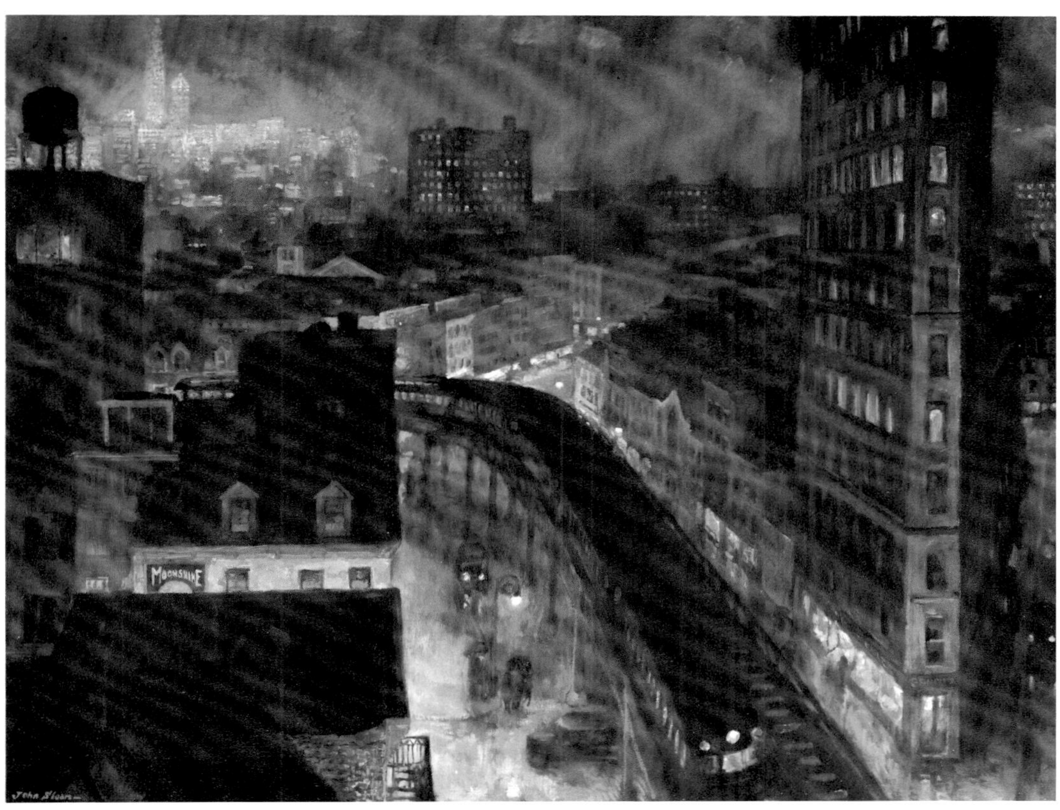

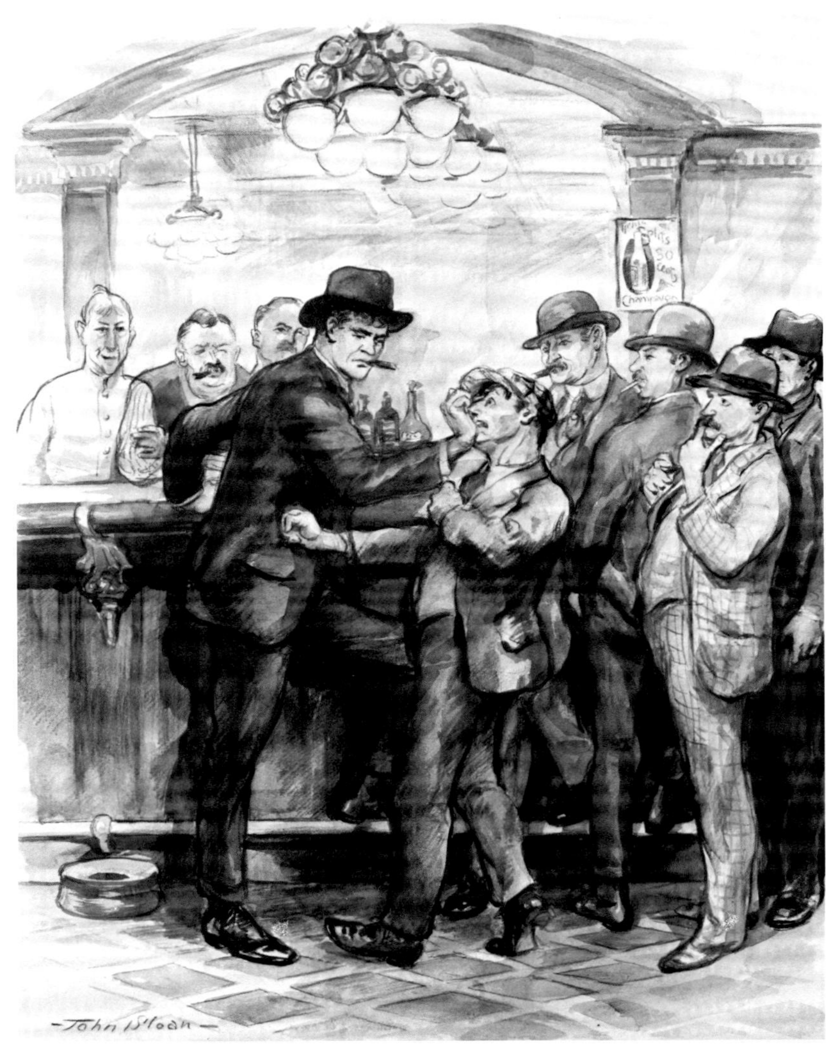

Mr. Dew was annoyed and showed it by applying the heel of his right hand suddenly under Mr. Smith's nose, nearly scraping that promontory off Mr. Smith's map, 1922
Crayon and wash on illustration board
23 x 16⅛ in
Published in Clifford Raymond, "Brothers Under the Sod," *Hearst's International,* August 1922, p. 52
Lent by the Delaware Art Museum, Gift of Helen Farr Sloan

Dew was a bully who organized unions and settled arguments with his fists or a gun.

Ella was a washtub woman **(also called *Family on Fire Escape*), *1922***
Ink wash, conte crayon, and graphite on paper board
17 x 23 in
Published in Clifford Raymond, "Brothers Under the Sod," *Hearst's International,* August 1922, p. 66
Lent by the Hood Museum of Art, Dartmouth College, Hanover, New Hampshire; Purchased through the Julia L. Whittier Fund

Dew and his family lived modestly until he was consumed with ambition and bought a grand house in a respectable part of Chicago.

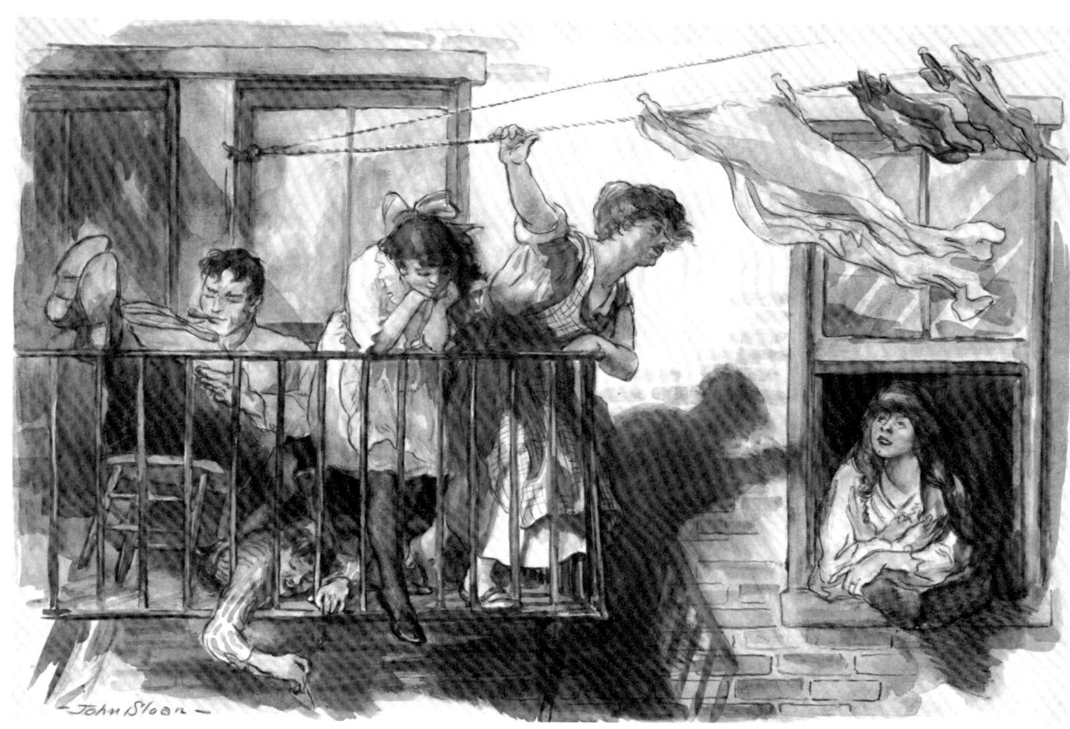

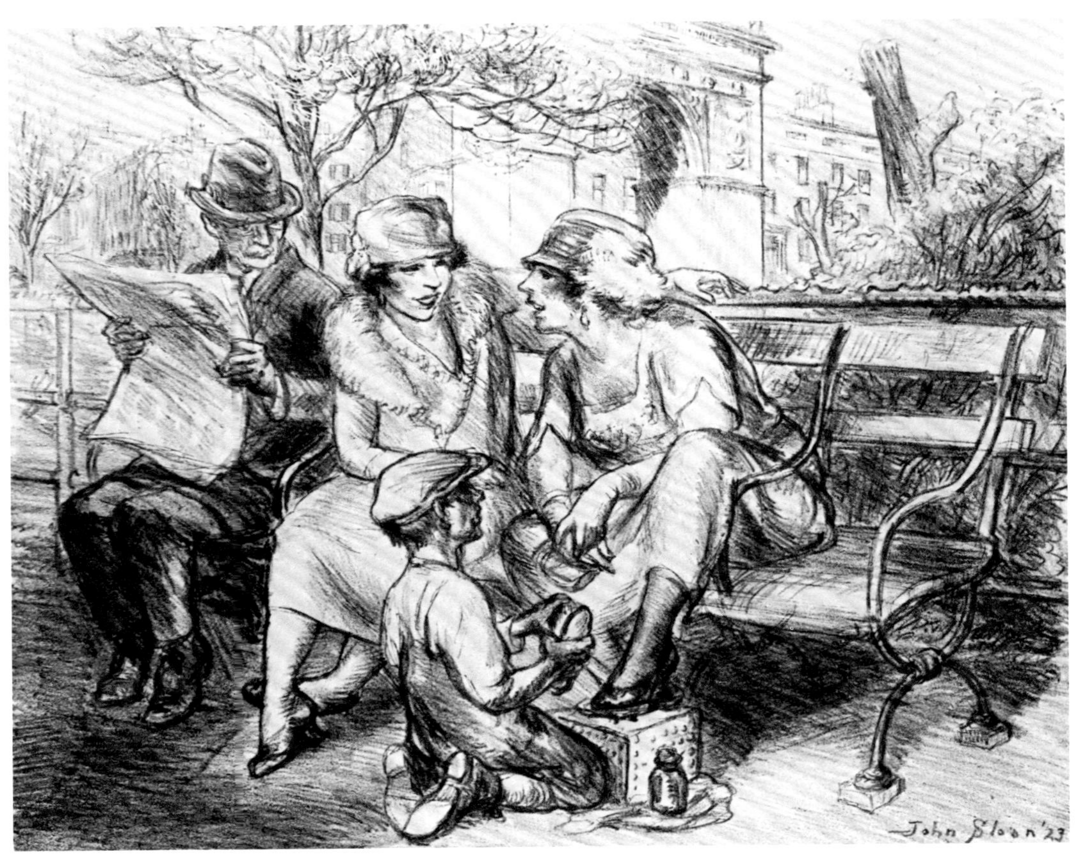

Shine, Washington Square, 1923
Lithograph
$7\frac{1}{4}$ x 9 in
Lent by the Delaware Art Museum, Gift of Helen Farr Sloan, 1965

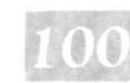

100 "It has been said that my work has been influenced by Cruikshank [the early nineteenth century English illustrator], but no critic has traced it to its true source, which is the work of John Leech [a somewhat later English illustrator]. . . . Cruikshank's people always have a quality of caricature."

Threshing Floor, Santa Fe, 1924–5
Oil on canvas
30⅛ x 40⅛ in
Courtesy of the Kraushaar Galleries, New York

101

In the summer of 1919 Sloan first visited Santa Fe, New Mexico, where he returned every summer but one until his last visit in 1950. Here, he shows the ancient threshing procedure of driving a herd of goats over the grain on sunbaked mud floor.

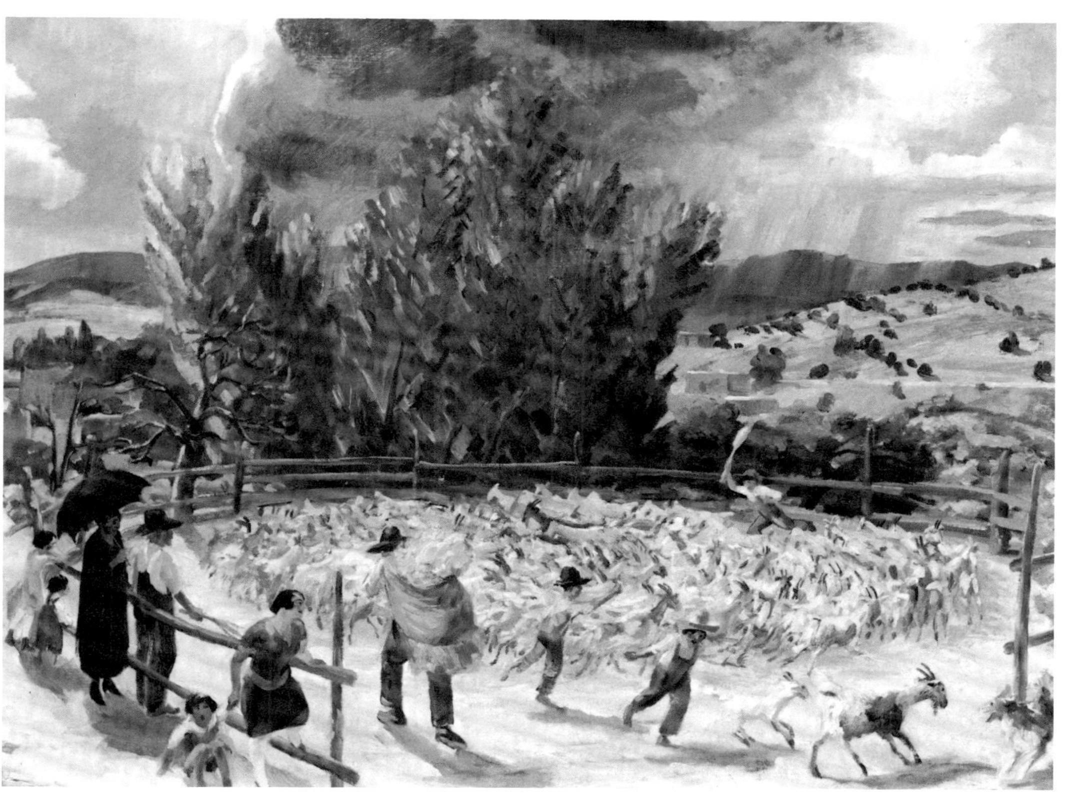

***Corpus Christi Procession*, 1925, 1932**
Oil on canvas
30 x 36 in
Lent from a New Jersey collection

102

The dances and religious ceremonies of the Indians and Hispanic natives of Santa Fe moved Sloan deeply, and he painted them on many occasions in the 1920s. Sketching and photography were not permitted at the Indian dances, so Sloan relied on his trained visual memory.

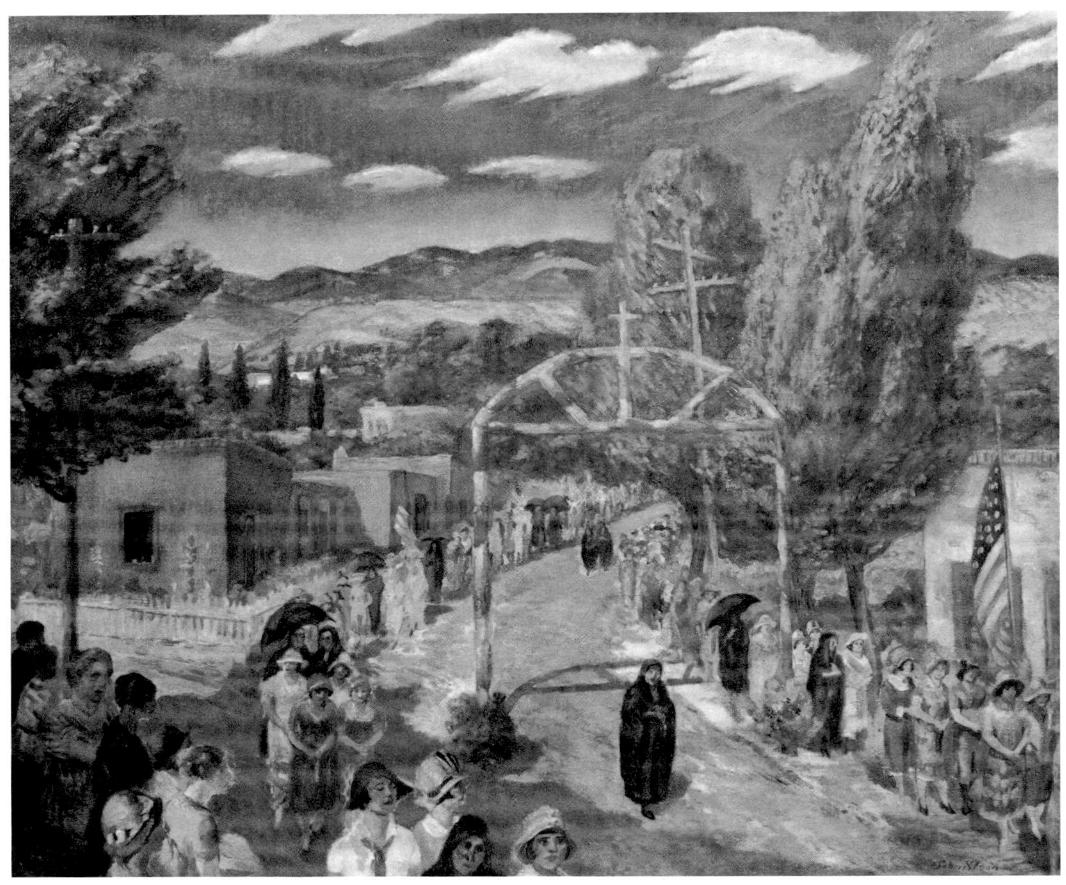

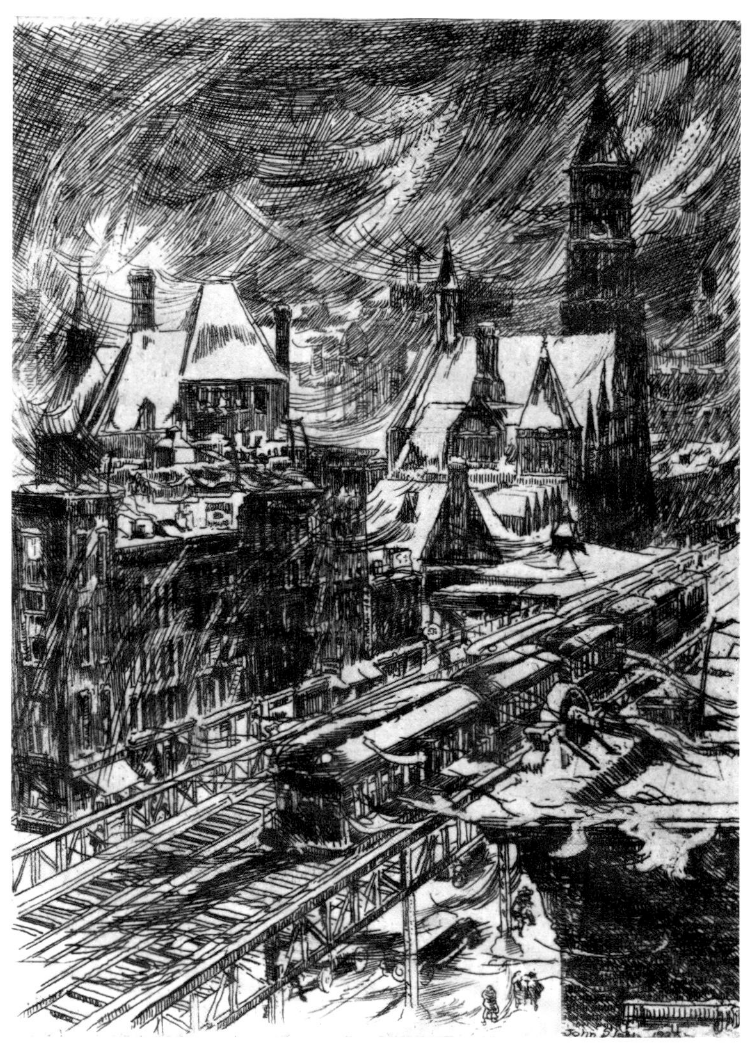

***Snowstorm in the Village*, 1925**
Etching
7 x 5 in
Lent by the Delaware Art Museum, Gift of Helen Farr Sloan, 1963

Made from the same vantage point as the painting *Jefferson Market, Sixth Avenue* (no. 90), Sloan's first state of this plate is dated February 1, 1925, three years after he had reworked the painting.

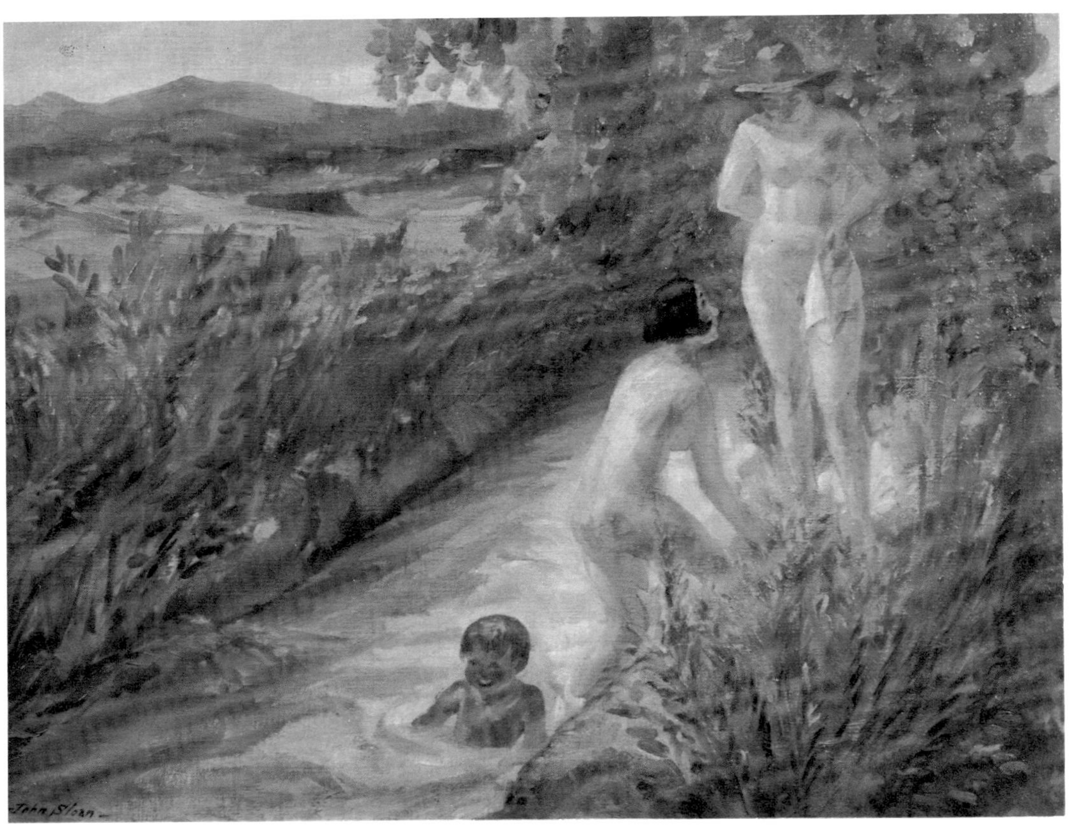

Bathers in the Acequia Madre, 1926
Oil on canvas
20⅛ x 26⅛ in
Lent anonymously

104

The Acequia Madre is an irrigation canal in the southeastern part of Santa Fe near Sloan's house. The figures are Dolly Sloan and Helen Shuster, the wife of the painter Will Shuster, and her son, Donald.

The White Way, 1926–7
Oil on canvas
30¼ x 32¼ in
Lent by the Philadelphia Museum of Art, Gift of Mrs. Cyrus McCormick, 1946, #46–10–2

105 "**A** sudden impulse to paint Broadway with its lights in a snowfall took me to Broadway and Fifty-third Street on this cold winter night. There I stood with pencil clutched in petrified fingers, making memoranda which resulted in this painting."

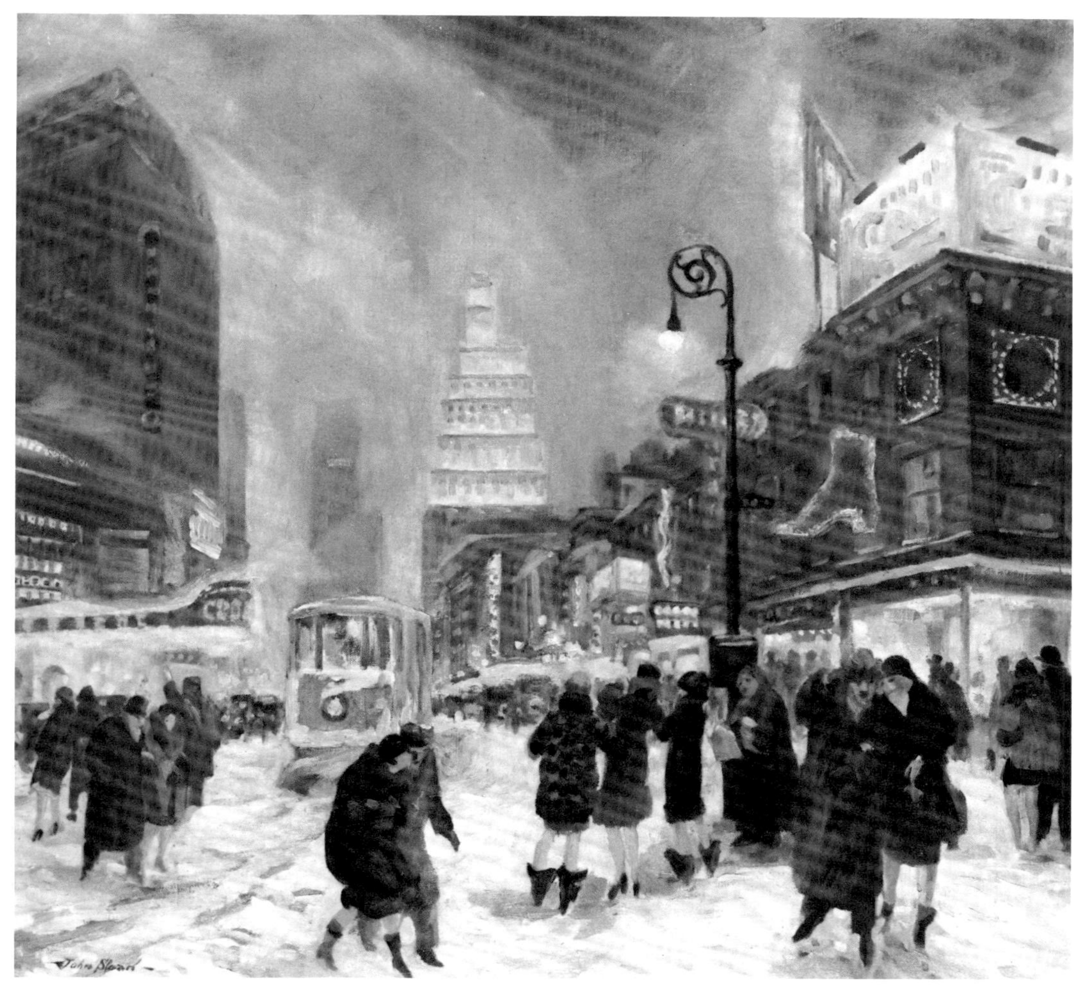

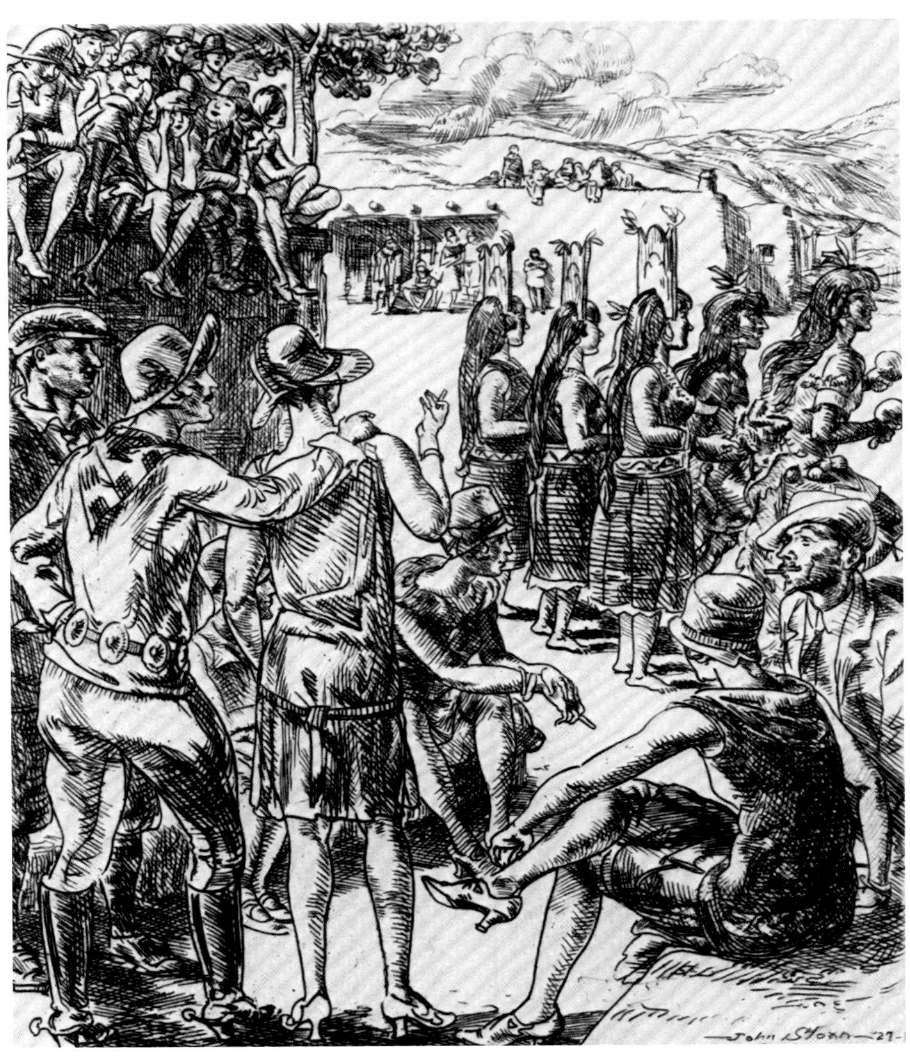

***Knees and Aborigines*, 1927**
Etching
7 x 6 in
Lent by the Delaware Art Museum, Gift of Helen Farr Sloan, 1963

Sloan's satirical bite is at its sharpest in this plate, which lampoons the rather witless and crude way that tourists are viewing the religious dances of the New Mexico Indians as just another form of entertainment, with no idea of their meaning.

The Fall of the Village Bastille, 1929
Flaxseed tempera underpaint, oil-varnish glaze on panel
30 x 24 in
Lent by the Kraushaar Galleries, New York

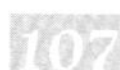

"The village, Greenwich, in New York City; the bastille being demolished was the ladies' jail and market of the Jefferson Market Court group. The foreground structure is a stairway of the Sixth Avenue elevated railway."

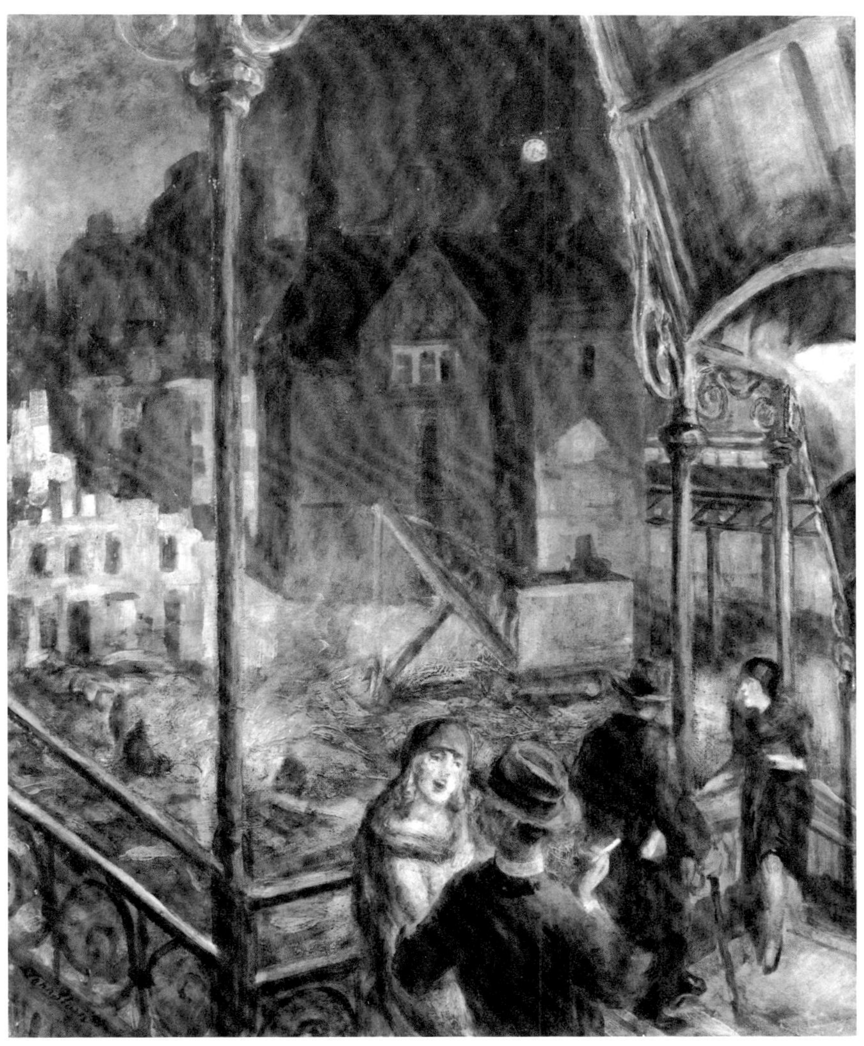

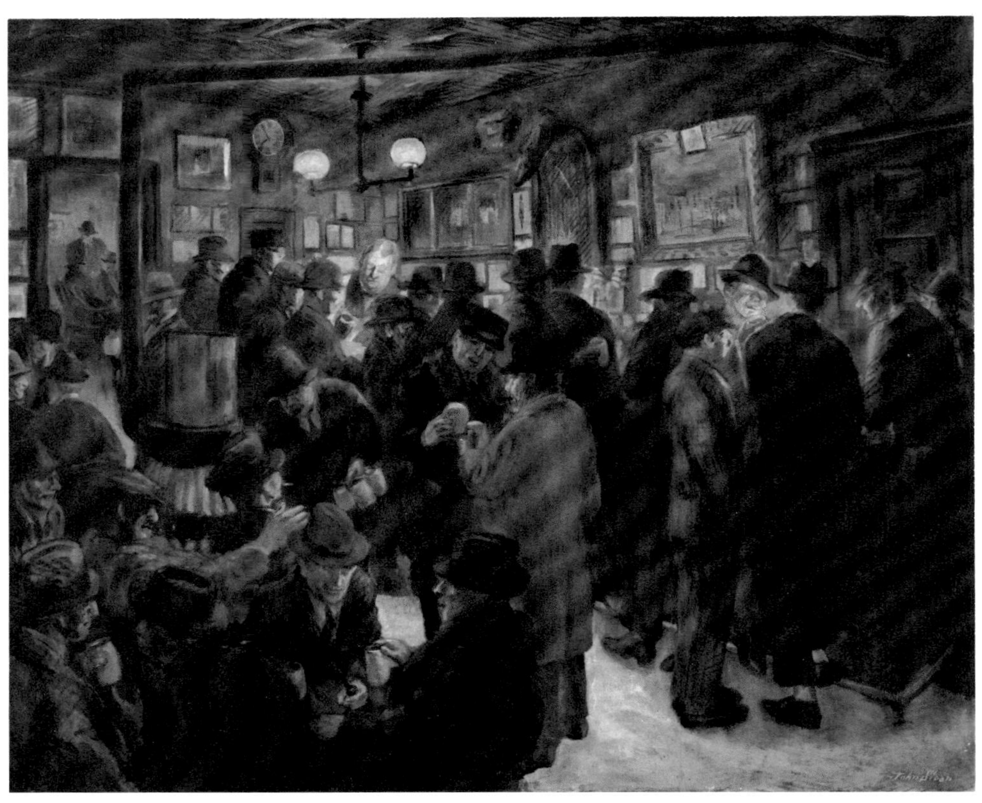

McSorley's Saturday Night, 1929–30, 1948
Oil underpaint, oil-varnish glaze on canvas
30¼ x 36¼ in
Lent by the Hirshhorn Museum and Sculpture Garden, Smithsonian Institution; Gift of Joseph H. Hirshhorn Foundation, 1966

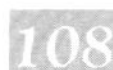

"Here we have McSorley's during the dark days of prohibition. Had all saloons been conducted with the dignity and decorum of McSorley's, prohibition could hever have been brought about... McSorley's never was closed... Painted from blessed memory."

Our Corner of the Studio, 1935
Tempera underpaint; oil-varnish glaze on panel
36 x 22¼ in
Lent anonymously

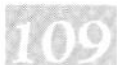

*I*n 1927 the Sloans moved to a studio-apartment at 53 Washington Square. Sloan wrote: "The picture has power, and the problems of chiaroscuro are well met. Its departure from visual representation is much greater than is apparent."

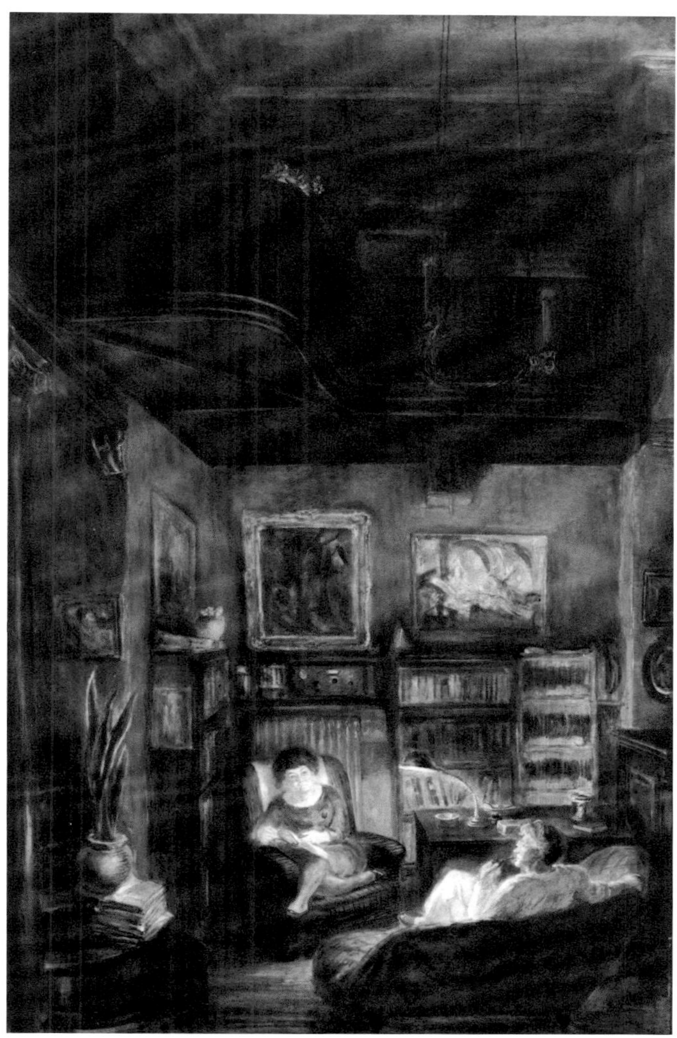

Flanagan...with wild shout leaped over the barrier, 1937
Etching
6 x 4 in
Published in W. Somerset Maugham, *Of Human Bondage* (New Haven, Connecticut: The Limited Editions Club, 1938), frontispiece
Lent by the Delaware Art Museum, Gift of Helen Farr Sloan, 1986

110

The protagonist, Philip Carey, handicapped by a club foot, went to Paris to study art and joined his friend Flanagan at the dance hall. Returning to London, Carey met a waitress, Mildred, and became obsessed with her.

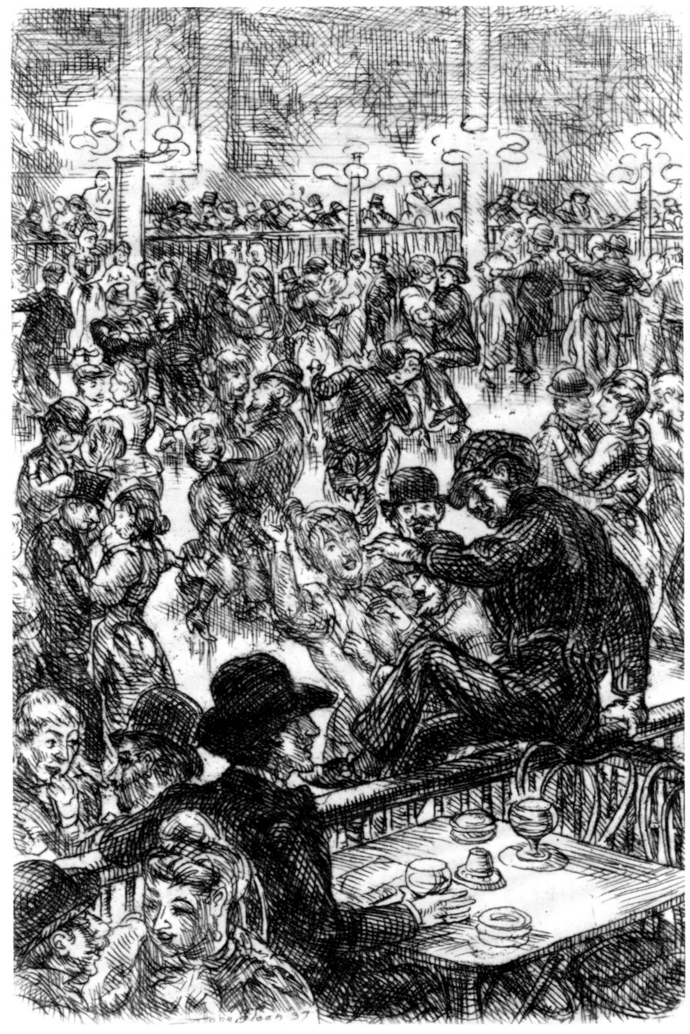

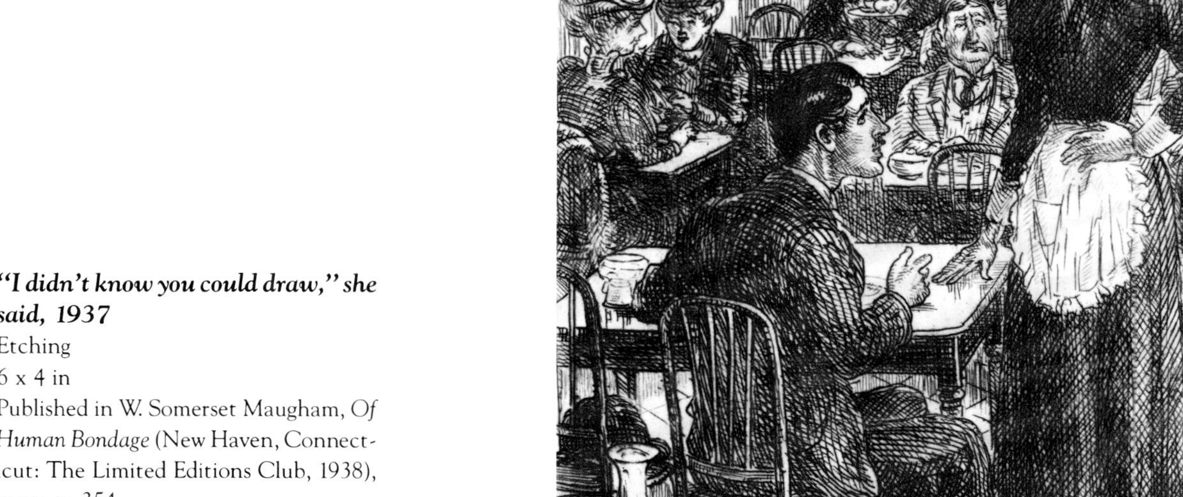

"I didn't know you could draw," she said, 1937
Etching
6 x 4 in
Published in W. Somerset Maugham, *Of Human Bondage* (New Haven, Connecticut: The Limited Editions Club, 1938), oppo. p. 354
Lent by the Delaware Art Museum, Gift of Helen Farr Sloan, 1986

In a letter Somerset Maugham praised Sloan's etchings: "To my mind you have caught wonderfully the tang of the period. They do what surely good illustration should do, excite the reader's interest and make him eager to know more about the people whose images the artist has shown him."

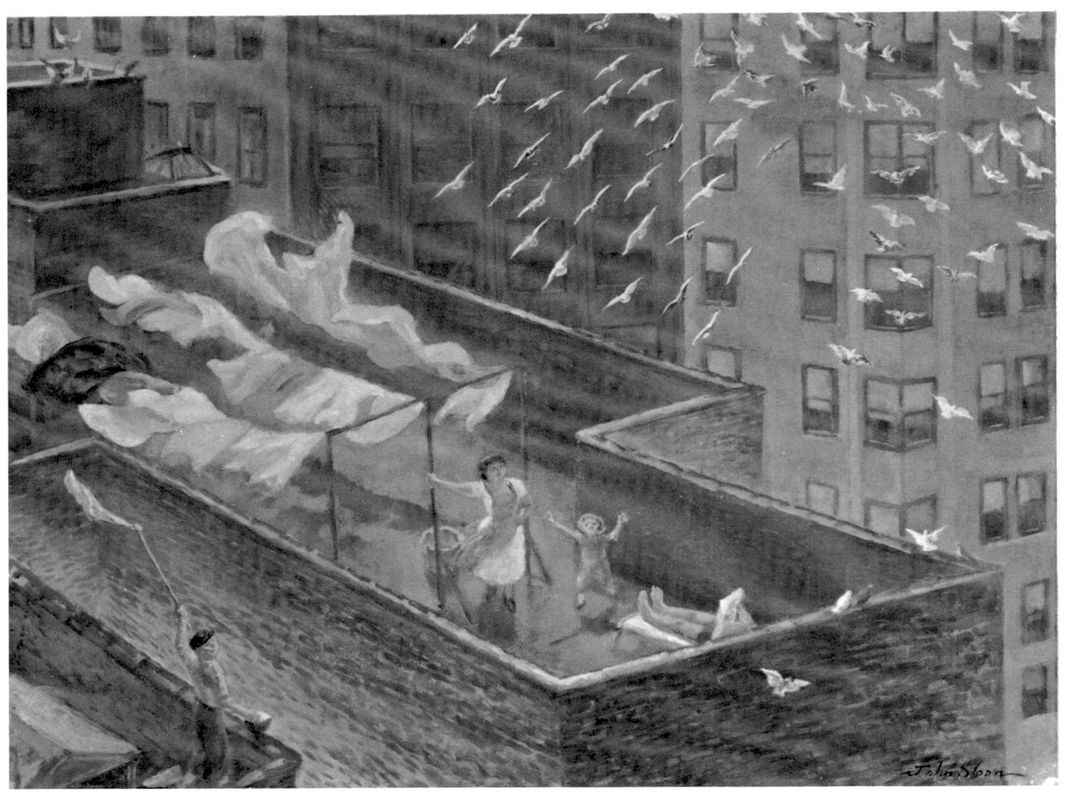

A *Roof in Chelsea*, 1940, 1945, 1951
Tempera underpaint, oil-varnish glaze on panel
20 x 26 in
Lent by the Hood Museum of Art, Dartmouth College, Hanover, New Hampshire; Purchased through the Julia L. Whittier Fund

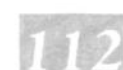

A *Roof in Chelsea* was one of the last of Sloan's New York City subjects. He began in 1940 and worked on it again five years later. In his last summer, spent in Hanover, New Hampshire, he worked on it again, completely repainting the flock of pigeons.

Monument in the Plaza, 1948, 1949
Tempera underpaint, oil-varnish glaze on panel
32 x 26 in
Courtesy of the Kraushaar Galleries, New York

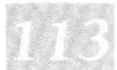

One of the most ambitious and complete compositions of Sloan's later years, this painting caused him much trouble over the year and a half he worked on it in Santa Fe and New York. After more than a year's work he remarked in his diary: "I worked a bit on the 'Plaza.' I might have built one by this time!"

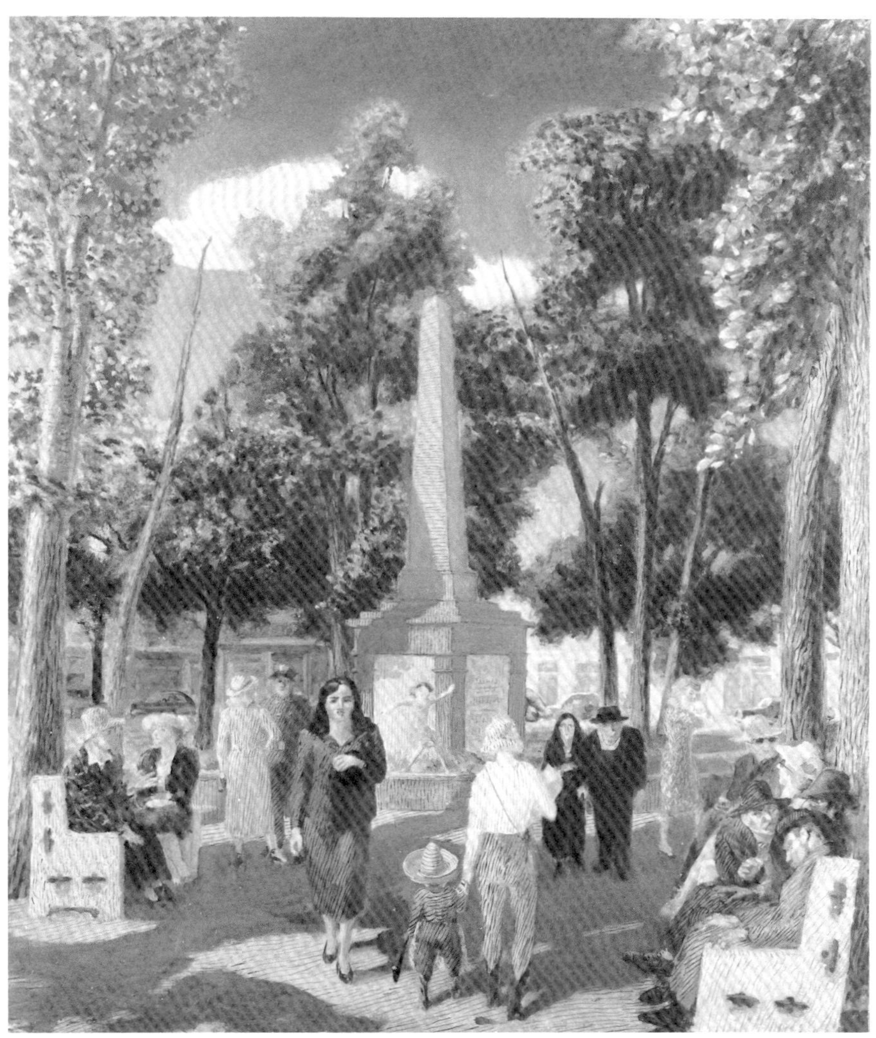

Photo Credits

References are to catalog numbers.

Amon Carter Museum, **28**

Oliver Baker, **104**

Bowdoin College Museum of Art, **61, 62**

Harold L. Brown Photography, **29**

The Butler Institute of American Art, **31**

Geoffrey Clements, **4, 15, 41, 64, 67, 76, 102, 107**

Columbus Museum of Art, **70**

The Corcoran Gallery of Art, **51**

Fogg Art Museum, **40, 80**

Judy Goffman Fine Art, **55**

Helga Photo Service, **94**

Hirshhorn Museum and Sculpture Garden, **58, 72, 108**

Hood Museum of Art, **17, 57, 83, 99, 112**

Indianapolis Museum of Art, **63**

Peter A. Juley and Son, **46, 48, 90, 92**

Raymond M. Kopcho, **3**

Jon McDowell, **1, 2, 7, 10, 11, 14, 18, 19, 22, 23, 24, 25, 26, 33, 34, 35, 44, 53, 54, 59, 60, 69, 84, 85, 86, 87, 88, 89, 96, 98, 100, 101, 103, 106, 109, 113**

McNay Art Museum, **43**

Richard Margolis, **45**

Munson-Williams-Proctor Institute, **52**

National Gallery of Art, **97**

National Museum of American Art, **40**

The Parrish Art Museum, **91**

Philadelphia Museum of Art, **38, 47, 105**

The Phillips Collection, **56**

Rollyn Puterbaugh, **50**

SKT Galleries, **42**

Soichi Sunami, **6, 39**

Joseph Szaszfai, **73**

The Toledo Museum of Art, **71**

University of Michigan Museum of Art, **66**

University of Nebraska Art Galleries, **81**

Typographers

Firenze & Company

Lithographers

Garamond Pridemark, Inc.

Design

Southam Associates, Inc.

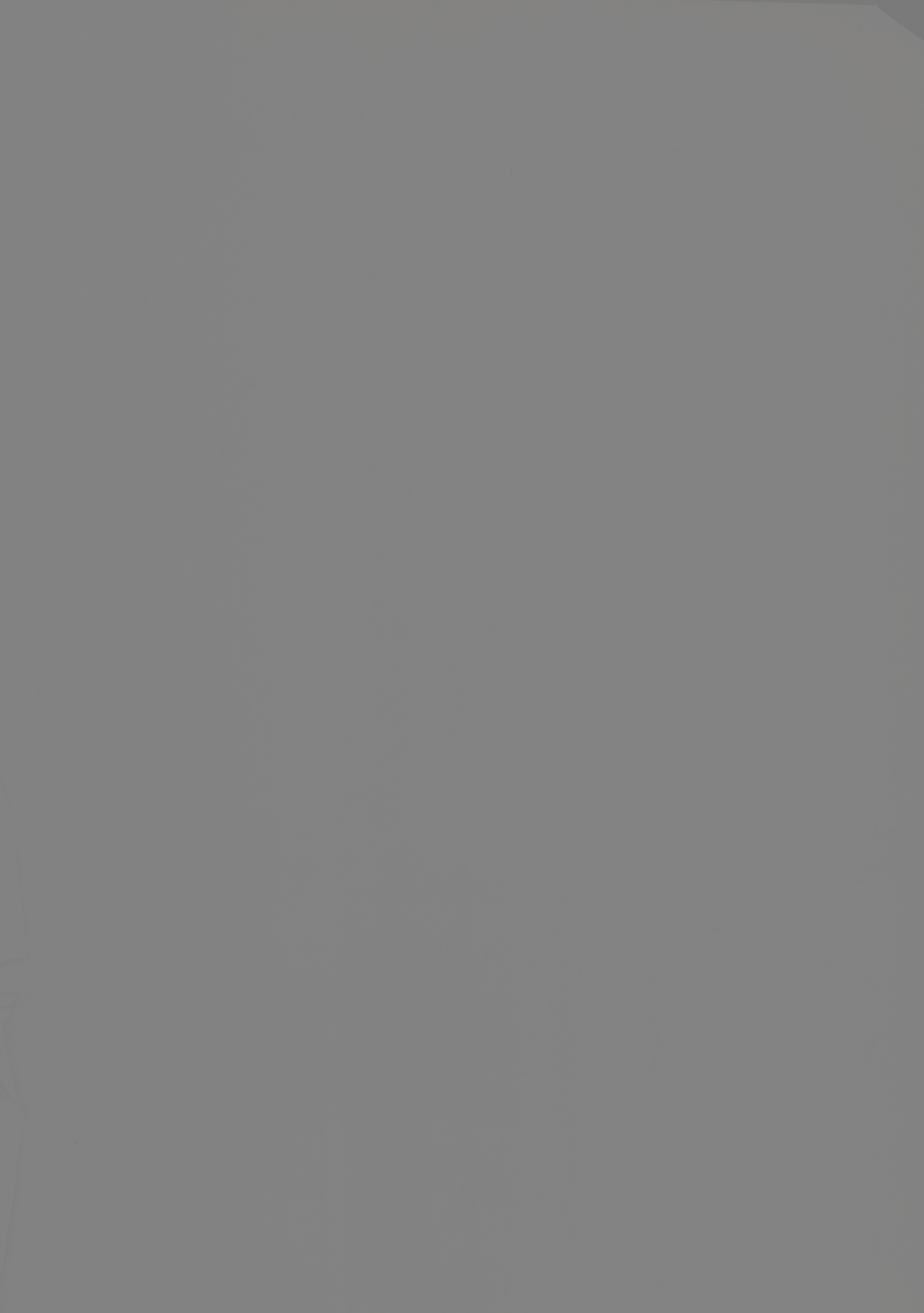

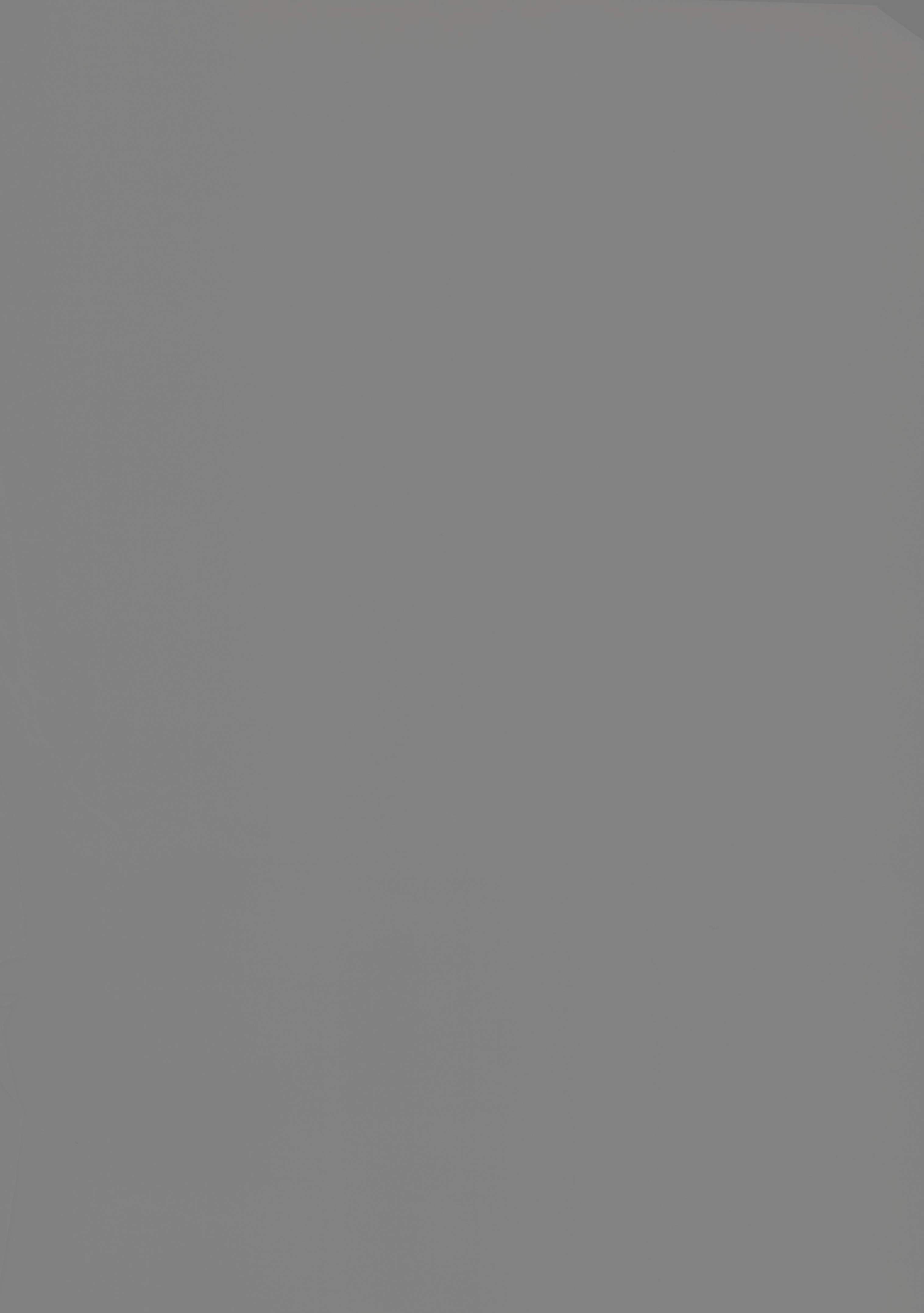